PLAN GRAPHICS

PLAN GRAPHICS

DAVID A. DAVIS
THEODORE D. WALKER

Fifth Edition

JOHN WILEY & SONS, INC.
New York Chichester Weinheim Brisbane Singapore Toronto

This publication is designed to provide accurate and authoritative
information in regard to the subject matter covered. It is sold with the
understanding that the publisher is not engaged in rendering professional
services. If professional advice or other expert assistance is required, the
services of a competent professional person should be sought.

Library of Congress Cataloging-in-Publication Data:
  Davis, David A.
    Plan graphics / David A. Davis and Theodore D. Walker. — 5th ed.
      p.   cm.
    Walker's name appears first on the earlier edition.
    "Published simultaneously in Canada."
    Includes index.
    ISBN 0-471-29221-4 (paper : acid-free paper)
    1. Architectural drawing. I. Walker, Theodore D. II. Walker,
  Theodore D. Plan graphics. III. Title.
  Arch. NA2700.W34 1999 2000
  720'.28'4—dc21
                                          98-51606

Printed in the United States of America.

10 9 8 7 6 5 4 3 2 1

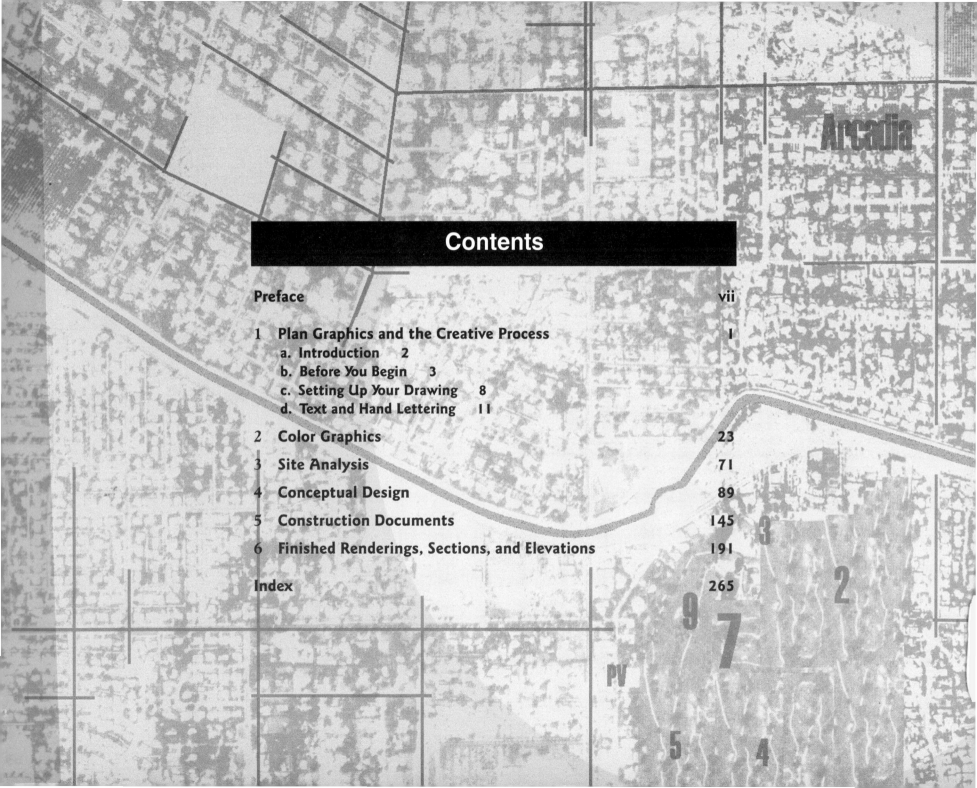

Contents

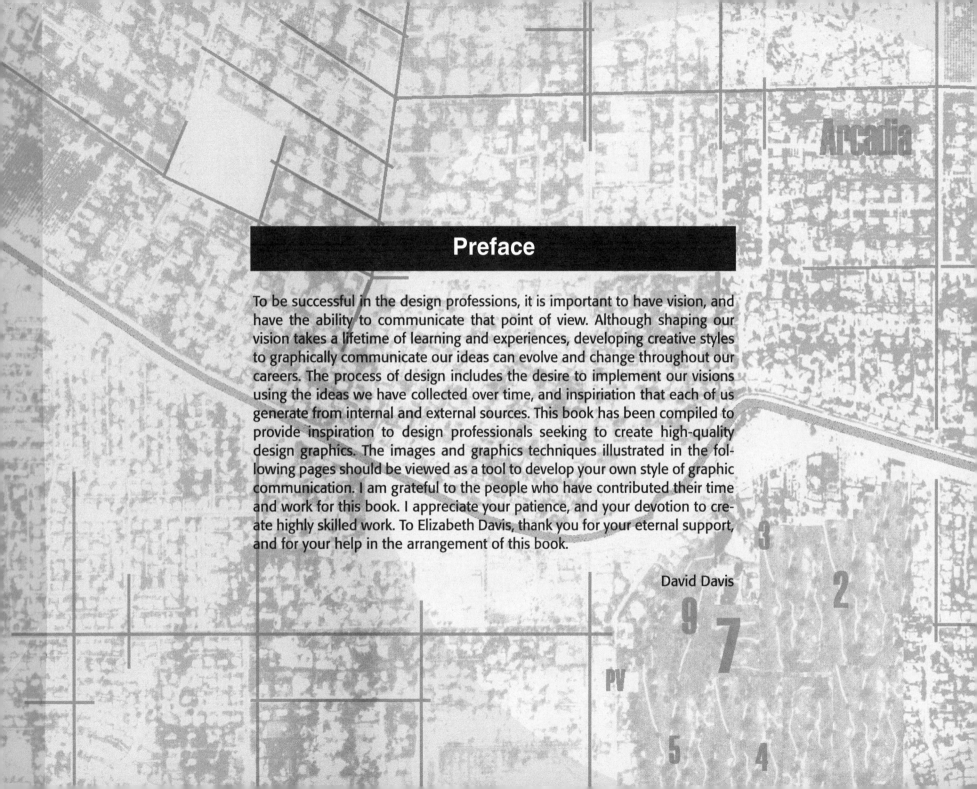

Preface

To be successful in the design professions, it is important to have vision, and have the ability to communicate that point of view. Although shaping our vision takes a lifetime of learning and experiences, developing creative styles to graphically communicate our ideas can evolve and change throughout our careers. The process of design includes the desire to implement our visions using the ideas we have collected over time, and inspiriation that each of us generate from internal and external sources. This book has been compiled to provide inspiration to design professionals seeking to create high-quality design graphics. The images and graphics techniques illustrated in the following pages should be viewed as a tool to develop your own style of graphic communication. I am grateful to the people who have contributed their time and work for this book. I appreciate your patience, and your devotion to create highly skilled work. To Elizabeth Davis, thank you for your eternal support, and for your help in the arrangement of this book.

David Davis

PLAN GRAPHICS

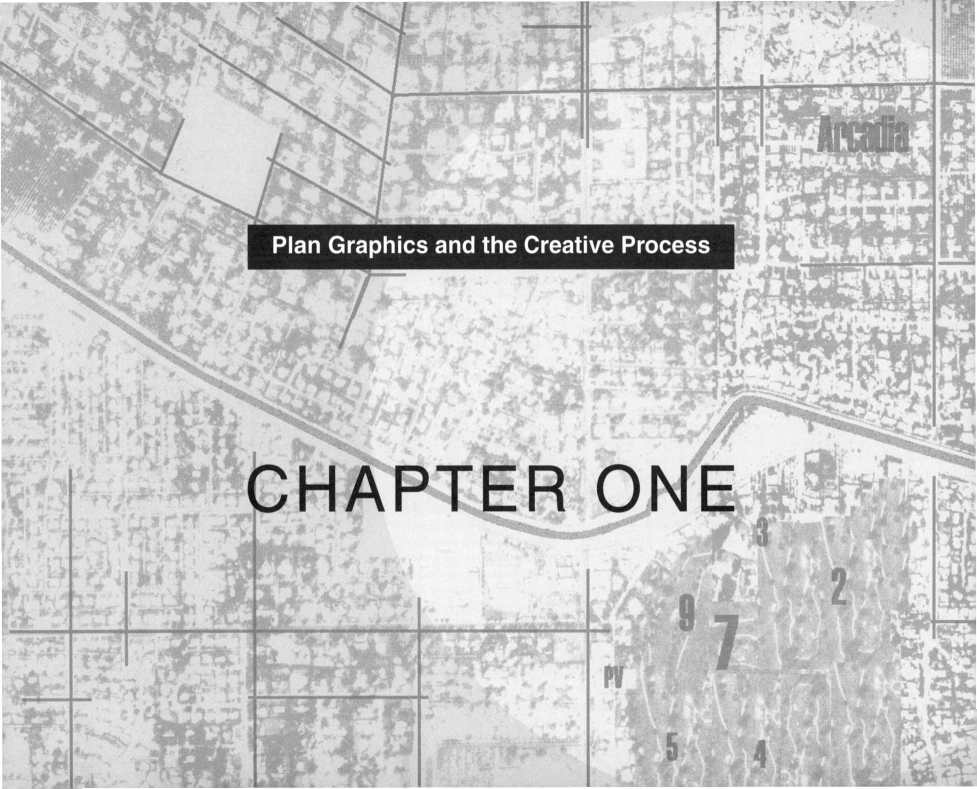

Plan Graphics and the Creative Process

CHAPTER ONE

Introduction

I have long believed that the design process is like a journey along a braided path. The path is marked by crossroads, difficult terrain, and barriers that are hard to negotiate. At times, the journey may seem impossible to complete because workable solutions to overcome obstacles are hard to conceive, and even harder to implement. At other times, the path is an enjoyable stroll through a process of research and discovery, conceptualization of design solutions, and the documentation of ideas. In either case, the process should be rewarding. It may also seem that the path is always going uphill—which is not to say that it is constantly difficult, but at any given point in the process it is easier to look back and see where you've been than to imagine what lies ahead of you in the future. Using your imagination to develop ideas and plan for the development of good quality graphics takes a great deal of skill, discipline, and practice. Exposure to the work of other professionals is a good way to help stimulate design thinking, which is why this edition of *Plan Graphics* is a valuable tool for designers. This compilation of work represents the graphic approaches of designers with unique backgrounds and experiences.

Fast forward yourself to the top of the hill, and look back at the design process. All along the path, you may be able to see different forms of graphic documentation that now constitute a newly created trail map. Each major phase of the design process is marked by design graphics that were used to summarize the journey to date and propose solutions to problems encountered. This book is organized in a similar fashion, beginning, at the bottom of the hill, with the documentation gained from research and analysis. At the midpoint of the journey are schematic and conceptual drawings. Near the top of the hill are construction documents and finished renderings. Select examples from each phase of the process are illustrated in color in Chapter 2.

Before You Begin

Before embarking on your journey, review the rest of this chapter to become familiar with the process of starting your design graphics. Before setting up your drawing, consider the following questions and ask yourself whether they apply to your work.

Recognizing the answers and issues related to these questions will help shape the decisions you will need to make when setting the format and style for the drawing.

What is the main idea you want the drawing to communicate?
One of the most subtle attributes of good-quality design graph-

Tools and Media Compatibility Checklist

Media Types	Tools: Color — Color Marker	Color Pencil	Pastels/Chalks	Clip Art/Collages	Watercolor Paints	Color Photographs	Charts and Tables	Color Film	Airbrushed Ink	Oil Paints/Acrylics	Computer Software	Non-Color — Ink (Hard Tip)	Ink (Felt Tip)	Graphite	Charcoal Pencils	Black/Grey Markers	Screen Film	Form-a-Line Tape	Computer Software
Bond (Opaque)		●	●	●		●	●	●			●	●	●	●	●	●	●	●	●
Bond (Transparent)		●	●	●		●	●	●			●	●		●	●		●	●	●
Mylar	●	●	●	●		●	●	●	●	●	●	●	●	●	●	●	●	●	●
Sepia Paper	●	●	●	●		●	●	●				●	●	●	●	●	●	●	
Ink Media		●	●	●		●	●	●			●	●	●	●	●	●	●	●	●
Presentation Blackline	●	●	●	●		●	●	●				●	●	●	●	●	●	●	
Presentation Brownline	●	●	●	●		●	●					●	●	●	●	●	●	●	
Watercolor Paper		●	●		●					●	●	●	●	●	●	●	●		●
Illustration Paper		●	●	●	●	●			●	●		●	●	●	●	●		●	
Kraft Paper	●					●	●	●	●		●	●	●	●	●			●	●
Vellum		●	●	●		●	●	●	●		●	●	●	●	●		●	●	●
Tracing Paper	●	●	●					●				●	●	●	●	●	●	●	
Butcher Paper		●	●	●		●	●	●			●	●	●	●	●		●	●	●
Canvas	●	●	●	●	●					●	●	●	●		●	●			●
Blueline		●	●				●	●				●	●	●	●		●	●	
Photographic Paper	●	●		●		●		●						●		●	●	●	
Cardboard	●	●	●	●		●		●	●			●	●	●		●	●	●	
Chip Board	●	●	●	●		●		●	●			●	●	●	●	●	●	●	
Rice Paper		●	●	●	●	●	●	●			●	●	●	●	●				●
Acetate	●			●		●	●	●	●							●	●	●	
Foam Core	●	●	●	●		●	●	●	●			●	●			●	●	●	
Use Your Imagination	●	●	●	●	●	●	●	●	●	●	●	●	●	●	●	●	●	●	●

Use this compatibility checklist as a guide in determining which media and tools best fit the style of graphics you are composing. Each solid circle represents compatibility between materials.

ics is that the viewer becomes very much aware of the primary concepts through clear graphic communication. Articulate the big ideas. Do not emphasize the extraneous clutter.

How will the drawings be viewed?

It is important to understand whether your drawings will be displayed and viewed at distances of less than 5 feet, between 5 and 15 feet, or greater than 15 feet. Additionally, how will the drawings be displayed? Will the originals be displayed, or will they be shown via slides or video? The overall format size, the size and spacing of text, and the amount of detail illustrated will differ depending on this distance. Generally, the closer the viewer is to the drawing, the greater the amount of detail expected.

Who is the audience?

The term *audience* refers here to the users of the drawings. Ask yourself, To whom do you intend to convey the information in the drawings? Is the intended audience a client who commissioned your work, a lay person representing the community, students, contractors, or other design professionals? Each audience group has a different understanding of the design process and, consequently, different expectations. For effective communication, design graphics should be tailored with the understanding that expectations may vary.

What phase of the design process do the drawings support?

Design graphics created in the early stages of the analysis and diagnostic evaluation process must be accurate, but can be developed in a less refined manner than those needed in technical drawings. Drawings of the conceptual nature tend to have accurate base data and are developed in a "looser" fashion. Conceptual drawings not only communicate the intent of the design solution, but can also make a statement about the image of the project or the designer. Construction drawings developed for implementation and archiving are developed clearly and accurately in order to communicate intent from the standpoint of constructability.

What is the potential for using a drawing in the future?

Is there a chance that your drawing will have a longer "shelf life" than others, or that it can be developed to serve as the basis for future drawings? If so, it may be wise to invest more time in such drawings to meet current and future expectations.

Have you explored a variety of media and tools available?

There are at least two schools of thought on how to stylize your design graphics. On one hand, you can develop a recognizable, and marketable, skill utilizing the same tools and media repeatedly. This often becomes the "brand" for which you are known. On the other hand, you have an opportunity to create drawings utilizing any number of media and tools available that may best match a style dictated by the project type. For example, you might hand draw a rendered site plan for an environmental showcase home on recycled paper, or choose to develop all your drawings using state-of-the-art software for a high-tech client.

Examples of using available media include hand drawing on vellum, mylar, bond, bristol board, trace paper, kraft, and, in some cases, canvas; computer plotting on bond, mylar, vellum, photographic paper, and special bond paper for color; hand rendering on presentation blacklines and brownlines, claycote, illustration board, watercolor paper, in addition to the aforementioned media; and applying notes, textures, or films on aerials, photographs, and presentation papers. An increasingly popular medium is found in the digital environment. Design graphics can be prepared on computers using text and graphic software; nondigital work can be scanned or photographed for digital enhancement and archiving. Transfer of electronic work for others to use or view is an excellent way to communicate efficiently. It's always a good idea to clarify copyright agreements prior to the transfer of digital work.

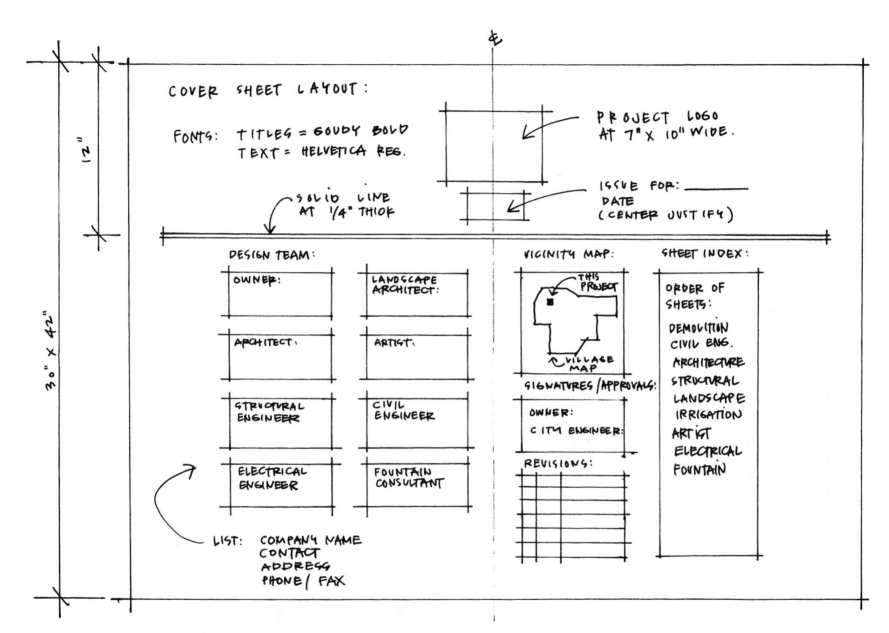

▌Cartoon example of a cover sheet.

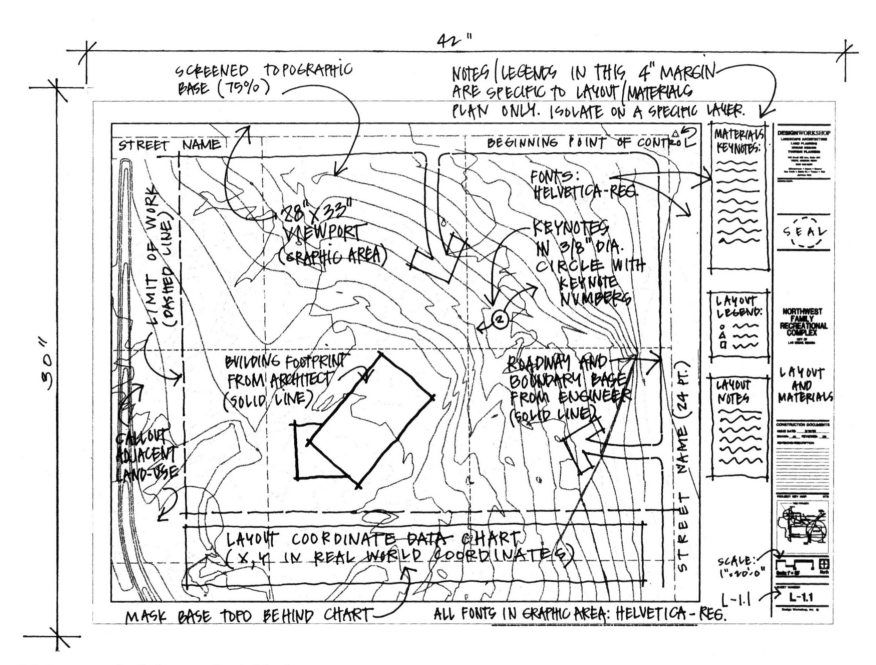

▌ Cartoon example of a layout and materials plan.

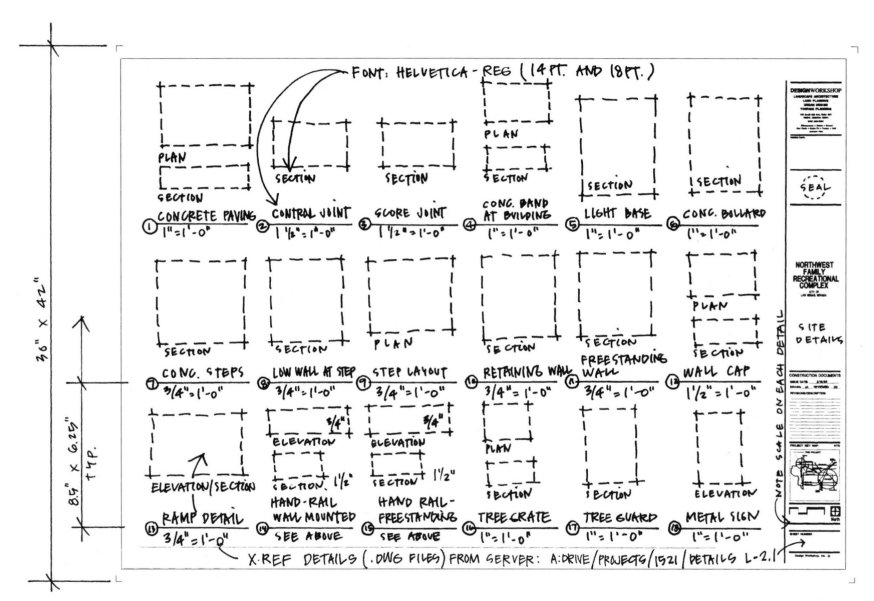

Cartoon example of a detail sheet.

Setting Up Your Drawing

After you have considered the preceding questions and before you start the actual drawing, practice one more planning technique. Invest the time to plan ahead and make key decisions on the structure and style of the drawing. Solving design problems requires some amount of preplanning; design graphics are no different. A small amount of time spent in preplanning at the beginning of the process will undoubtedly pay off with good-quality end products. Consider the following elements of design graphics.

Composition

For the purposes of this book, composition will refer to the arrangement of two-dimensional graphic and text elements of the drawing. Preplanning the graphic layout is an essential step in the process of developing quality design drawings. Composing the drawing to balance the weight of the elements on the sheet, and organizing the placement of the text and titles for aesthetic value and clarity are of primary importance for presentation drawings. The scale of the drawing and how much context to show should also be considered. For construction drawings, the emphasis is on clarity and efficiency. Although aesthetic value is important, construction documents must communicate the graphic and written instructions for implementation clearly and concisely.

"Cartoon diagrams" are reduced-scale storyboards created prior to preparing any family of graphic exhibits. An example of a cartoon set for construction drawings is illustrated above. The cartoon set identifies the format by sheet size, scale, location of notes and legends, and order of sheets in the set. In addition, details and enlarged plans can be identified and planned into the set layout. Think of the cartoon diagram as a graphic instruction for the design team to follow throughout the design process.

Establishing rules and preparing a mock-up

Developing a graphic standard prior to beginning your drawing and preparing a realistic mock-up are part of being a disciplined designer. One of the goals in preparing presentation-quality drawings is to be consistent and to not rely on making quick decisions on the fly when you are in the middle of preparing a drawing. Following these standards, which can be customized per drawing, throughout the process allows you to work in a more efficient manner and allows others to assist you once they know the rules.

Line work

Line weight and line quality are measured in thickness and consistency, respectively. Selecting line weights for plan graphics is slightly different from assigning line weights for elevations and sections. In plan graphics the designer has some flexibility in making lines thicker or thinner, based on the importance of the object. In creating a site plan where the building forms are the most important element in communicating the spatial character

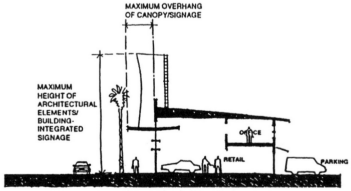

West End One/Two-Story Commercial

This one- or two-story commercial building type may include retail, restaurants and professional offices. Building height may not exceed two stories. Parking is at-grade.

This simple section effectively uses text and textures to create a clear and balanced exhibit.

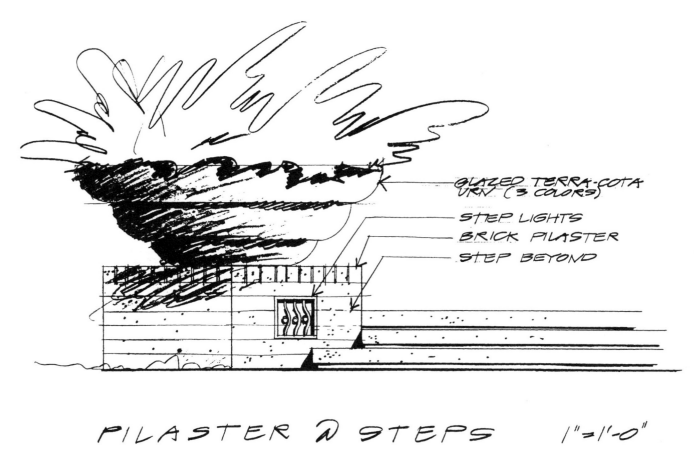

GLAZED TERRA-COTA
URN (3 COLORS)

STEP LIGHTS
BRICK PILASTER
STEP BEYOND

PILASTER @ STEPS   1"=1'-0"

| Design vignettes can be hand drawn to create a warm, craftsman style.
Clarity is achieved by a variety of clear and consistent line types.

of the design, the building lines should be bold and shadows pronounced. In drawing a planting plan where the trees and shrub massings are the focus of the graphic, then the building lines and shadows should recede. In elevation and section drawings, the selection of line weights is generally based on the depth of the object in view. Thicker lines, or profile lines, are used to define changes in object depth.

Line quality is an issue related primarily to hand-drawn graphics and text. If computer-drawing methods are used cor-

rectly, then good line quality should not be hard to achieve. Line weight consistency and line connections will be accurate and clear. For hand drawings, special care should be given to ensure that lines do not fluctuate greatly in thickness and that connecting lines overlap slightly. To achieve consistent line weights using a lead holder, practice twirling the lead holder as you draw. This will keep the lead tip sharp, thus saving you time by not requiring the constant use of a lead sharpener. Overlapping connecting lines ensures accuracy and clarity in a drawing.

Textures and patterns

Patterns in your drawings have a way of communicating changes in the ground plane treatments or illustrating positive/negative relationships. The use of hatching, stippling, color films, or color markers and pencils is an effective way to clearly delineate areas to be popped-out or recessed. Remember that patterns should not dominate the drawing (unless the idea is to make it look like a piece of tapestry), but should complement the composition, balance, and lines. Patterns should be kept light enough as not to block out important information or cause confusion in the clarity of the drawing.

Texturing a drawing usually applies to presentation-style drawings that require added levels of detail to communicate your ideas or to enhance the artistic quality of the rendering. For example, illustrating roof textures and building "caps" adds a finished quality and sense of realism to a drawing. Furthermore, when rendering a drawing with color pencils, pastels, charcoal, or graphite, you might place a textured board below the drawing. The contrasting effect is pronounced when your drawing tools highlight the raised portions of the textured board and barely cover the depressed portions. Illustration board, watercolor paper, and chipboard are good examples of textured bases.

Shadows

Shadows are used to give two-dimensional plan graphics a quasi-three-dimensional quality. Location, depth, and darkness of shadows should be considered carefully. It is a rare occasion when plan graphics do not use some form of shadowing. Decide how prominent the shadows should be in the drawing, then explore the options available to achieve the desired effect. Bottom-side (left or right) shadows tend to lift objects off the page, enhancing the three-dimensional effect. The length of shadows should be related to the actual height of the real object for accuracy, but this is a graphic effect that should not

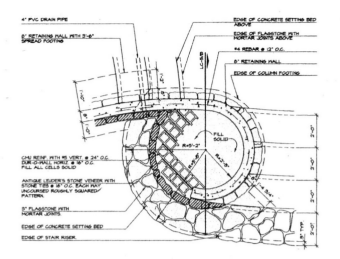

C LOWER ENHANCED COLUMN PLAN SECTION
SCALE: 1/2"=1'-0"

▍ This design development detail uses text to frame the graphic.

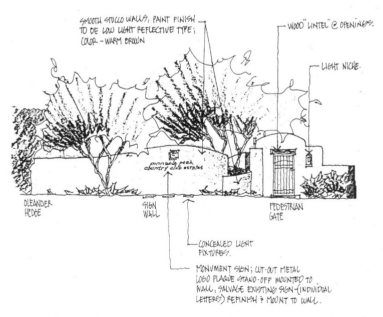

▍Hand-lettered text can be customized to fit the style of graphic it supports.

cover the essential elements of the proposed design. Find a way to provide effective shadows without affecting the clarity of the drawing. Determining the lengths of the graphic shadows depends on the size and complexity of the drawing.

Text and Hand Lettering

The selection of graphic examples in this book was based on the quality of composition, color, clarity of delineation, line work, and text style and layout. Although the images catch our eye first and are regarded as being of primary importance, the written notation adds a level of detail and information the images cannot represent. In most cases, when notation is needed we should think about how to integrate the words, or block of words, into the entire composition. For example, the positive image a paragraph creates when viewed is of a geometric shape, which should be carefully incorporated into the plan graphic. Another example concerns the possible dual function of titles within the composition. The most important of these functions is to provide project identity, but a title may secondarily function may as an element of the graphic composition. Sometimes text style or color can be used effectively to create a positive first impression. Throughout this book we have illustrated not only the importance of design graphics but also the importance of the text within the composition.

The following paragraphs focus on developing hand-lettering techniques. Before you begin to add handwritten notes to your work, take a short time to decide what role your notation

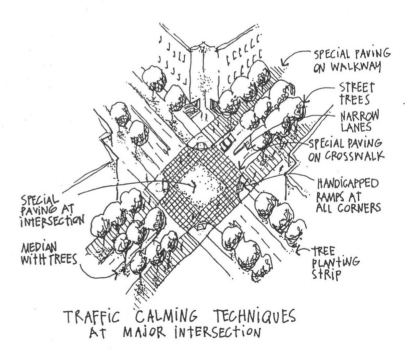

| Hand-drawn graphic for technical communication relies on clarity and efficiency of information presented.

| Graphic diagrams can be quickly prepared in a loose style, without sacrificing clarity.

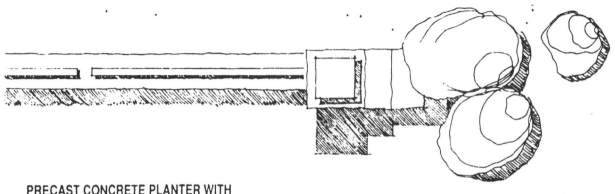

PRECAST CONCRETE PLANTER WITH
NATURAL GREY COLOR

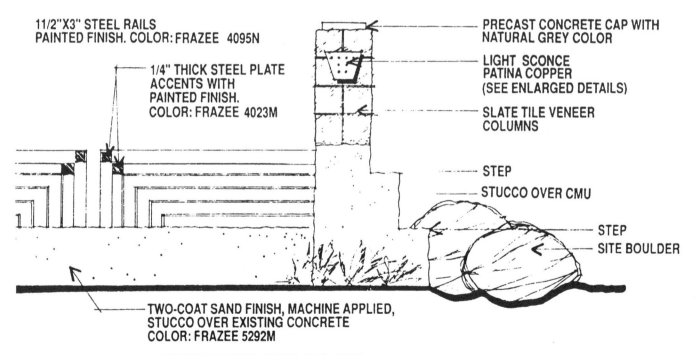

11/2"X3" STEEL RAILS
PAINTED FINISH. COLOR: FRAZEE 4095N

1/4" THICK STEEL PLATE
ACCENTS WITH
PAINTED FINISH.
COLOR: FRAZEE 4023M

PRECAST CONCRETE CAP WITH
NATURAL GREY COLOR

LIGHT SCONCE
PATINA COPPER
(SEE ENLARGED DETAILS)

SLATE TILE VENEER
COLUMNS

STEP

STUCCO OVER CMU

STEP

SITE BOULDER

TWO-COAT SAND FINISH, MACHINE APPLIED,
STUCCO OVER EXISTING CONCRETE
COLOR: FRAZEE 5292M

1 1/2" SQUARE TUBE STEEL RAIL WITH
PAINTED FINISH COLOR: FRAZEE 4095N

Hand-drawn design graphics can be formalized using typed text. In this case, text
layout is structured in an organized fashion to accentuate the contrast of styles.

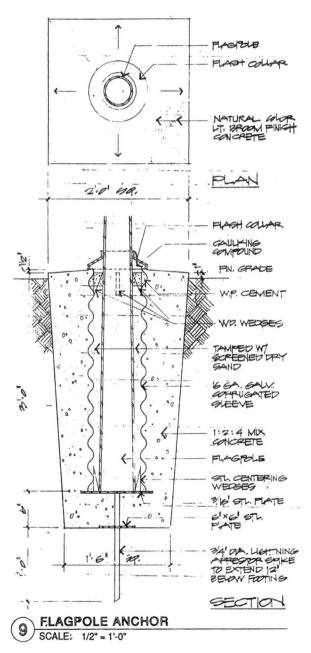

PLAN

2'-0" DIA.

FLASH COLLAR

CAULKING COMPOUND

FIN. GRADE

W.P. CEMENT

WD. WEDGES

TAMPED W/ SCREENED DRY SAND

16 GA. GALV. CORRUGATED SLEEVE

1:2:4 MIX CONCRETE

FLAGPOLE

STL. CENTERING WEDGES

3/16" STL. PLATE

6"x6" STL. PLATE

3/4" DIA. LIGHTNING ARRESTOR SPIKE TO EXTEND 12" BELOW FOOTING

FLAGPOLE

FLASH COLLAR

NATURAL COLOR LT. BROOM FINISH CONCRETE

SECTION

9 **FLAGPOLE ANCHOR**
SCALE: 1/2" = 1'-0"

▎**Hand-drawn detail style.**

has within the plan graphic. Usually, notation on conceptual and design development-style work is causally drafted and precisely worded, and its placement is a predetermined element of the final composition. Conversely, in preparing construction documents or details, notation is usually drafted firmly with a straight-edge, consisting of technical information and general notes. Whenever possible, its placement should attempt to complement the overall composition.

Determine the media best suited for your purposes. Generally, graphite or plastic lead on mylar or vellum is best in drafting construction documents because it is quickly applied and easily erased. Ink is an effective medium for presentation-style drawings owing to its boldness, crisp lines, and ability to reproduce more clearly than graphite.

Decide which form of hand lettering, freehand or hard-line, you should use and what size is appropriate. There are no rules when it comes to conceptual and design development drawings. Freehand, hard-line, or digitally prepared text is always appropriate. Give some thought to the style of drawing when selecting a style of text. Generally, freehand text is quickly applied and will complement a loose style of image. A refined style of hard-line or digital text should be used on all construction documents and final details. The size of the letters will be determined by the designer, based on the importance of the notes within the plan and overall legibility.

The last item of consideration, mainly in presentation work, is what notation is necessary and where it is to be placed. To decide, simply place a piece of tracing paper over the entire plan and map out your notes. By doing so, you can design the layout of notes around the graphic elements, strengthening the overall composition. Aligning blocks of text to complement the composition of the graphics is represented throughout this book.

Remember: Consistency is the key to successful hand lettering. Once you have determined the style, shape, size, and

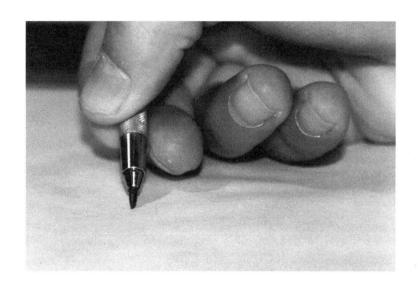

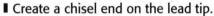
■ Create a chisel end on the lead tip.

location of notation, maintain these elements of hand lettering throughout the entire plan graphic.

One of the best overall techniques is to use guidelines to achieve clear, consistent lettering. Guidelines are horizontal and vertical lines drawn lightly with a hard lead, 3H or 4H, or non-photo pencil to aid in the construction of letters and numerals. Nonphoto pencils work well in situations where it is important that the guidelines are not produced in the final image.

Use a soft lead pencil for lettering, as it will be easier to control than a hard lead and will glide more easily over the surface of the paper or mylar. To start, try an H or HB lead. Later, as you

become more proficient, experiment with various leads so that you can eventually use the appropriate leads for the different drawing surfaces available.

Before you begin, flatten the lead on a piece of scrap paper or sandpaper block to produce a chisel point. You can create both thick and thin lines by twirling the lead holder between your thumb and fingers. The flat edge of the chisel point is used for thick lines, and the side edge for thin vertical lines.

In hand lettering it is important to develop your own style of lettering, and to understand the unique spacing relationships for each letter (kerning). Practice making quick decisions on kern-

Use the thin edge of the chisel for vertical lines, and the flat edge for all others.

ing based on visual relationships. Most letters should maintain equal heights to achieve a consistent appearance. The letters "C, G, O, S, and Q" should project slightly above and below the guidelines to avoid appearing too short.

To draw each letter accurately with matched heights, always use horizontal guidelines. It also should be noted that hand-lettered notation is easier to read when the designer provides adequate spacing between letters, words, and sentences.

Another very successful technique is to ensure that all crossbars connect at the same point in each letter. To begin, practice using three hori-zontal guidelines for each line of text. After drawing the upper and lower guidelines, add a third horizontal guideline at a point slightly above the midpoint between the first two guidelines. All crossbars should connect at points along this middle guideline.

Your objective when hand lettering is to be sure the notation is accurate and legible. To ensure accuracy, you must understand the content and always check for incorrect spelling. A common problem that compromises legibility is the smearing of letters. To avoid smudging the graphite, it is best to begin at the top of the plan and work down from the left to the right,

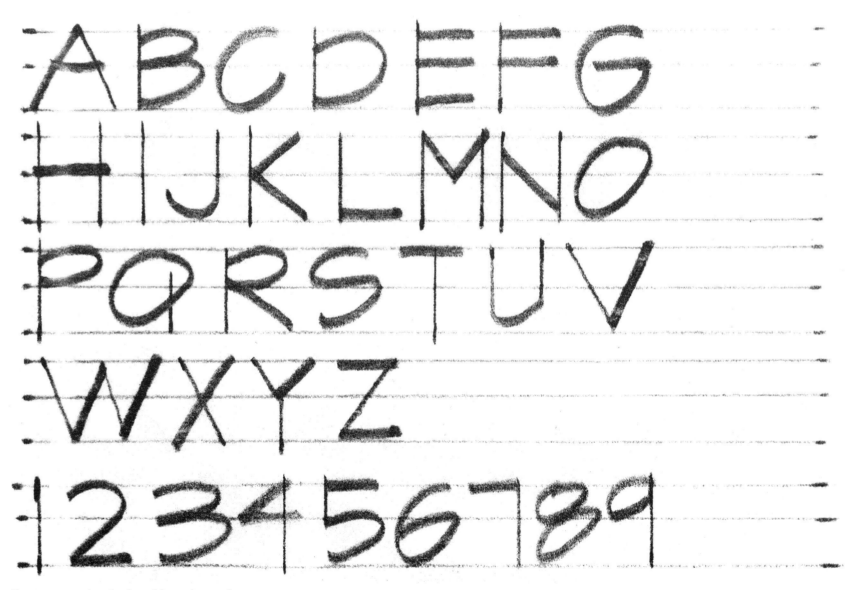

ABCDEFG
HIJKLMNO
PQRSTUV
WXYZ
123456789

❚ One example of a hand-lettering style.

when possible. Even when working left to right, it is common to drag your arm or triangle across the fresh graphite, causing it to smear. To avoid this problem, practice lettering with the guide triangle on the right side of the lead holder as opposed to the left side, which seems so much more natural for right-handed persons. Simply wrap your left arm over the top of the parallel rule and place your thumb and forefinger on the top of the guide triangle, gliding it across the parallel rule as you write.

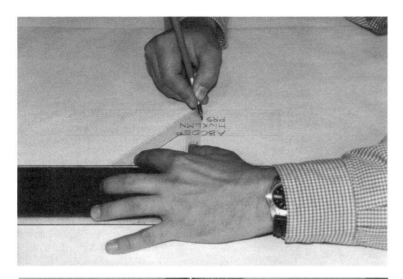

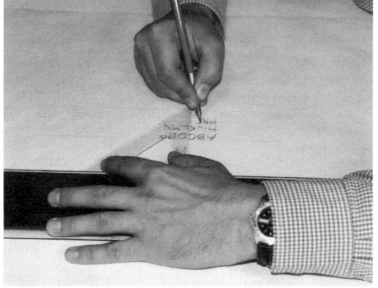

Hand positions for right-handed people using a parallel rule and a straight edge.

SMOOTH MASONRY FINISH. PAINT
TO MATCH SIGNAGE & PLANTER
WALL. COLOR TO BE APPROVED
BY LANDSCAPE ARCH/OWNER

HAND TROWELLED CONTROL JOINT
1/4" RADIUS FROM EDGE - SEE PLAN
FOR PATTERN AND LOCATION

8"x8" #8 W.W.M CENTERED, 12" MIN.
FROM EDGES.

1 1/2" HIGH DENSITY RIGID BOARD INSULATION

1/2" PREFORMED FIBER EXPANSION JOINT
W/ BACKER ROD AND SEALANT.

6" CONCRETE SLAB W/ BROOM FINISH

6" COMPACTED ROADBASE

COMPACTED SUBGRADE

HYDRONIC SNOWMELT COIL, TIE TO W.W.M
2" MAX. FROM TOP OF CONCRETE, LOOP
UNDER JOINTS. SEE MECHANICAL DRAWINGS
FOR PIPING LAYOUT AND SYSTEMS
SPECIFICATIONS.

Grouping notes will also strengthen the overall plan graphic. Not only do grouped notes provide mass to the composition, they also make it easier for the reader to pick out information. The reader does not have to search the entire plan for single "floating" notes.

In all graphic communications, including hand lettering, the line is a fundamental element. In drafting any line, the empha-sis is always on the end points of the line. Avoid letting up or decreasing pressure at the end of your stroke. Verticals are drawn with thin lines, whereas horizontals are drawn boldly with thick lines. Such lines are achieved by twirling the lead holder as you write. As you gain experience, you will notice that when using this technique with a soft lead and maintaining the chisel point, the need to sharpen the lead point is minimized.

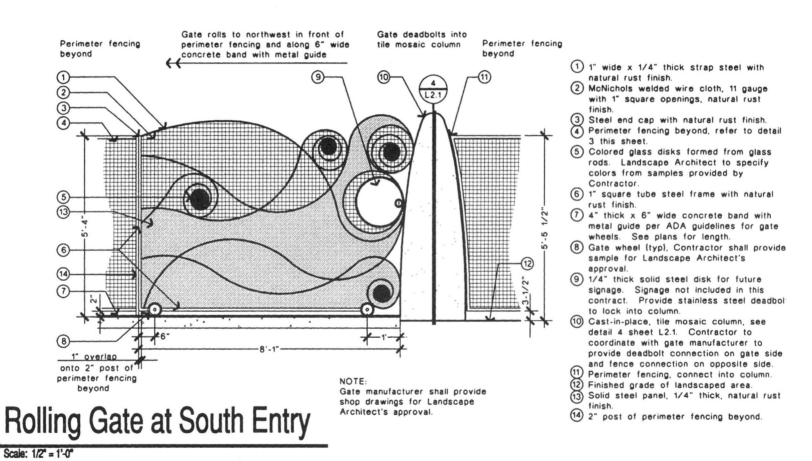

Perimeter fencing beyond

Gate rolls to northwest in front of perimeter fencing and along 6" wide concrete band with metal guide

Gate deadbolts into tile mosaic column

Perimeter fencing beyond

1 1" wide x 1/4" thick strap steel with natural rust finish.
2 McNichols welded wire cloth, 11 gauge with 1" square openings, natural rust finish.
3 Steel end cap with natural rust finish.
4 Perimeter fencing beyond, refer to detail 3 this sheet.
5 Colored glass disks formed from glass rods. Landscape Architect to specify colors from samples provided by Contractor.
6 1" square tube steel frame with natural rust finish.
7 4" thick x 6" wide concrete band with metal guide per ADA guidelines for gate wheels. See plans for length.
8 Gate wheel (typ). Contractor shall provide sample for Landscape Architect's approval.
9 1/4" thick solid steel disk for future signage. Signage not included in this contract. Provide stainless steel deadbol to lock into column.
10 Cast-in-place, tile mosaic column, see detail 4 sheet L2.1. Contractor to coordinate with gate manufacturer to provide deadbolt connection on gate side and fence connection on opposite side.
11 Perimeter fencing, connect into column.
12 Finished grade of landscaped area.
13 Solid steel panel, 1/4" thick, natural rust finish.
14 2" post of perimeter fencing beyond.

1" overlap onto 2" post of perimeter fencing beyond

NOTE: Gate manufacturer shall provide shop drawings for Landscape Architect's approval.

2 Rolling Gate at South Entry
Scale: 1/2" = 1'-0"

For clarity, numeric keynotes can be used to separate the text from an image, without diminishing the level of information to be communicated.

ABCDEFGHIJKLMNOPQRSTUVWXYZ
1234567890   ₵ ₵ $ ¢ # and/or

abcdefghijklmnopqrstuvwxyz 1234567890
american society of landscape architects

ABCDEFGHIJKLMNOPQRSTUVWXYZ   1234567890
AMERICAN SOCIETY OF LANDSCAPE ARCHITECTS

ABCDEFGHIJKLMNOPQRSTUVWXYZ 1234567810
AMERICAN SOCIETY of LANDSCAPE ARCHITECTS

REMOVE SECONDARY WALLS, ORNAMENTATION &
LIGHT FIXTURES — REFINISH WALL TO MATCH
PROPOSED IMPROVEMENTS.

RELOCATED PLANTER FOR BETTER
VEHICULAR ACCESS. w/ LOW PLANTINGS &
SPECIMEN TREE.

NEW MASONRY SIGN WALL TO MIMIC EAST SIDE
OF ENTRY DRIVE.

PAINTED LANE DIVIDER.

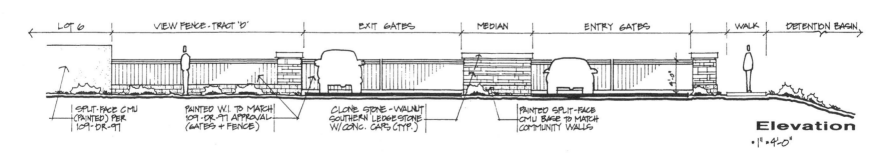

LOT 6 | VIEW FENCE - TRACT 'D' | EXIT GATES | MEDIAN | ENTRY GATES | WALK | DETENTION BASIN

SPLIT-FACE CMU (PAINTED) PER 109-DR-97

PAINTED W.I. TO MATCH 109-DR-97 APPROVAL (GATES + FENCE)

CLONE STONE - WALNUT SOUTHERN LEDGESTONE W/CONC. CAPS (TYP.)

PAINTED SPLIT-FACE CMU BASE TO MATCH COMMUNITY WALLS

Elevation
1" = 4'-0"

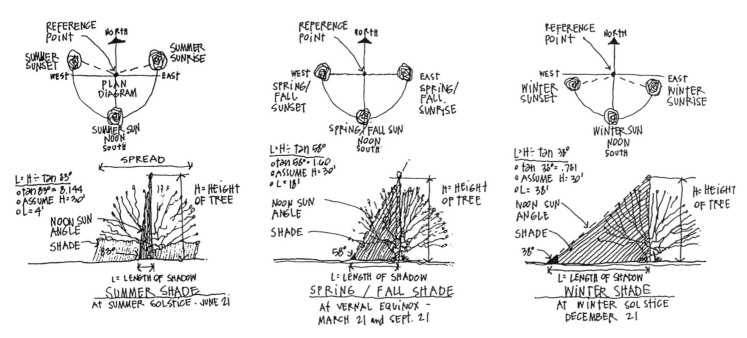

Summer (left diagram):

REFERENCE POINT

NORTH

SUMMER SUNSET
WEST

SUMMER SUNRISE

PLAN DIAGRAM

EAST

SUMMER SUN
NOON
SOUTH

SPREAD

$L = H \div \tan 83°$
- $\tan 83° = 8.144$
- ASSUME $H = 30'$
- $L = 4'$

H = HEIGHT OF TREE

NOON SUN ANGLE

SHADE

$83°$

L = LENGTH OF SHADOW

SUMMER SHADE
AT SUMMER SOLSTICE - JUNE 21

Spring/Fall (middle diagram):

REFERENCE POINT

NORTH

WEST SPRING/FALL SUNSET

EAST SPRING/FALL SUNRISE

SPRING/FALL SUN
NOON
SOUTH

$L = H \div \tan 58°$
- $\tan 58° = 1.60$
- ASSUME $H = 30'$
- $L = 18'$

NOON SUN ANGLE

SHADE

H = HEIGHT OF TREE

$58°$

L = LENGTH OF SHADOW

SPRING / FALL SHADE
AT VERNAL EQUINOX -
MARCH 21 and SEPT. 21

Winter (right diagram):

REFERENCE POINT

NORTH

WEST WINTER SUNSET

EAST WINTER SUNRISE

WINTER SUN
NOON
SOUTH

$L = H \div \tan 38°$
- $\tan 38° = .781$
- ASSUME $H = 30'$
- $L = 38'$

NOON SUN ANGLE

SHADE

H = HEIGHT OF TREE

$38°$

L = LENGTH OF SHADOW

WINTER SHADE
AT WINTER SOLSTICE
DECEMBER 21

Freehand analysis vignettes with a high level of environmental data are clear, quick, and to the point. These types of vignettes can be recycled during the design process and used on final design graphics or within text to support the analysis.

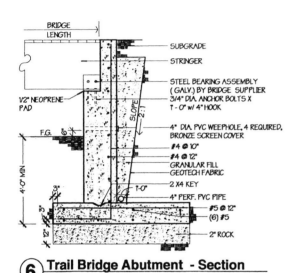

BRIDGE
LENGTH

SUBGRADE

STRINGER

STEEL BEARING ASSEMBLY
(GALV.) BY BRIDGE SUPPLIER
3/4" DIA. ANCHOR BOLTS X
1'- 0" w/ 4" HOOK

1/2" NEOPRENE
PAD

F.G.

SLOPE 2:1

4'-0" MIN

4" DIA. PVC WEEPHOLE, 4 REQUIRED,
BRONZE SCREEN COVER

#4 @ 10"
#4 @ 12"
GRANULAR FILL
GEOTECH FABRIC

2 X 4 KEY

1'- 0"

4" PERF. PVC PIPE

#5 @ 12"
(6) #5

2" ROCK

(6) Trail Bridge Abutment - Section
1/2" = 1' - 0"

▌Computer-generated graphic detail with dimensions on left
side, and notes on right.

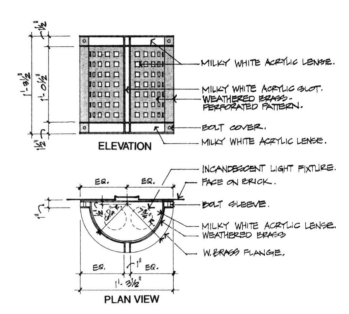

ELEVATION

MILKY WHITE ACRYLIC LENSE.

MILKY WHITE ACRYLIC SLOT.
WEATHERED BRASS-
PERFORATED PATTERN.

BOLT COVER.

MILKY WHITE ACRYLIC LENSE.

INCANDESCENT LIGHT FIXTURE.

FACE ON BRICK.

BOLT SLEEVE.

MILKY WHITE ACRYLIC LENSE.
WEATHERED BRASS

W. BRASS FLANGE.

EQ.   EQ.

1"

EQ.   1"   EQ.

1'- 3½"

PLAN VIEW

▌Hand-drawn graphic detail with clear separation of text and dimensions.

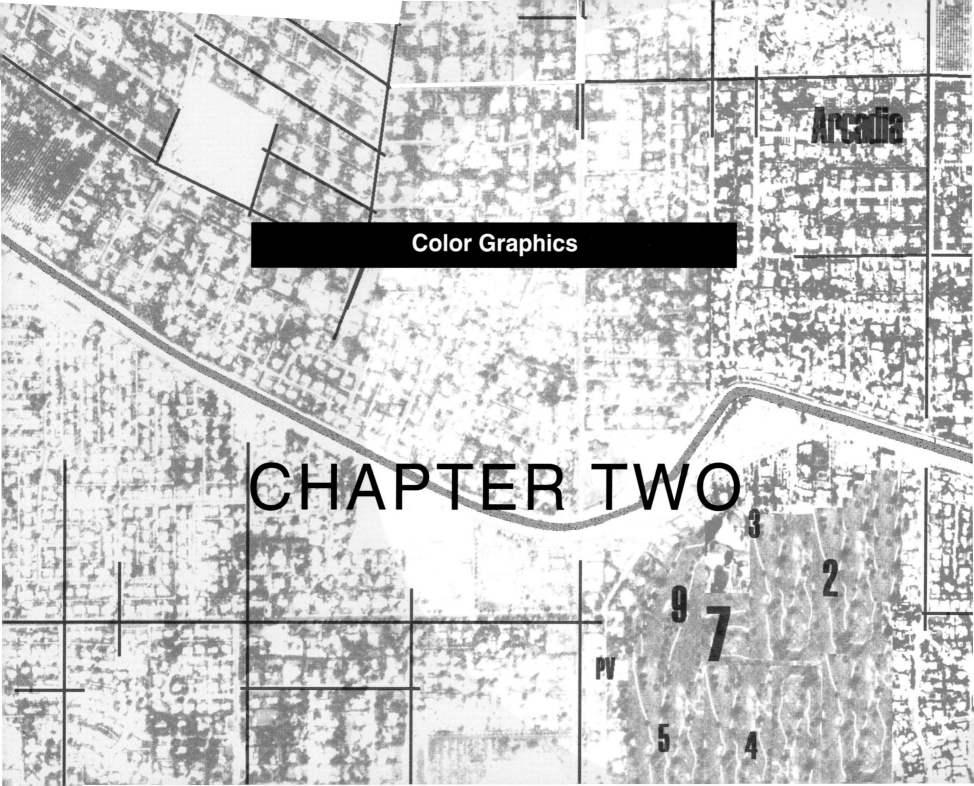

Color Graphics

CHAPTER TWO

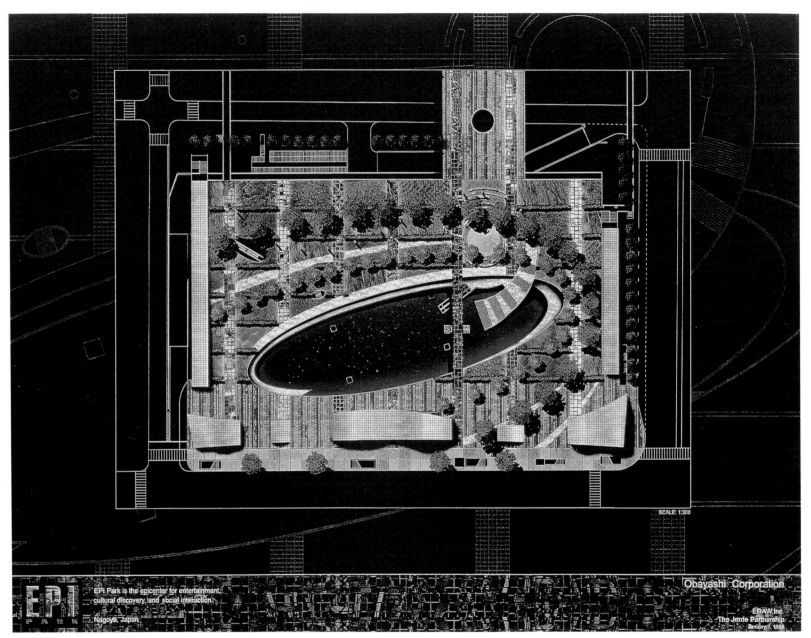

Obayashi Corporation. Computer-generated rendering plotted from Quark Express. The base drawing is created in AutoCADD and saved to Adobe Photoshop as a postscript file where it is rendered. The rendered image is saved into Quark Express, where text and titles are added.

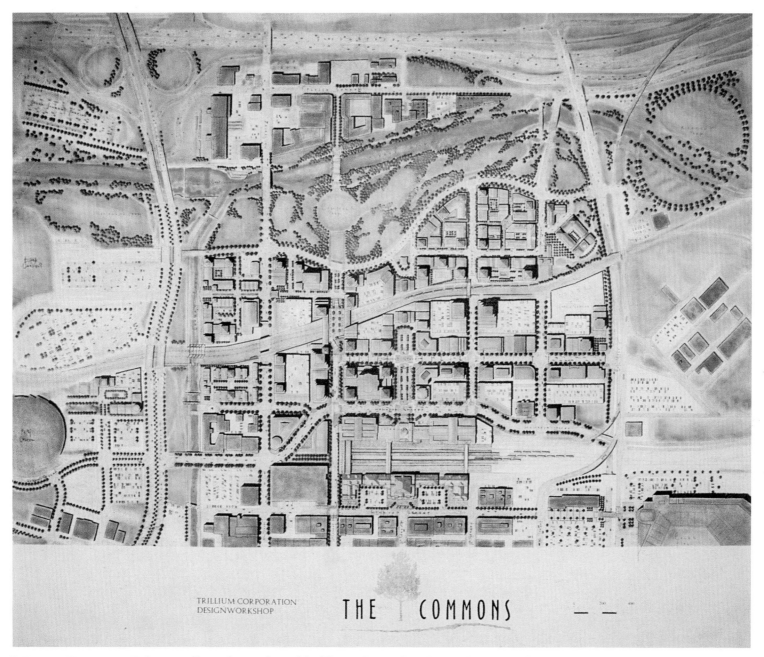

TRILLIUM CORPORATION
DESIGNWORKSHOP

THE COMMONS

Denver Commons. Color pencils and pastels on blackline print on bond. Pastels are used for foundation color in large areas. Color pencils are used in detail areas and to highlight key elements.

ENTRY EXPERIENCE CONCEPT
SCALE : 1" = 20'-0"

Anthem
COUNTRY CLUB

Anthem Country Club. Color pencil on kraft paper. The base is hand-drawn using ink on vellum with a computer-generated title block. Text callouts are computer-generated and added to the vellum base with sticky-back material. Note that clarity is achieved with hand-drawn style by maintaining a consistency of the line strokes and shadows.

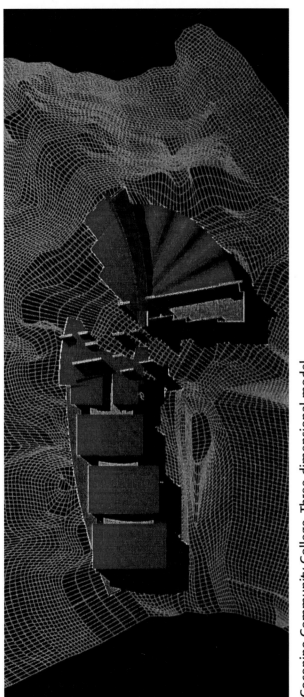

Coconino Community College. Three-dimensional model created and rendered in AutoCADD on a Macintosh.

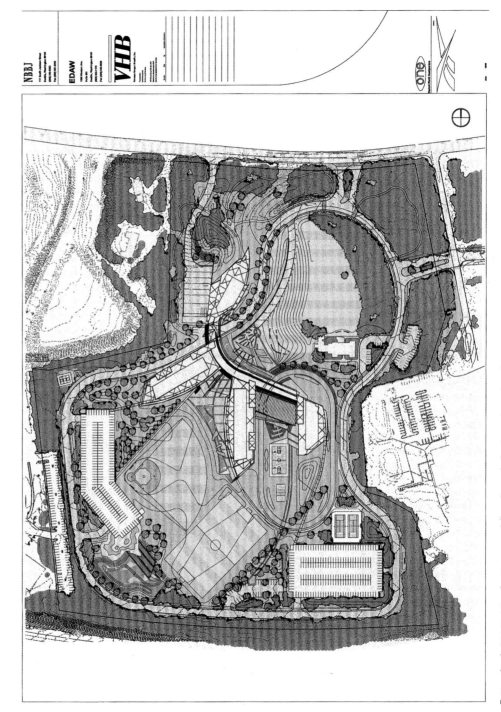

Reebok/W.G. Hook. Scanned freehand design drawing is imported into AutoCADD to be composited with the base drawing. The composite digital file is then imported into ArcView and rendered.

RIO SALADO CROSSING

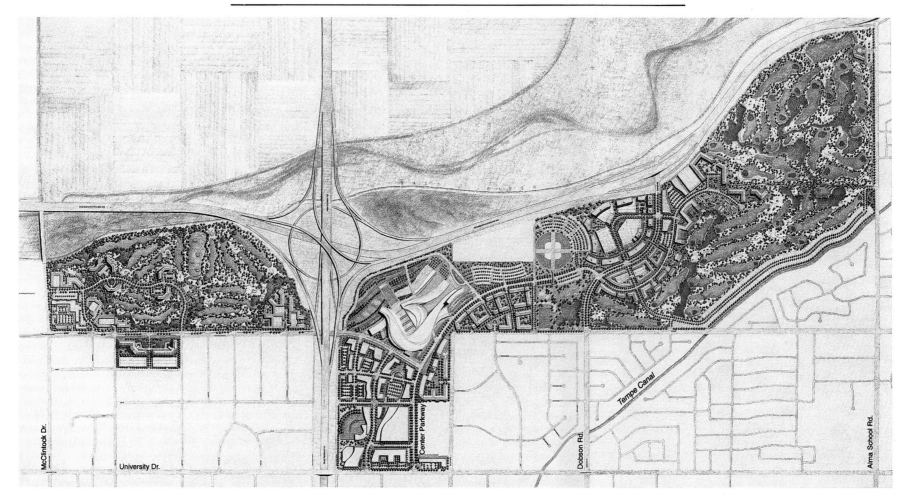

Rio Salado Crossing. Color pencil on white bond. The base drawing is created in Auto-CADD on a PC platform and ink jet plotted onto bond. Once rendered, the image is then scanned and imported into Quark Express. In Quark Express, the composition is refined and text is added. The size of the original document is 6 feet wide by 3 feet high.

RIO SALADO CROSSING

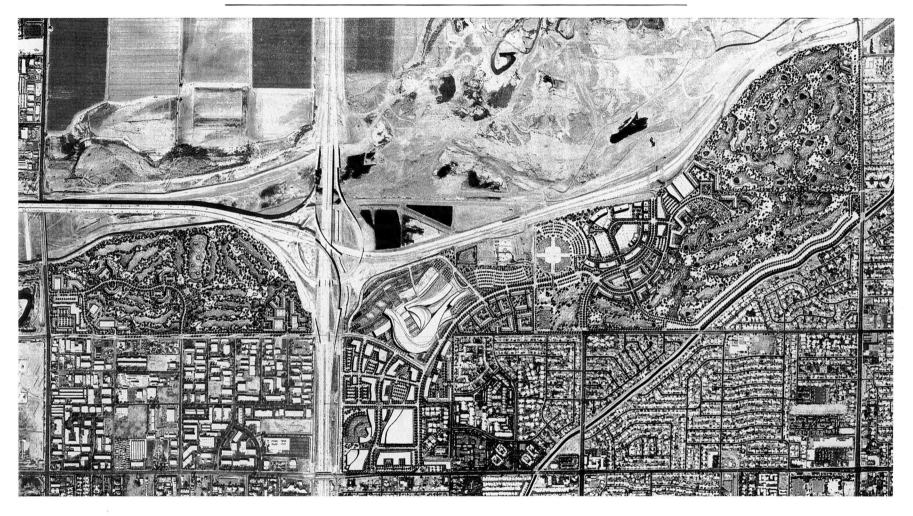

CONTEXT PLAN

NORTH

Rio Salado Crossing. Scanned color pencil rendering and scanned aerial of the adjacent properties are composited in Adobe Photoshop. The composite is imported into a title block template in Quark Express.

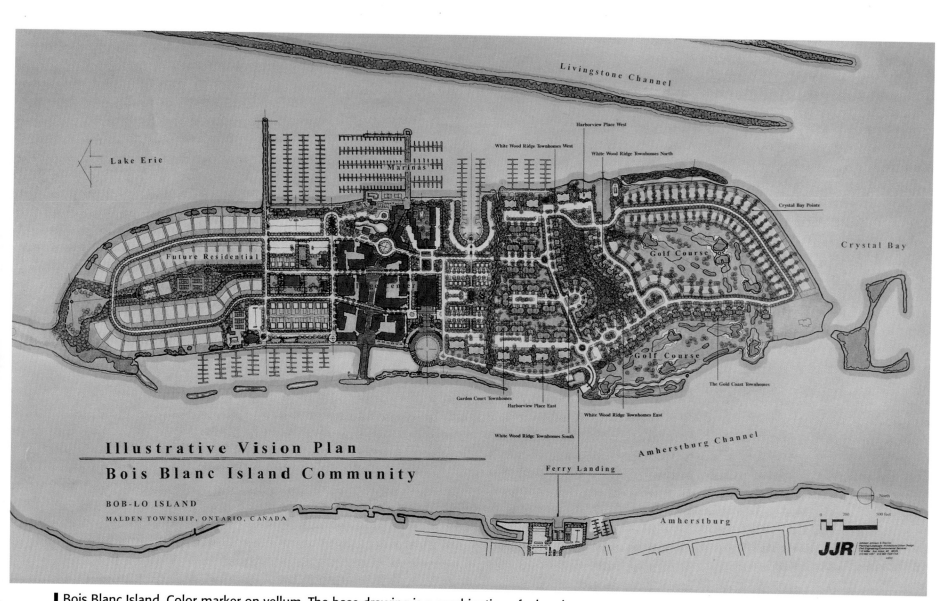

Livingstone Channel

Lake Erie

Harborview Place West

White Wood Ridge Townhomes West

White Wood Ridge Townhomes North

Marinas

Crystal Bay Pointe

Future Residential

Golf Course

Crystal Bay

Golf Course

The Gold Coast Townhomes

Garden Court Townhomes

Harborview Place East

White Wood Ridge Townhomes East

White Wood Ridge Townhomes South

Amherstburg Channel

Illustrative Vision Plan
Bois Blanc Island Community

BOB-LO ISLAND

MALDEN TOWNSHIP, ONTARIO, CANADA

Ferry Landing

Amherstburg

North

JJR

Bois Blanc Island. Color marker on vellum. The base drawing is a combination of a hand-drawn site plan and computer-generated text and titles. Text is added manually to the base prior to printing the final vellum.

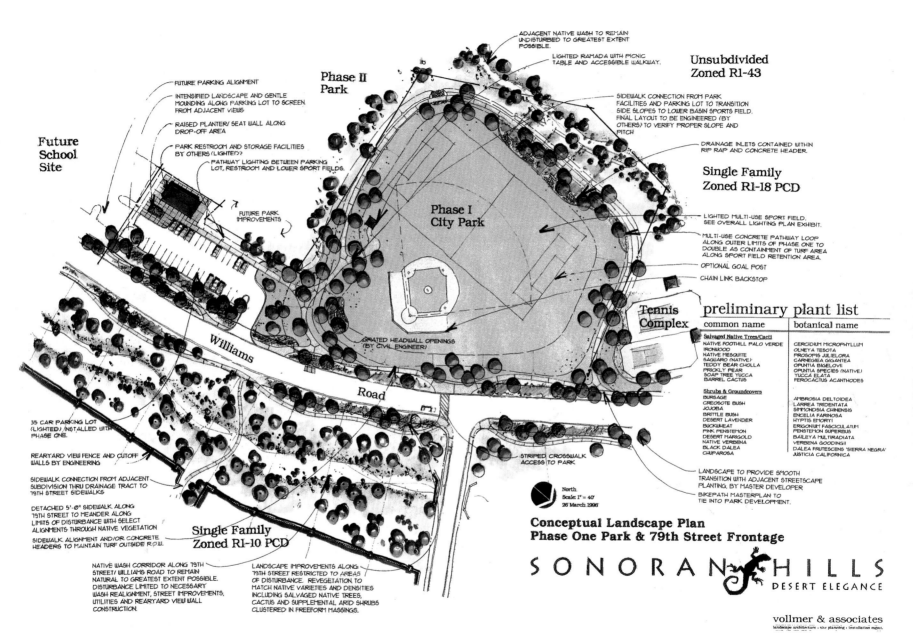

FUTURE PARKING ALIGNMENT

INTENSIFIED LANDSCAPE AND GENTLE MOUNDING ALONG PARKING LOT TO SCREEN FROM ADJACENT VIEWS

RAISED PLANTER/ SEAT WALL ALONG DROP-OFF AREA

PARK RESTROOM AND STORAGE FACILITIES BY OTHERS (LIGHTED)

PATHWAY LIGHTING BETWEEN PARKING LOT, RESTROOM AND LOWER SPORT FIELDS.

Phase II Park

Future School Site

FUTURE PARK IMPROVEMENTS

ADJACENT NATIVE WASH TO REMAIN UNDISTURBED TO GREATEST EXTENT POSSIBLE.

LIGHTED RAMADA WITH PICNIC TABLE AND ACCESSIBLE WALKWAY.

Unsubdivided Zoned R1-43

SIDEWALK CONNECTION FROM PARK FACILITIES AND PARKING LOT TO TRANSITION SIDE SLOPES TO LOWER BASIN SPORTS FIELD. FINAL LAYOUT TO BE ENGINEERED (BY OTHERS) TO VERIFY PROPER SLOPE AND PITCH

DRAINAGE INLETS CONTAINED WITHIN RIP RAP AND CONCRETE HEADER.

Single Family Zoned R1-18 PCD

Phase I City Park

LIGHTED MULTI-USE SPORT FIELD. SEE OVERALL LIGHTING PLAN EXHIBIT.

MULTI-USE CONCRETE PATHWAY LOOP ALONG OUTER LIMITS OF PHASE ONE TO DOUBLE AS CONTAINMENT OF TURF AREA ALONG SPORT FIELD RETENTION AREA.

OPTIONAL GOAL POST

CHAIN LINK BACKSTOP

Williams

Road

GRATED HEADWALL OPENINGS (BY CIVIL ENGINEER)

Tennis Complex

STRIPED CROSSWALK ACCESS TO PARK

35 CAR PARKING LOT (LIGHTED) INSTALLED WITH PHASE ONE.

REARYARD VIEW FENCE AND CUTOFF WALLS BY ENGINEERING

SIDEWALK CONNECTION FROM ADJACENT SUBDIVISION THRU DRAINAGE TRACT TO 79TH STREET SIDEWALKS

DETACHED 5'-0" SIDEWALK ALONG 79TH STREET TO MEANDER ALONG LIMITS OF DISTURBANCE WITH SELECT ALIGNMENTS THROUGH NATIVE VEGETATION

SIDEWALK ALIGNMENT AND/OR CONCRETE HEADERS TO MAINTAIN TURF OUTSIDE R.O.W.

Single Family Zoned R1-10 PCD

NATIVE WASH CORRIDOR ALONG 79TH STREET/ WILLIAMS ROAD TO REMAIN NATURAL TO GREATEST EXTENT POSSIBLE. DISTURBANCE LIMITED TO NECESSARY WASH REALIGNMENT, STREET IMPROVEMENTS, UTILITIES AND REARYARD VIEW WALL CONSTRUCTION.

LANDSCAPE IMPROVEMENTS ALONG 79TH STREET RESTRICTED TO AREAS OF DISTURBANCE. REVEGETATION TO MATCH NATIVE VARIETIES AND DENSITIES INCLUDING SALVAGED NATIVE TREES, CACTUS AND SUPPLEMENTAL ARID SHRUBS CLUSTERED IN FREEFORM MASSINGS.

North
Scale: 1" = 40'
26 March 1996

LANDSCAPE TO PROVIDE SMOOTH TRANSITION WITH ADJACENT STREETSCAPE PLANTING, BY MASTER DEVELOPER

BIKEPATH MASTERPLAN TO TIE INTO PARK DEVELOPMENT.

preliminary plant list

common name	botanical name
Salvaged Native Trees/Cacti	
NATIVE FOOTHILL PALO VERDE	CERCIDIUM MICROPHYLLUM
IRONWOOD	OLNEYA TESOTA
NATIVE MESQUITE	PROSOPIS JULIFLORA
SAGUARO (NATIVE)	CARNEGIEA GIGANTEA
TEDDY BEAR CHOLLA	OPUNTIA BIGELOVII
PRICKLY PEAR	OPUNTIA SPECIES (NATIVE)
SOAP TREE YUCCA	YUCCA ELATA
BARREL CACTUS	FEROCACTUS ACANTHODES
Shrubs & Groundcovers	
BURSAGE	AMBROSIA DELTOIDEA
CREOSOTE BUSH	LARREA TRIDENTATA
JOJOBA	SIMMONDSIA CHINENSIS
BRITTLE BUSH	ENCELIA FARINOSA
DESERT LAVENDER	HYPTIS EMORYI
BUCKWHEAT	ERIOGONUM FASCICULATUM
PINK PENSTEMON	PENSTEMON SUPERBUS
DESERT MARIGOLD	BAILEYA MULTIRADIATA
NATIVE VERBENA	VERBENA GOODINGII
BLACK DALEA	DALEA FRUTESCENS 'SIERRA NEGRA'
CHUPAROSA	JUSTICIA CALIFORNICA

Conceptual Landscape Plan
Phase One Park & 79th Street Frontage

SONORAN HILLS
DESERT ELEGANCE

vollmer & associates
landscape architecture · site planning · installation mgmt.

Sonoran Hills. Color marker on presentation blackline. The base drawing is hand-drawn on mylar, with text and titles added manually with sticky-back. The character and composition of this plan is enhanced by the contrast of the loose drawing and formatted typed text.

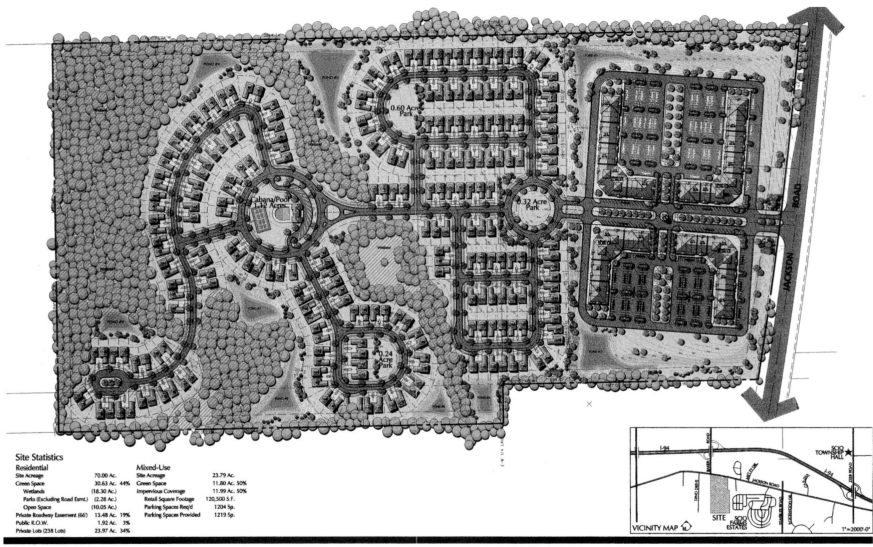

Site Statistics

Residential
Site Acreage	70.00 Ac.
Green Space	30.63 Ac. 44%
Wetlands	(18.30 Ac.)
Parks (Excluding Road Esmt.)	(2.28 Ac.)
Open Space	(10.05 Ac.)
Private Roadway Easement (66')	13.48 Ac. 19%
Public R.O.W.	1.92 Ac. 3%
Private Lots (238 Lots)	23.97 Ac. 34%

Mixed-Use
Site Acreage	23.79 Ac.
Green Space	11.80 Ac. 50%
Impervious Coverage	11.99 Ac. 50%
Retail Square Footage	120,500 S.F.
Parking Spaces Req'd	1204 Sp.
Parking Spaces Provided	1219 Sp.

VICINITY MAP

Site Development Plan

Hometown Village

of Scio

SCALE 1"=100'-0"

June, 1998

JJR Incorporated

Hometown Village. Computer-generated rendering from Micro-station. Printed on bond.

A Trailhead / Cool Zone
B Future Exhibit

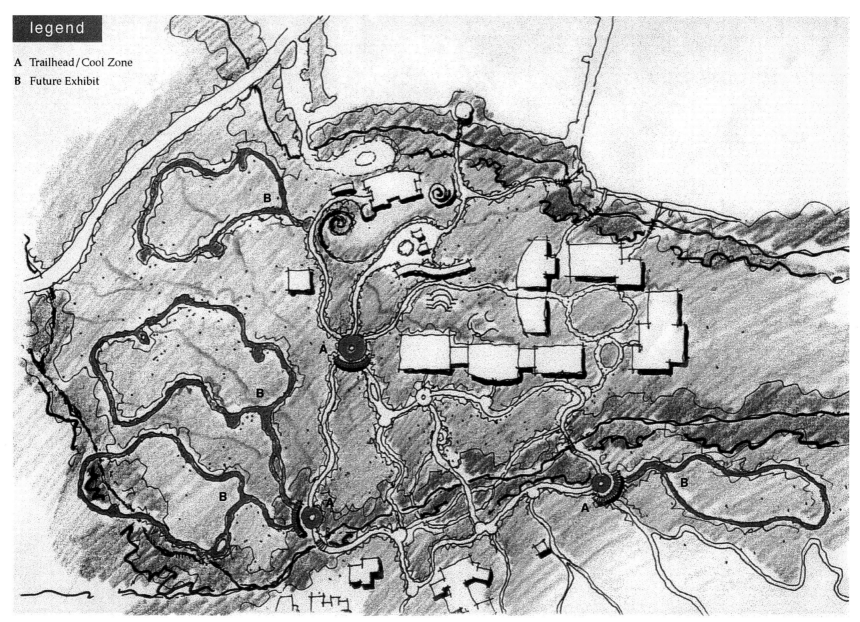

Future Exhibits and Cool Zones

Desert Botanical Garden. Color pencil over blackline print on bond. The base line work is drawn freehand over a topographic map. The rendered site plan is scanned and imported into Quark Express, where key callouts, legends, and titles are composed.

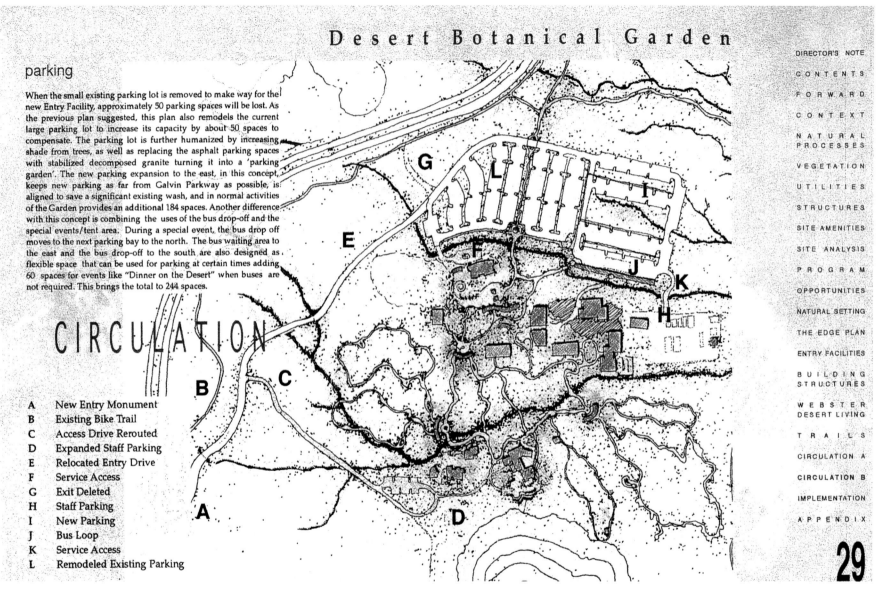

parking

When the small existing parking lot is removed to make way for the new Entry Facility, approximately 50 parking spaces will be lost. As the previous plan suggested, this plan also remodels the current large parking lot to increase its capacity by about 50 spaces to compensate. The parking lot is further humanized by increasing shade from trees, as well as replacing the asphalt parking spaces with stabilized decomposed granite turning it into a 'parking garden'. The new parking expansion to the east, in this concept, keeps new parking as far from Galvin Parkway as possible, is aligned to save a significant existing wash, and in normal activities of the Garden provides an additional 184 spaces. Another difference with this concept is combining the uses of the bus drop-off and the special events/tent area. During a special event, the bus drop off moves to the next parking bay to the north. The bus waiting area to the east and the bus drop-off to the south are also designed as flexible space that can be used for parking at certain times adding 60 spaces for events like "Dinner on the Desert" when buses are not required. This brings the total to 244 spaces.

CIRCULATION

A New Entry Monument
B Existing Bike Trail
C Access Drive Rerouted
D Expanded Staff Parking
E Relocated Entry Drive
F Service Access
G Exit Deleted
H Staff Parking
I New Parking
J Bus Loop
K Service Access
L Remodeled Existing Parking

29

Desert Botanical Garden. Color pencil over blackline print on bond. The base linework is drawn freehand over a topographic map. The rendered site plan is scanned and imported into Quark Express, where text, key callouts, legends, and titles are composed. Note that this exhibit is one of many in a larger master plan document that includes numerous exhibits, tables, and text. In the right-hand margin is a simplified listing of the table of contents, with the current exhibit highlighted in blue ink.

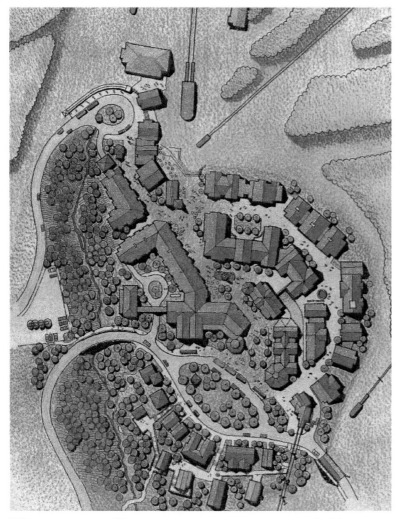

VILLAGE CORE

Killington Village. Color pencil on presentation blackline. The base drawing is hand-drawn on mylar using a topographic map as a guide. The rendering is scanned and imported into Quark Express to compose with a uniform title block consistent throughout the document.

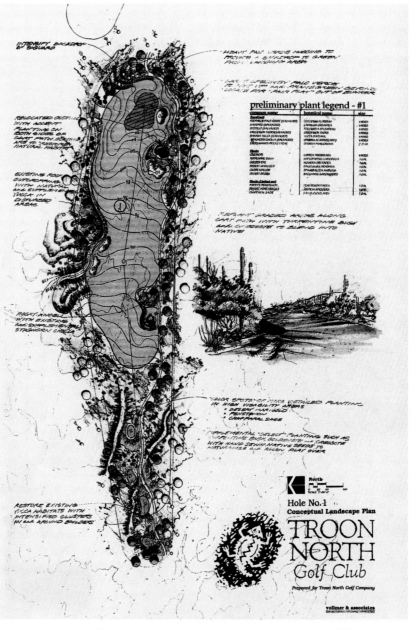

preliminary plant legend - #1

Hole No. 1
Conceptual Landscape Plan

TROON NORTH
Golf Club
Prepared for Troon North Golf Company

vollmer & associates

Troon North Golf Club. Color marker on presentation blackline. The base drawing is hand-drawn on mylar, with the legend and titles added manually with sticky-back. The hand-drawn perspective and text are added to the base drawing.

35

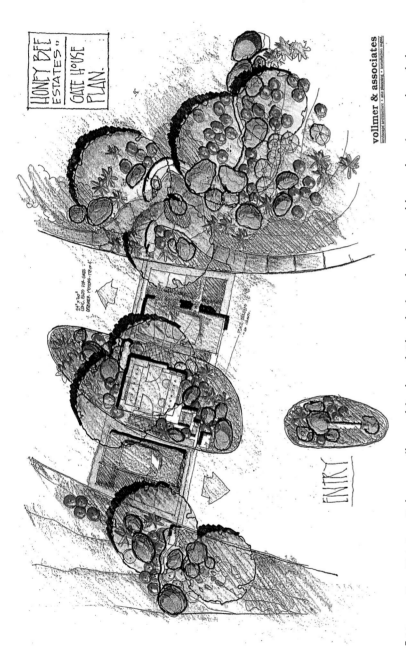

vollmer & associates
landscape architecture • land planning • installation mgmt

Honey Bee Estates. Color pencil on white bond. The design drawing and base drawing are hand-drawn. Hand-lettering of the text and titles adds to the quality of the craftsmanship.

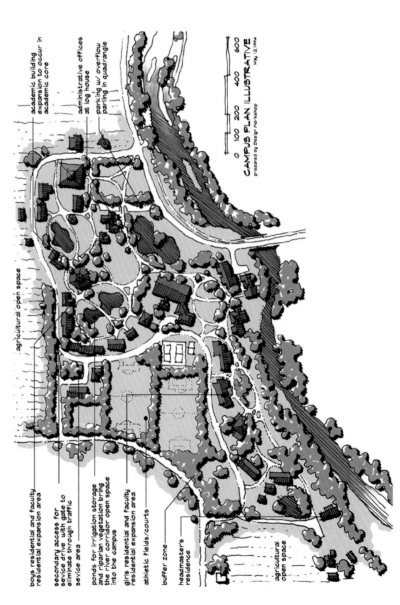

academic building expansion to occur in academic core

administrative offices at log house

parking w/ overflow parking in quadrangle

CAMPUS PLAN ILLUSTRATIVE
May 12,1994
prepared by Design Workshop

0   100 200   400   600

agricultural open space

boys residential and faculty residential expansion area

secondary access for sevice drive with gate to eliminate through traffic

service area

ponds for irrigation storage and riparian vegetation bring the river corridor open space into the campus

girls residential and faculty residential expansion area

athletic fields/courts

buffer zone

headmaster's residence

agricultural open space

Colorado Rocky Mountain School. Color marker on presentation blackline. The finished rendering is scanned without text and imported into AutoCADD. In AutoCADD, the text and titles are added to complete the composition.

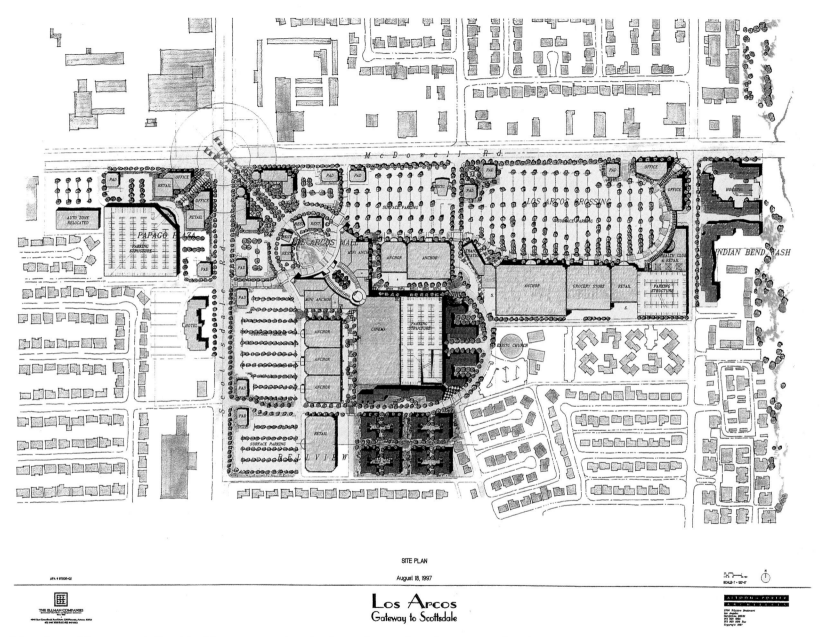

Los Arcos. The presentation blackline was rendered using color marker, then scanned and printed with a bubblejet printer. This process works well when multiple reproductions are required.

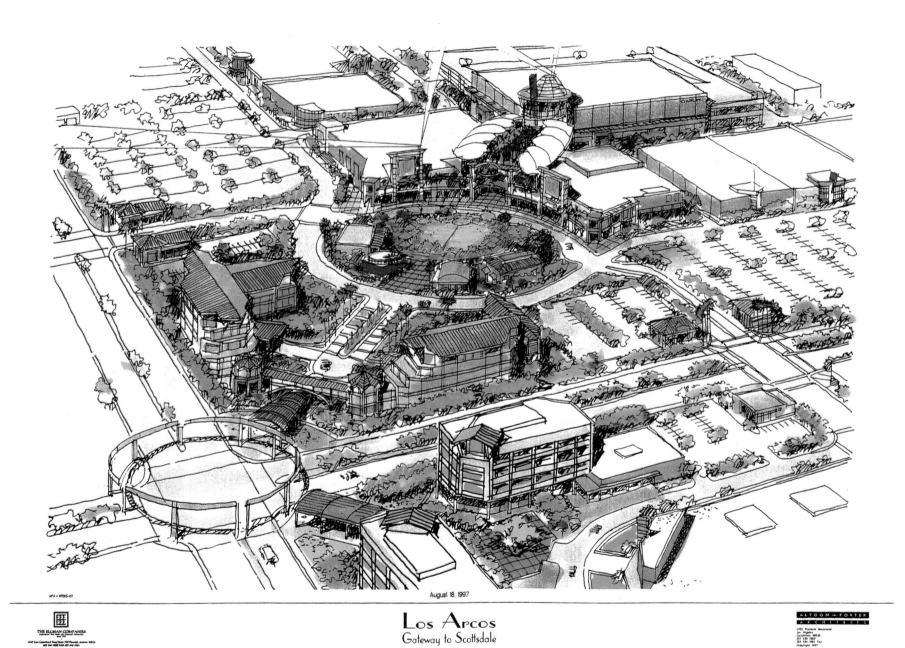

August 18, 1997

Los Arcos
Gateway to Scottsdale

Los Arcos. Perspective view of preceding site plan. Color marker on presentation blackline.
Note that this rendering was created freehand, using hard-line guidelines as a basis.

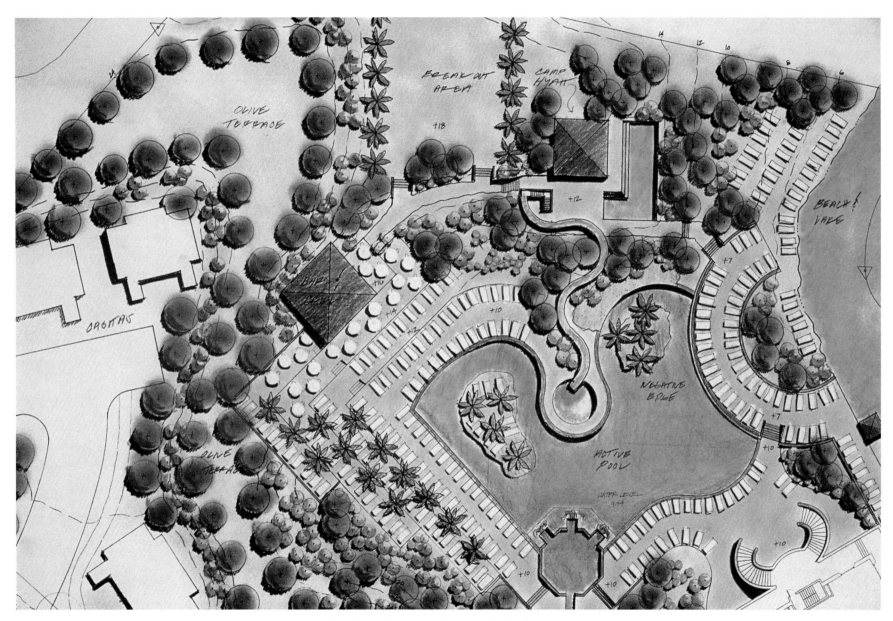

Hyatt at Lake Las Vegas. Pastels, color pencil, and black marker on white bond. The base line work is created in AutoCADD, with proposed design hand-drawn on vellum. Pastel colors are applied by hand using soft tissues.

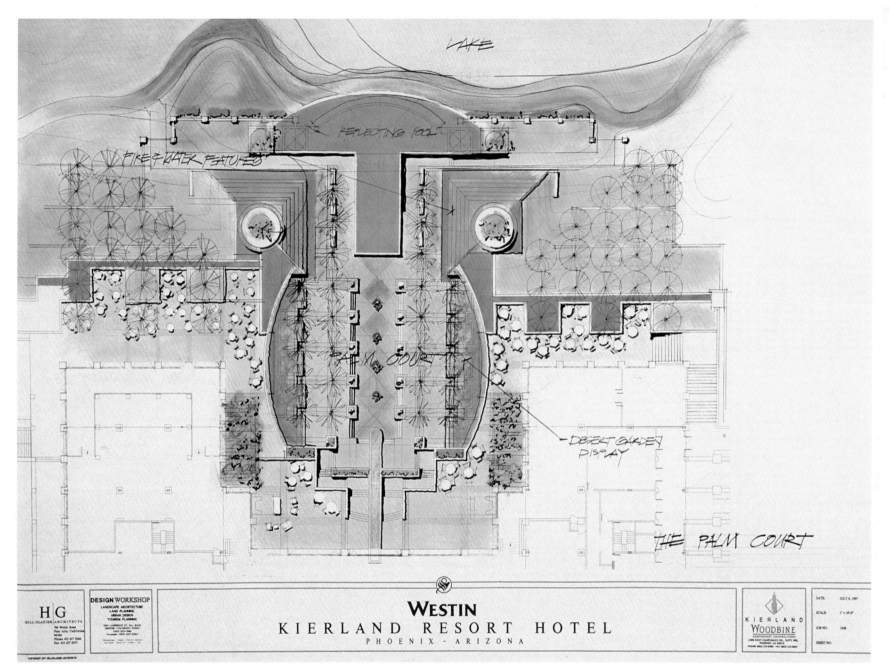

Kierland Resort Hotel. Pastels, color pencil, and black marker on white bond. The base line work is created in AutoCADD, with proposed design hand-drawn on vellum. Pastel colors are applied by hand using soft tissues.

Within the rendering, the following hand-lettered labels appear:

- *LAKE*
- *ADVENTURE POOL COMPLEX*
- *"PALM COURT"*
- *TENNIS COURT*
- *FITNESS COURT*
- *ARRIVAL COURT*
- *SERVICE*
- *BALLROOM ENTRY*

WESTIN
KIERLAND RESORT HOTEL
PHOENIX · ARIZONA

KIERLAND
WOODBINE

DATE: JULY 3, 1997
SCALE: 1"=40'-0"
JOB NO: 1645
SHEET NO:

Kierland Resort Hotel. Pastels, color pencil, and black marker on presentation blackline. This rendering is generated using an architectural site plan as a base, with color added on the blackline print. Note that the hand-lettered text is large and minimal. Only key spatial areas are identified.

41

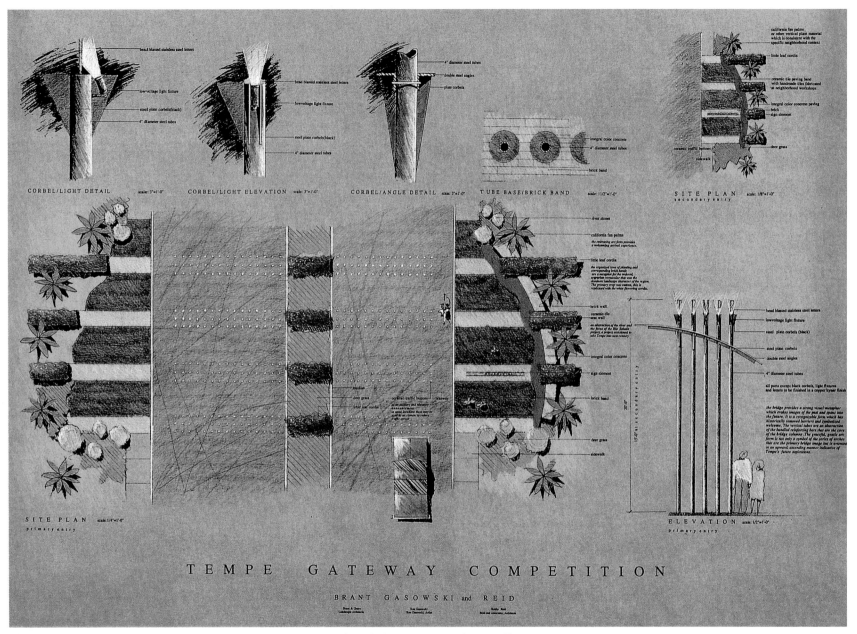

Tempe Gateway. Color pencil on kraft paper. The base is hand-drawn using ink on vellum, with a computer-generated title block. Text callouts are computer-generated and added to the vellum base with sticky-back material. Note the use of white and light color pencils to highlight the drawing.

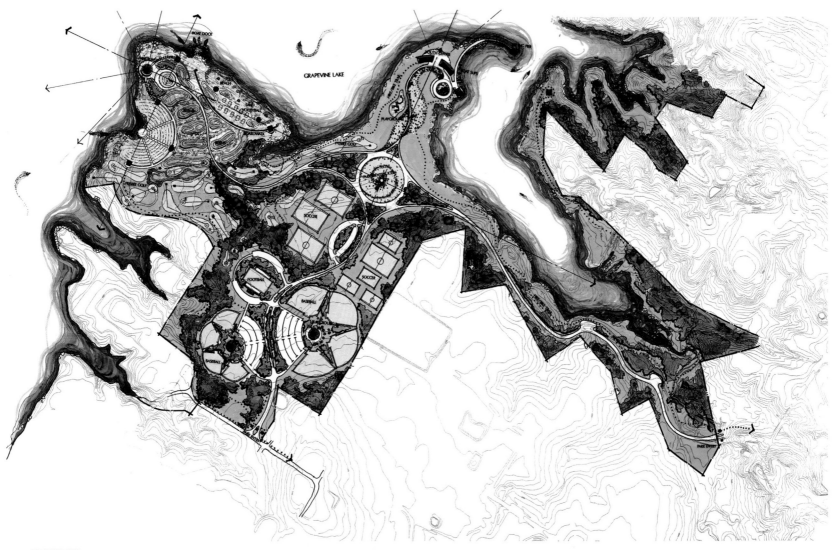

PREPARED FOR:

CITY OF GRAPEVINE
PARKS AND RECREATION
GRAPEVINE, TEXAS 76099

CONCEPTUAL MASTER PLAN SCHEME A

MEADOWMERE PARK

GRAPEVINE, TEXAS

AUGUST 28, 1998

NORTH

SCALE: 1" = 200'-0"

PREPARED BY:

MESA
DESIGN GROUP

Meadowmere Park. Color marker on white trace paper over
computer-generated base.

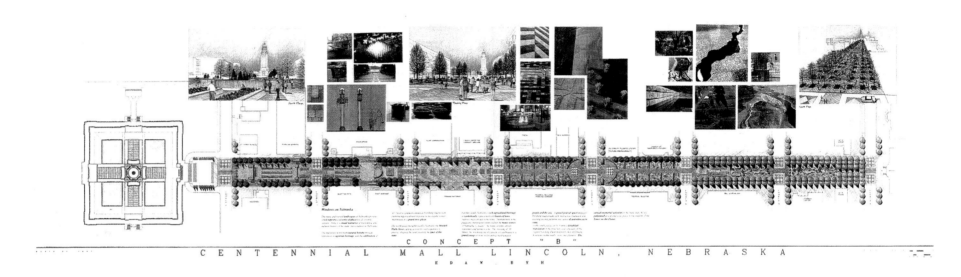

CENTENNIAL MALL LINCOLN, NEBRASKA

Centennial Mall. Color pencil on presentation blackline, with color images mounted directly on the original. The base drawing is freehand, using a CADD base as a guide.

banco seating, arbor and fireplace

palm container & metal grill

palm armature

urn and pilaster

central court plan
scale: 1/8" = 1'-0

MISSION PALMS
Hotel & Conference Center

Brant & Grovy
Landscape Architects

February 25, 1988

Tempe Mission Palms. Color pencil on kraft paper. The elevational views may not directly correspond to the plan drawing for reference, but they are laid out in a very simple fashion. Note that the elevation titles align in each direction.

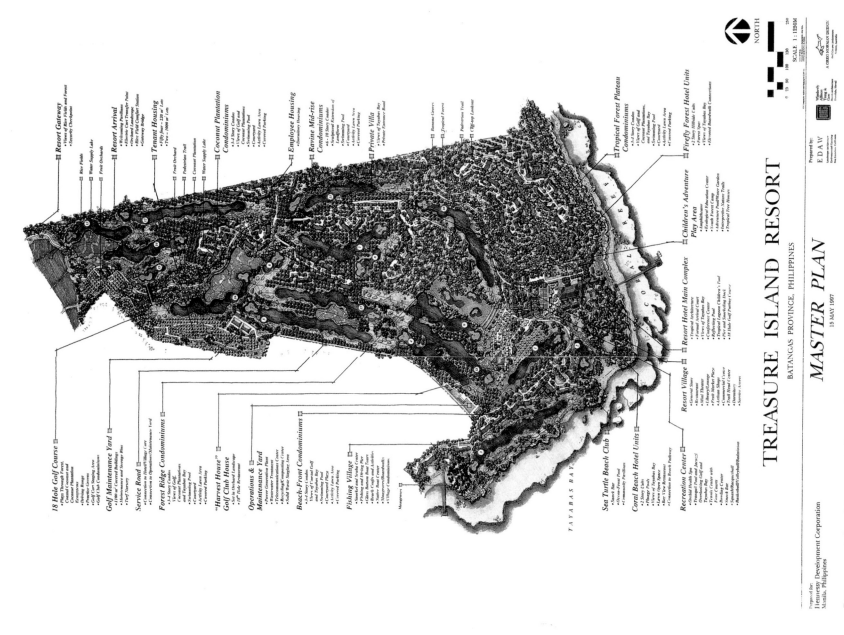

Resort Gateway
- Views of Rice Fields and Forest
- Security Checkpoint

Resort Arrival
- Welcome Pavilion
- Electric Cart Transfer Point
- Orchard Landscape
- Rice Field Comfort Station
- Gateway Bridge

Tenant Housing
- Fifty-four – 220 m² Lots
- Two – 1000 m² Lots

Rice Fields
Water Supply Lake
Fruit Orchards

Coconut Plantation Condominiums
- 3-4 Story Condos
- Coconut Plantations
- Swimming Pool
- Courtyard
- Activity Lawn Area
- Covered Parking

Fruit Orchard
Coconut Plantation
Pedestrian Trail
Water Supply Lake

Employee Housing
- Dormitory Housing

Ravine Mid-rise Condominiums
- 6 - 10 Story Condos
- Sculptural Extension of Landform
- Swimming Pool
- Courtyard
- Activity Lawn Area
- Covered Parking

Private Villa
- 1-2 Story Condos
- Views of Golf and Tayabas Bay
- Activity Lawn Area
- Covered Parking
- Private Entrance Road

Tropical Forest Plateau Condominiums
- 3-4 Story Condos
- Views of Golf and Coconut Plantation, and Tayabas Bay
- Swimming Pool
- Courtyard
- Activity Lawn Area
- Covered Parking

Firefly Forest Hotel Units
- 2 Story Hillside Units
- Forest Spa
- Views of Tayabas Bay
- Elevated Boardwalk Connectors

Banana Grove
Tropical Forest
Pedestrian Trail
Hilltop Lookout

Children's Adventure Play Area
- Amphitheatre
- Ecological Education Center
- Youth Forest Camp
- Adventure Pool/Water Garden
- Interpretive Nature Trails
- Tropical Tree Houses

Resort Hotel Main Complex
- Tropical Architecture
- Formal Arrival Court
- Views of Tayabas Bay
- Conference Center
- Reflecting Pool
- Tropical Lagoon Children's Pool
- Pier and Snorkeling Dock
- 18 Hole Golf Putting Course

Resort Village
- General Store
- Restaurant
- Mini Theater
- Library/Lounge
- Fresh Market Place
- Artisan Shops
- Commercial Center
- Trail Head Center
- Dormitory
- Service Access

18 Hole Golf Course
- Plays Through Forest, Coastal Coconut and Coastal Plantation Ecosystems
- Driving Range
- Practice Greens
- Golf Cart Staging Area
- Golf Club Condominiums

Golf Maintenance Yard
- 1100 m² Covered Buildings
- Maintenance and Sewage Plant
- Turf Nursery

Service Road
- Connection to Hotel/Village Core
- Connection to Operations/Maintenance Yard

Forest Ridge Condominiums
- 3-4 Story Condos
- Views of Golf, Coconut Plantation and Tayabas Bay
- Swimming Pool
- Courtyard
- Activity Lawn Area
- Covered Parking

"Harvest House" Golf Club House
- Sits in Coconut Landscape
- 18th Hole Relaxation

Operations & Maintenance Yard
- Power Generation Plant
- Wastewater Treatment
- Telecommunication Center
- Recycling/Composting Center
- Solid Waste Supplier, Area

Beach-Front Condominiums
- 3-4 Story Condos
- Views of Coastal Golf and Tayabas Bay
- Swimming Pool
- Courtyard Plaza
- Activity Lawn Area
- Covered Parking

Fishing Village
- Snorkel and Scuba Center
- Fishing and Diving Pier
- Glass Bottom Boat Tours
- Beach Crafts and Activities
- Native Boat Center
- Bowling Center
- Snack Bar
- Squash/Racquetball
- Basketball/Volleyball/Badminton

Recreation Center
- Orchid Health Spa
- Tropical Pool and Jacuzzi Overlooking Golf and Tayabas Bay
- Tennis Center
- Fitness Center
- Snack Bar
- Village Condominiums

Coral Beach Hotel Units
- 2 Story Units
- Plunge Pools
- Views of Tayabas Bay
- Lawn Open Space
- Bar/View Restaurant
- Connection to Beach Pathway

Mangroves

Sea Turtle Beach Club
- Snack Bar
- Ocean-Front Pool
- Community Pavilions

TAYABAS BAY

NORTH

SCALE 1 : 1250M
0 25 50 100 150 250

Prepared for:
Hennessy Development Corporation
Manila, Philippines

Prepared by:
E D A W

TREASURE ISLAND RESORT
BATANGAS PROVINCE, PHILIPPINES

MASTER PLAN
15 MAY 1997

A GREG NORMAN DESIGN

Treasure Island Resort. Color marker and color pencil on presentation blackline. The design drawing is freehand over a base, plotted from AutoCADD, which includes text, title block, and screened line work.

46

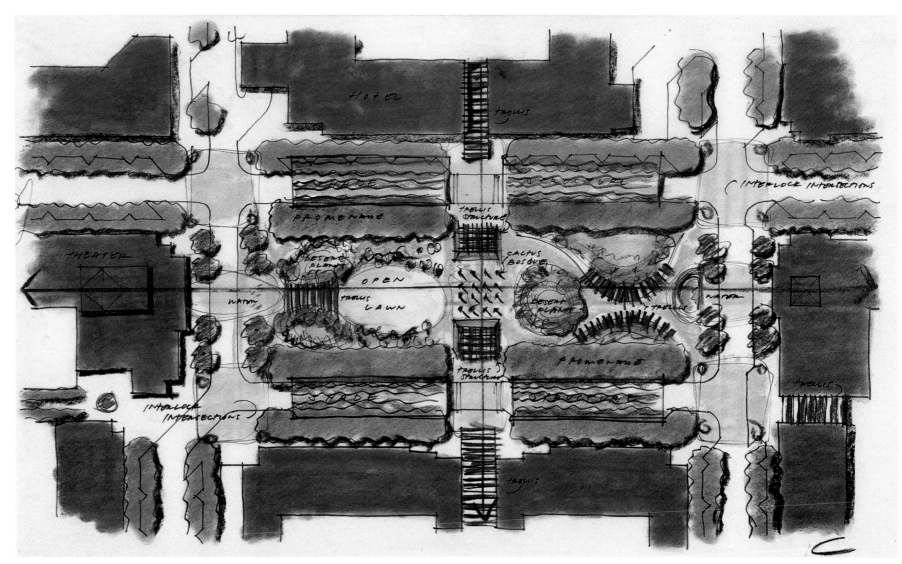

Kierland Commons. Black marker and pastels on white tracing paper. The base line work in black marker is drawn accurately, using tracing paper over an architectural site plan. Dark shadows help give depth to the drawing even at a very schematic level.

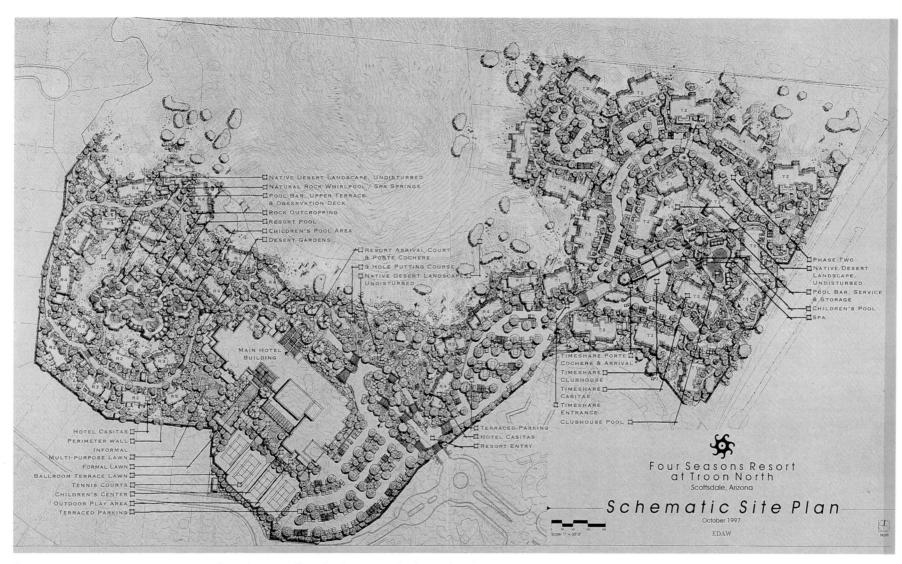

Within the site plan image, the following labels appear:

NATIVE DESERT LANDSCAPE, UNDISTURBED
NATURAL ROCK WHIRLPOOL / SPA SPRINGS
POOL BAR, UPPER TERRACE & OBSERVATION DECK
ROCK OUTCROPPING
RESORT POOL
CHILDREN'S POOL AREA
DESERT GARDENS

RESORT ARRIVAL COURT & PORTE COCHERE
9 HOLE PUTTING COURSE
NATIVE DESERT LANDSCAPE, UNDISTURBED

MAIN HOTEL BUILDING

HOTEL CASITAS
PERIMETER WALL
INFORMAL MULTI-PURPOSE LAWN
FORMAL LAWN
BALLROOM TERRACE LAWN
TENNIS COURTS
CHILDREN'S CENTER
OUTDOOR PLAY AREA
TERRACED PARKING

TERRACED PARKING
HOTEL CASITAS
RESORT ENTRY

PHASE TWO NATIVE DESERT LANDSCAPE, UNDISTURBED
POOL BAR, SERVICE & STORAGE
CHILDREN'S POOL
SPA

TIMESHARE PORTE COCHERE & ARRIVAL
TIMESHARE CLUBHOUSE
TIMESHARE CASITAS
TIMESHARE ENTRANCE
CLUBHOUSE POOL

Four Seasons Resort
at Troon North
Scottsdale, Arizona

Schematic Site Plan

October 1997

EDAW

Scale: 1" = 30'-0"

North

Four Seasons Resort at Troon North. Color pencil on kraft paper. The base drawing was created in AutoCADD to accurately show topographic and engineering aspects. The proposed design is freehand with black ink. Text is created in AutoCADD; the leaders are added in freehand on the rendering.

Four Seasons Resort at Troon North. Color pencil on kraft paper. The freehand section is scanned and imported into AutoCADD. The photographs are color reductions, spray mounted to the final rendering. Text is created in AutoCADD; the leaders are added in freehand on the rendering.

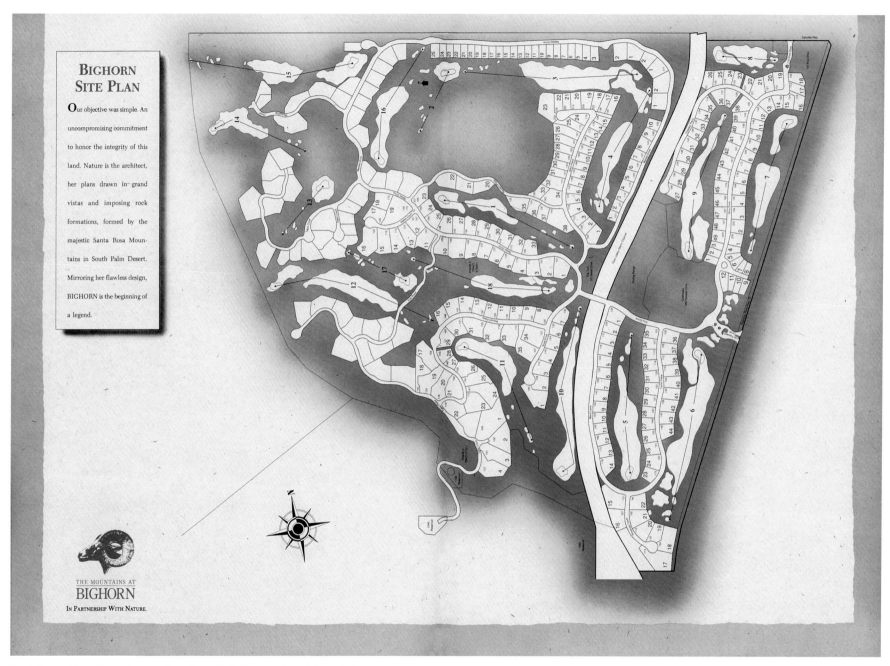

THE MOUNTAINS AT
BIGHORN
IN PARTNERSHIP WITH NATURE.

Bighorn Site Plan. CADD drawing digitally rendered in Adobe
Photoshop.

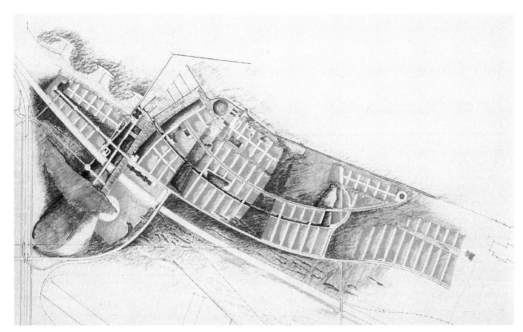

Gary Waterfront. Color pencil on vellum. The base drawing is hand-drawn ink on vellum, using a straightedge, a compass, and french curves. Color is applied directly onto the original base. Note that the absence of text and title blocks is a weakness in these renderings.

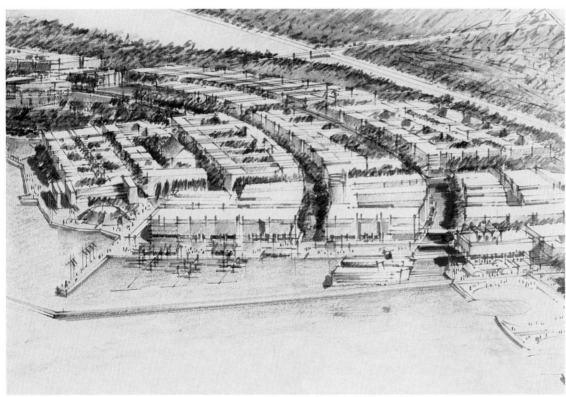

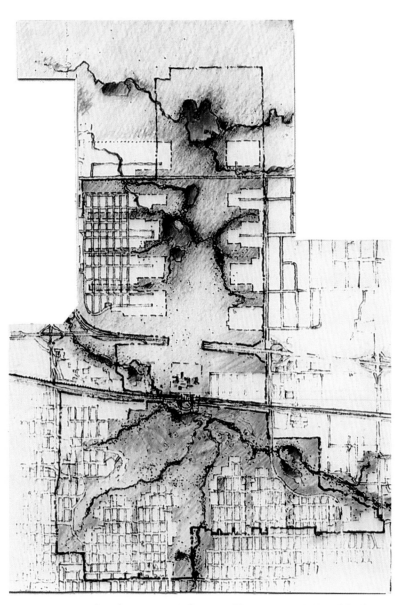

Stapleton Redevelopment. Color pencil on presentation black-line over freehand base. The base drawing is created by tracing the roadway network on an aerial. The rendering illustrates the open space between developed properties.

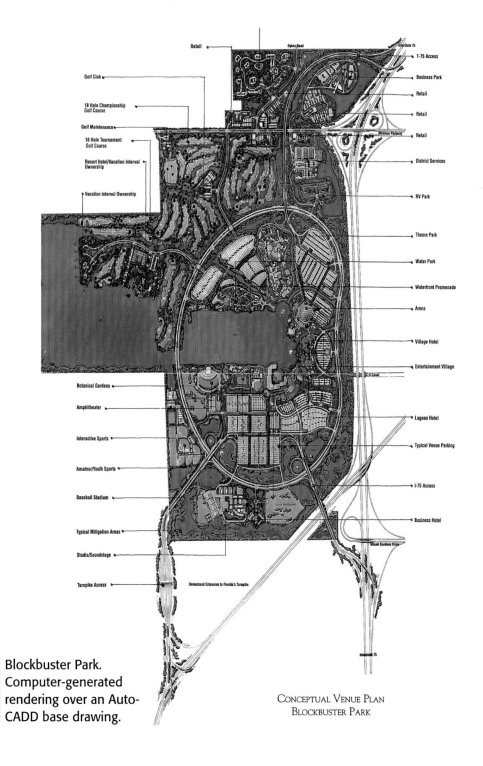

Retail
Golf Club
18 Hole Championship Golf Course
Golf Maintenance
18 Hole Tournament Golf Course
Resort Hotel/Vacation Interval Ownership
Vacation Interval Ownership
Botanical Gardens
Amphitheater
Interactive Sports
Amateur/Youth Sports
Baseball Stadium
Typical Mitigation Areas
Studio/Soundstage
Turnpike Access

Dykes Road
Interstate 75
I-75 Access
Business Park
Retail
Retail
Miramar Parkway
Retail
District Services
RV Park
Theme Park
Water Park
Waterfront Promenade
Arena
Village Hotel
Entertainment Village
Lagoon Hotel
Typical Venue Parking
I-75 Access
Business Hotel
Miami Gardens Drive
Homestead Extension to Florida's Turnpike
Interstate 75

CONCEPTUAL VENUE PLAN
BLOCKBUSTER PARK

Blockbuster Park. Computer-generated rendering over an Auto-CADD base drawing.

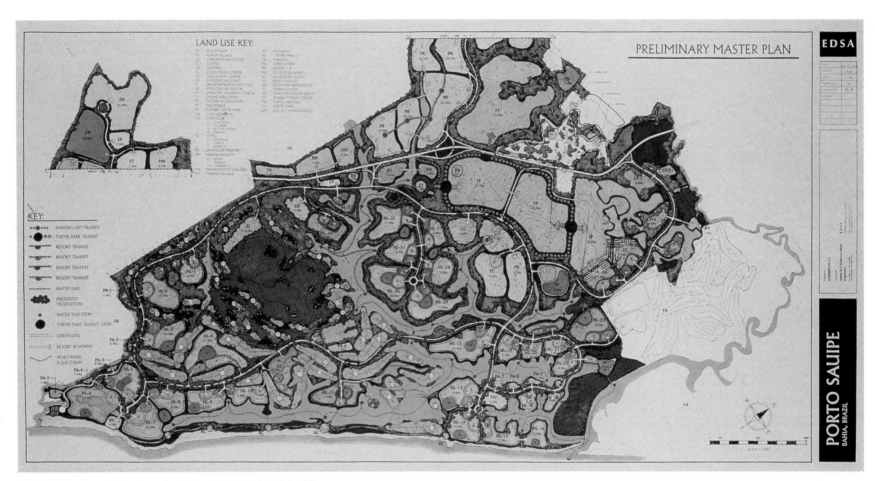

Porto Sauipe. Color marker on presentation blackline over computer-generated base.

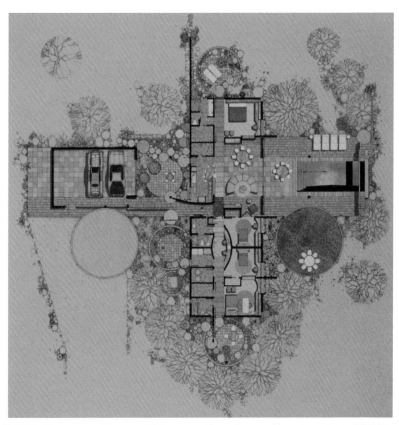

APS Showcase House. Color pencil on brownline over AutoCADD base drawing.

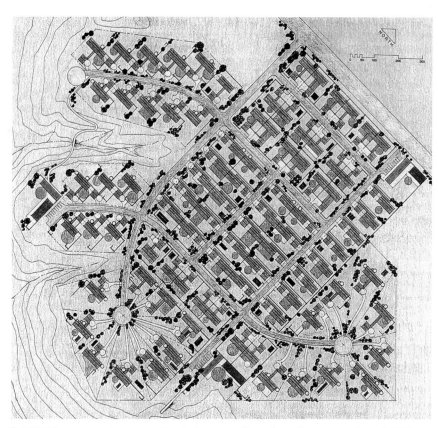

APS Showcase Community. Color pencil on bond over an AutoCADD base drawing.

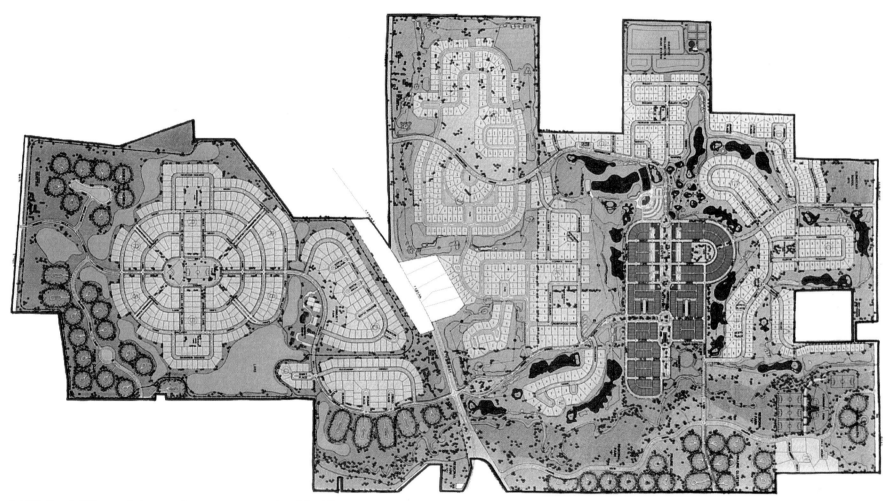

❚ Mill Creek Village. Color marker on presentation blackline.

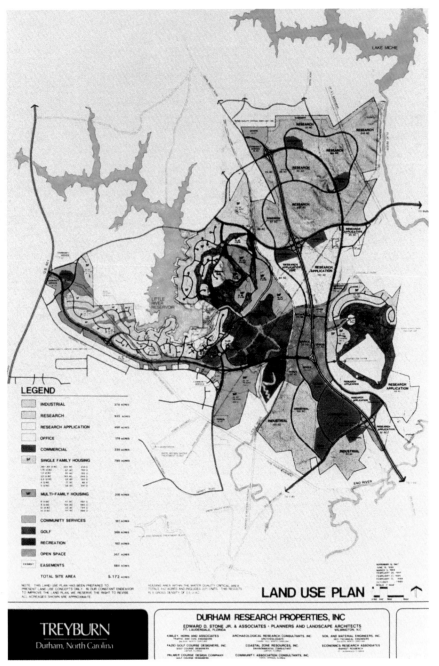

Treyburn. Color marker on presentation blackline over an Auto-CADD base.

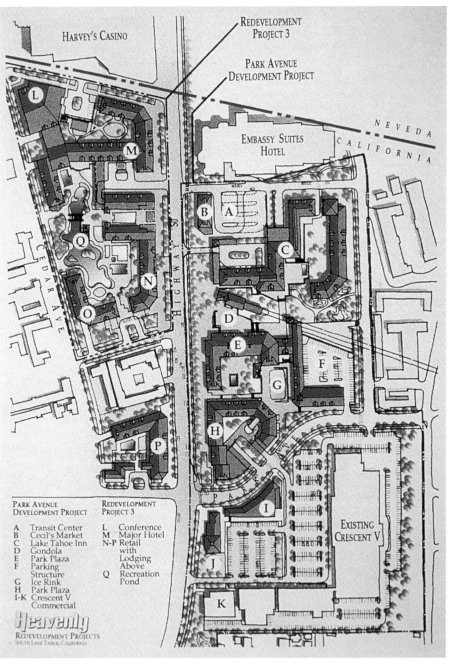

Heavenly. Color marker on presentation blackline over Auto-CADD base.

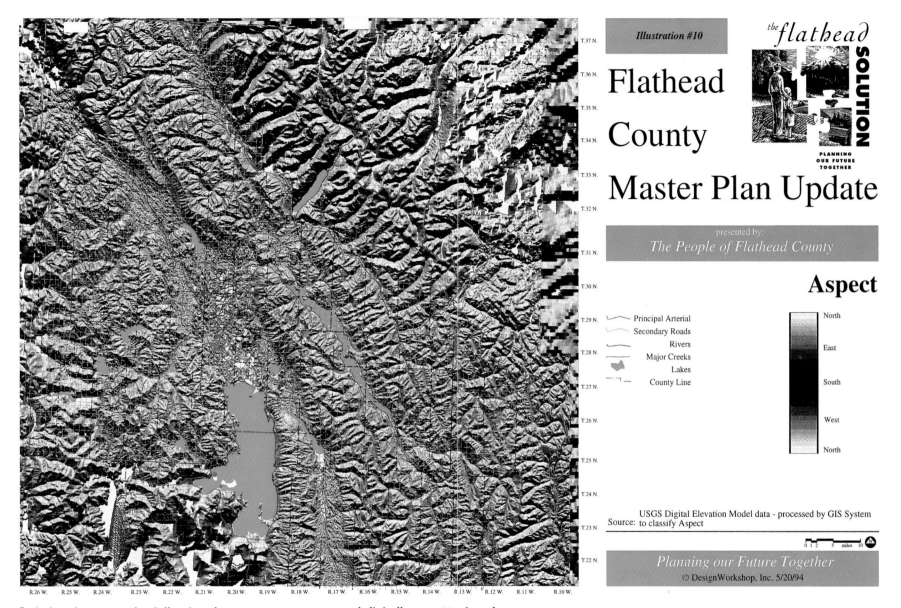

Illustration #10

the *flathead*

SOLUTION

PLANNING OUR FUTURE TOGETHER

Flathead County Master Plan Update

presented by:
The People of Flathead County

Aspect

Principal Arterial
Secondary Roads
Rivers
Major Creeks
Lakes
County Line

North

East

South

West

North

USGS Digital Elevation Model data - processed by GIS System
Source: to classify Aspect

0 1 2   5   miles   10

Planning our Future Together
© DesignWorkshop, Inc. 5/20/94

Flathead County. The following three maps are composed digitally on a Macintosh. Because of the immense size of the study area, and the complexity of planning issues, massive amounts of facts were collected and values expressed during the planning process. For these reasons, two software programs, MacGIS and MiniCAD 4, were used to create a series of analysis, inventory, and planning maps based on factual data.

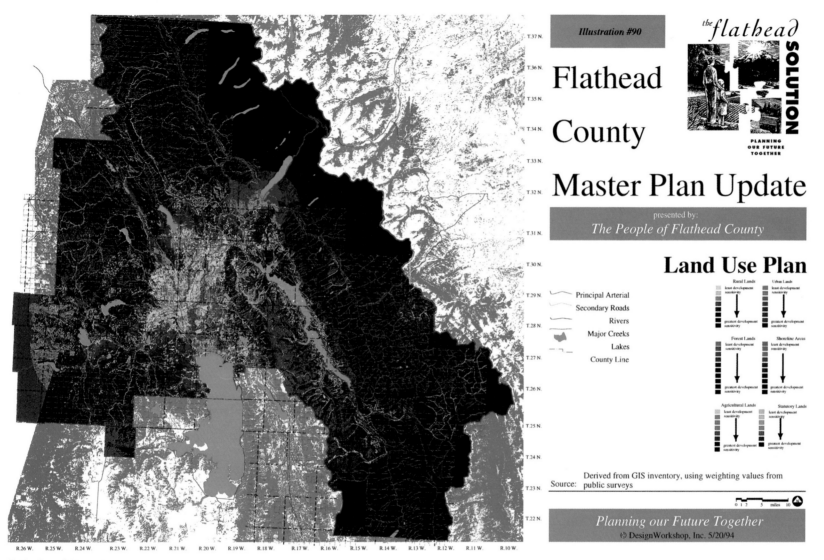

Illustration #90

Flathead County

the **flathead**
SOLUTION

**PLANNING
OUR FUTURE
TOGETHER**

Master Plan Update

presented by:
The People of Flathead County

Land Use Plan

Rural Lands	Urban Lands
least development sensitivity	least development sensitivity
↓	↓
greatest development sensitivity	greatest development sensitivity

Forest Lands	Shoreline Areas
least development sensitivity	least development sensitivity
↓	↓
greatest development sensitivity	greatest development sensitivity

Agricultural Lands	Statutory Lands
least development sensitivity	least development sensitivity
↓	↓
greatest development sensitivity	greatest development sensitivity

Principal Arterial
Secondary Roads
Rivers
Major Creeks
Lakes
County Line

Source: Derived from GIS inventory, using weighting values from public surveys

0 1 2   5   miles   10

Planning our Future Together
DesignWorkshop, Inc. 5/20/94

❚ Flathead County.

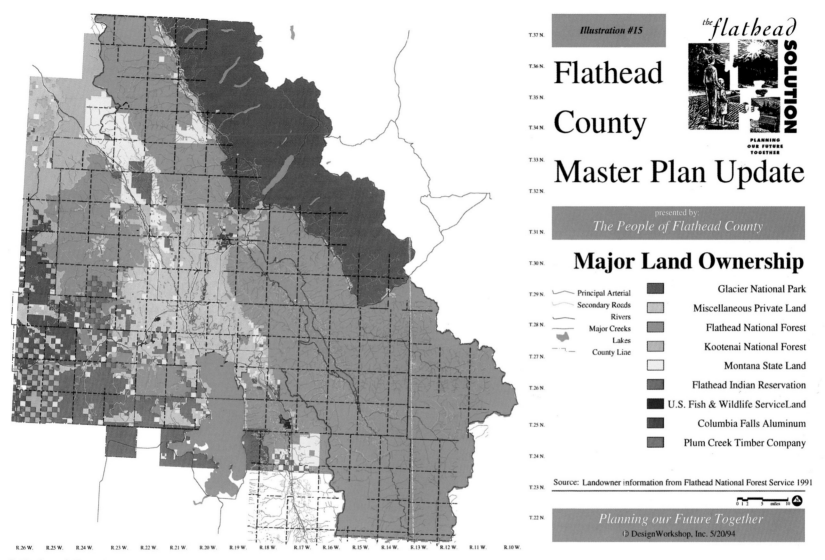

Illustration #15

Flathead County Master Plan Update

the *flathead* **SOLUTION**

PLANNING OUR FUTURE TOGETHER

presented by:
The People of Flathead County

Major Land Ownership

Principal Arterial	Glacier National Park
Secondary Roads	Miscellaneous Private Land
Rivers	Flathead National Forest
Major Creeks	Kootenai National Forest
Lakes	Montana State Land
County Line	Flathead Indian Reservation
	U.S. Fish & Wildlife ServiceLand
	Columbia Falls Aluminum
	Plum Creek Timber Company

Source: Landowner information from Flathead National Forest Service 1991

0 1 2   5   miles   10

Planning our Future Together
© DesignWorkshop, Inc. 5/20/94

❚ Flathead County.

LEGEND

ENTRY FEATURE DRIVE 1
ARRIVAL PLAZA 2
PARKING GARAGE ENTRY/EXIT 3
AMPHITHEATER 4
ROOMS 5
BACK OF HOUSE 6
RESTAURANT 7
BREEZEWAY 8
POOL AND DECK 9
SERVICE 10
PARKING GARAGE EXIT 11
VILLA UNITS 12
TENNIS/FITNESS CENTER 13
OUTDOOR EVENTS/COOKOUT AREA 14
HORSE STABLES AND TACK ROOM 15
SCENIC OVERLOOK 16

SITE PLAN

D E S E R T   S T A R   R E S O R T
A T   S T A R R   P A S S
T U C S O N   A R I Z O N A

DEV-CON ASSOCIATES
350 BAY STREET, SUITE 1200
TORONTO, CANADA. M5H 2S6

ALLEN & PHILP ARCHITECTS
7000 E. CAMELBACK RD. SUITE 300
SCOTTSDALE, ARIZONA. 85251

Desert Star Resort. Color marker on blackline. The concentration of color and detail in the center of the drawing is used to highlight the heart of the conceptual site plan. The viewer's focus is intended to be drawn to the center of the design concept.

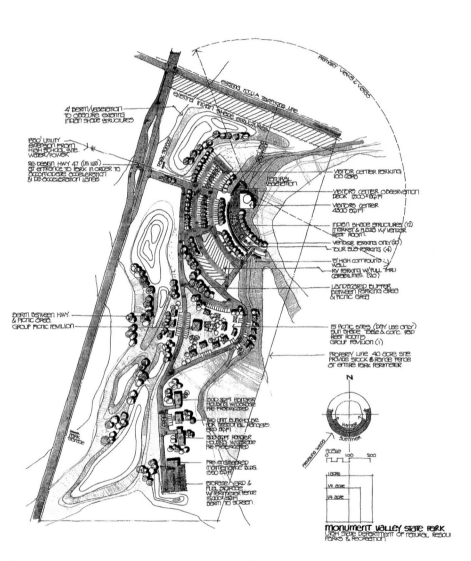

Monument Valley State Park. Color pencil on bond with hand-lettered text.

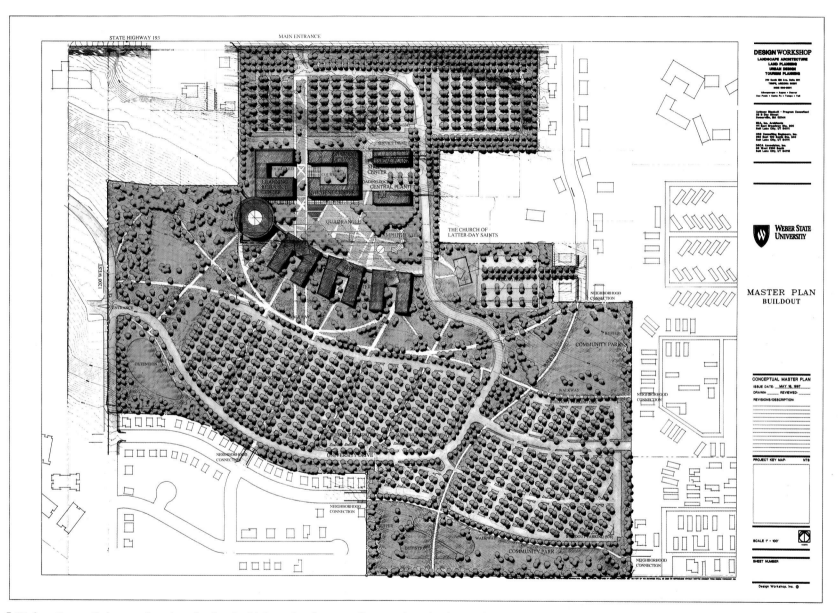

Weber State. Color marker (on the back side) and color pencil on mylar. The base plot, from an AutoCADD file, is printed on single-sided frosted mylar. Ink baselines and color marker are applied to the back, nonfrosted side. Color pencil is applied to the front, frosted side.

Summerlin. Color pencil on overexposed sepia paper. Photographs and postprint images are manually applied to the rendered graphic.

Walnut Creek. Color pencil and photographs in collage format on brownline paper.

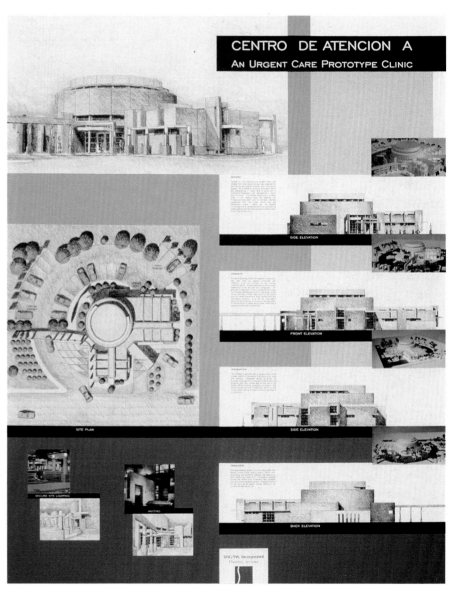

Urgent Care Prototype. Color pencil renderings scanned and formatted in Adobe Pagemaker and plotted on special paper.

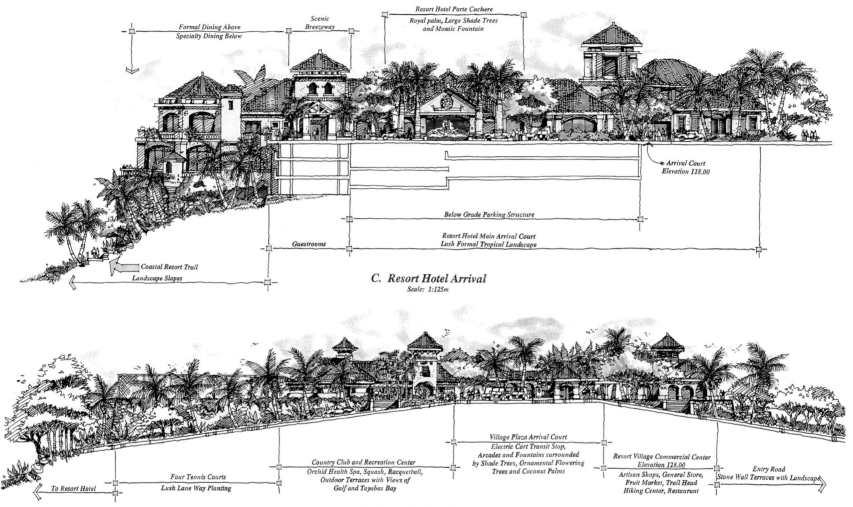

Formal Dining Above
Specialty Dining Below

Scenic
Breezeway

Resort Hotel Porte Cochere
Royal palm, Large Shade Trees
and Mosaic Fountain

Arrival Court
Elevation 118.00

Below Grade Parking Structure

Guestrooms

Resort Hotel Main Arrival Court
Lush Formal Tropical Landscape

Coastal Resort Trail
Landscape Slopes

C. Resort Hotel Arrival
Scale: 1:125m

Village Plaza Arrival Court
Electric Cart Transit Stop,
Arcades and Fountains surrounded
by Shade Trees, Ornamental Flowering
Trees and Coconut Palms

Resort Village Commercial Center
Elevation 128.00
Artisan Shops, General Store,
Fruit Market, Trail Head
Hiking Center, Restaurant

Entry Road
Stone Wall Terraces with Landscape

Country Club and Recreation Center
Orchid Health Spa, Squash, Racquetball,
Outdoor Terraces with Views of
Golf and Tayabas Bay

Four Tennis Courts
Lush Lane Way Planting

To Resort Hotel

D. Resort Village Square
Scale: 1:125m

TREASURE ISLAND RESORT

BATANGAS PROVINCE, PHILIPPINES

Prepared for:
Hennessy Development Corporation
Manila, Philippines

MASTER PLAN
15 MAY 1997

Prepared by:

EDAW
Landscape Architecture
Environmental Planning
San Francisco, California

Wimberly
Allison
Tong &
Goo
Resort Architecture
Honolulu, Hawaii

A GREG NORMAN DESIGN
Golf Course Architecture
Sydney, Australia

Treasure Island MP. Color marker and color pencil on presentation blackline. The design
drawing is freehand over a base, plotted from AutoCADD, which includes text, title block,
and screened line work.

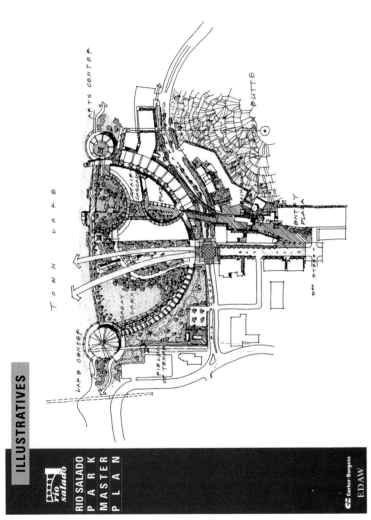

Rio Salado Park. Color pencil freehand original is scanned into AutoCADD and plotted with color title block.

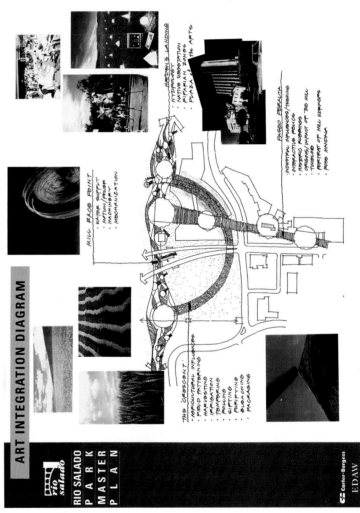

Rio Salado Park. Color pencil freehand original is scanned into AutoCADD and plotted with color title block. The photographs are scanned images, imported into AutoCADD, and plotted with color sketches.

NBBJ
VHB
McNamara/Salvia
Cosentini
EDAW
Turner

Aerial View

The Reebok World Headquarters

Reebok World Headquarters. Watercolor paint on watercolor paper over a wire-frame base. A three-dimensional wire-frame base in a CADD program is used to establish desired perspective views and aid in the creation of an accurate freehand line drawing.

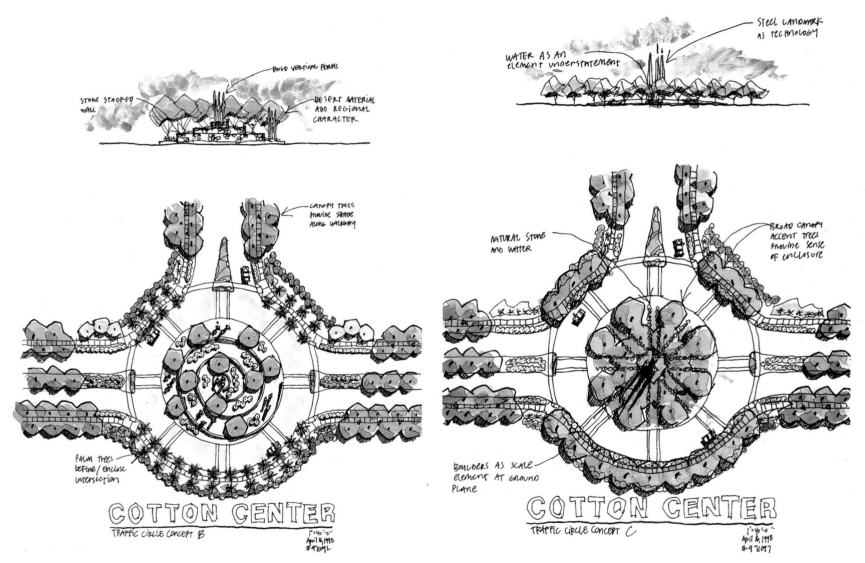

STEEL LANDMARK
AS TECHNOLOGY

WATER AS AN
ELEMENT UNDERSTATEMENT

BOLD VERTICAL FORMS

STONE STACKED
WALL

DESERT MATERIAL
ADD REGIONAL
CHARACTER

NATURAL STONE
AND WATER

BROAD CANOPY
ACCENT TREES
PROVIDE SENSE
OF ENCLOSURE

CANOPY TREES
PROVIDE SHADE
ALONG WALKWAY

PALM TREES
DEFINE / ENCLOSE
INTERSECTION

BOULDERS AS SCALE
ELEMENTS AT GROUND
PLANE

COTTON CENTER

TRAFFIC CIRCLE CONCEPT B

COTTON CENTER

TRAFFIC CIRCLE CONCEPT C

▌Cotton Center. Freehand in ink on tracing paper with color marker on original.

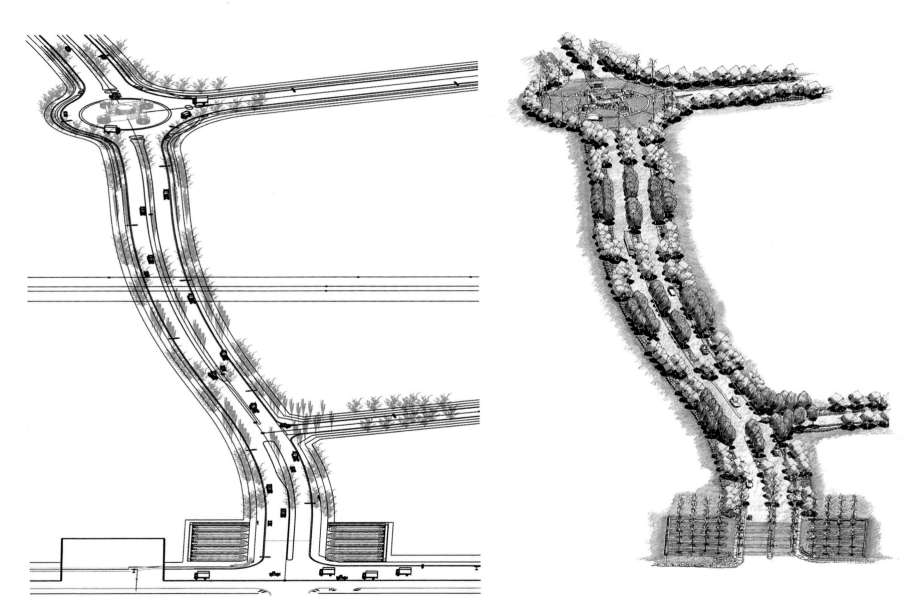

Cotton Center. Color pencil on presentation blackline. The base drawing was created in AutoCADD using 3-D modeling. A plot of the base bird's-eye view was traced freehand and printed on presentation blackline prior to rendering.

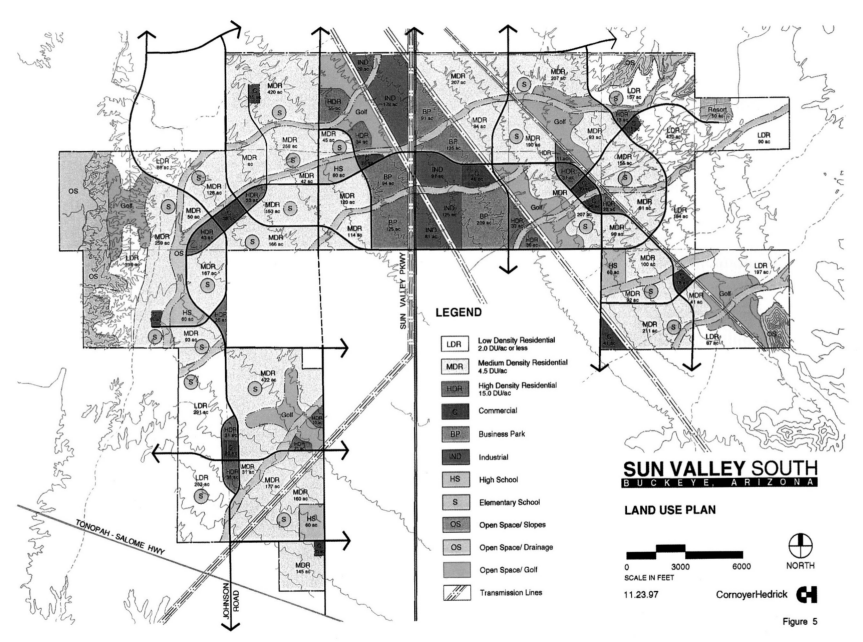

LEGEND

LDR	Low Density Residential 2.0 DU/ac or less
MDR	Medium Density Residential 4.5 DU/ac
HDR	High Density Residential 15.0 DU/ac
C	Commercial
BP	Business Park
IND	Industrial
HS	High School
S	Elementary School
OS	Open Space/ Slopes
OS	Open Space/ Drainage
	Open Space/ Golf
	Transmission Lines

SUN VALLEY SOUTH
B U C K E Y E ,   A R I Z O N A

LAND USE PLAN

0   3000   6000
SCALE IN FEET

NORTH

11.23.97   CornoyerHedrick

Figure 5

▌ Sun Valley South. Rendering in Adobe Illustrator over AutoCADD base.

69

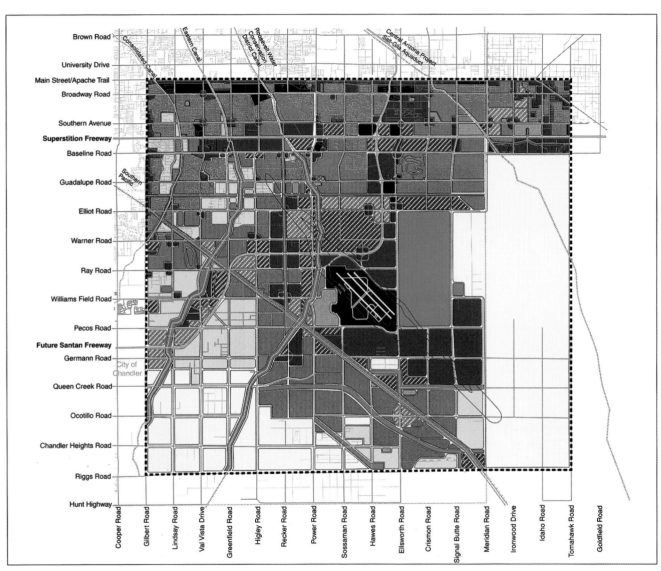

WRPS Land Use Plan

Rural Residential (0-1 DU/AC)
Maricopa County: Rural Residential (0-1 DU/AC)
Mesa: Low Density Residential (0-1 DU/AC)
Queen Creek: Very Low Density Residential (0-1 DU/AC)

Low Density Residential (1-2 DU/AC)
Gilbert: Low Residential (0-3 DU/AC)
Maricopa County: Suburban Residential (0-2 DU/AC)
Mesa: Medium-Low Density Residential (1-2 DU/AC)
Queen Creek: Low Density Residential (1-2 DU/AC)

Medium Density Residential (2-5 DU/AC)
Gilbert: Medium Residential (0-4 DU/AC)
Maricopa County: Urban Residential/Low (0-6 DU/AC)
Mesa: Medium Density Residential (2-5 DU/AC)
Queen Creek: Medium Density Residential (2-6 DU/AC)

Medium-High Density Residential (5-15 DU/AC)
Gilbert: Medium-High Residential (4-8 DU/AC)
Maricopa County: Urban Residential/Medium (0-12 DU/AC)
Mesa: Medium-High Density Residential (5-15 DU/AC)

High Density Residential (15+ DU/AC)
Maricopa County: Urban Residential/High (0-25 DU/AC)
Mesa: High Density Residential (15+ DU/AC)

Mixed Use
(High Density Residential, Commercial, Office, Commerce Park)
Gilbert: Multi-Use Employment
Maricopa County: Mixed Use Center
Mesa: Commercial/Office
Queen Creek: Town Center

Commercial/Office
Gilbert: Multi-Use Commercial
Queen Creek: Town Center

Commercial
Gilbert: Community Commercial
Mesa: Regional, Community and Neighborhood Commercial

Proving Grounds

Commerce Park/Agri-Business
Mesa: Commerce Park
Queen Creek: Employment-Type B

Industrial/Agri-Business
Maricopa County: Light Industrial Center
Mesa: General Industrial
Queen Creek: Employment-Type A

Aviation Related Industrial

Public/Quasi-Public
Gilbert: Public/Institutional
Mesa: Public/Semi-Public/School
Queen Creek: Public/Quasi-Public

Open Space
Gilbert: Open Space
Maricopa County: Open space
Mesa: Park/Open Space
Queen Creek: Open Space

- - - Noise Contours

▪▪▪▪ WRPS Study Area Boundary

WILLIAMS REGIONAL PLANNING STUDY

Source: BRW, Inc. November 28, 1995

0 FT   4800   9,600   14,400

B R W

Williams Regional Plan Study. Computer-generated land use plan plotted from Adobe Freehand. The base drawing is built in AutoCADD from numerous sources. The AutoCADD file is converted to Adobe Illustrator using "Cadmover" software, then exported into Adobe Freehand.

Site Analysis

Project research and site analysis generally constitute the first phase of the design process. The purpose of site analysis is to collect, verify, and examine all physical, environmental, cultural, and legal data available that affects a subject site. Understanding a site's relationship to the surrounding context is an important part of the analysis. In establishing the limits of the base map, be sure to include enough of the context that will affect the site development. The graphic representation of a site analysis will likely be accompanied by written documentation in greater detail covering the cultural, social, economic, and market analyses. A key objective of a site analysis plan is to identify clearly the opportunities and constraints of potential development.

CHAPTER THREE

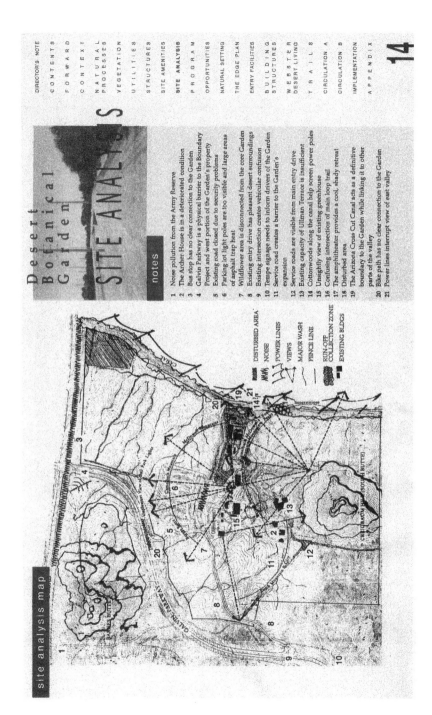

DIRECTOR'S NOTE
CONTENTS
FORWARD
CONTEXT
NATURAL PROCESSES
VEGETATION
UTILITIES
STRUCTURES
SITE AMENITIES
SITE ANALYSIS
PROGRAM
OPPORTUNITIES
NATURAL SETTING
THE EDGE PLAN
ENTRY FACILITIES
BUILDING STRUCTURES
WEBSTER DESERT LIVING
TRAILS
CIRCULATION A
CIRCULATION B
IMPLEMENTATION
APPENDIX

14

Desert Botanical Garden

SITE ANALYSIS

notes

1. Noise pollution from the Army Reserve
2. The Archer House is in a deteriorated condition
3. Bus stop has no clear connection to the Garden
4. Galvin Parkway is a physical barrier to the Boundary Project and west portion of the Garden's property
5. Existing road closed due to security problems
6. Parking lot light poles are too visible and large areas of asphalt trap heat
7. Wildflower area is disconnected from the core Garden
8. Existing entry drive has pleasant desert surroundings
9. Existing intersection creates vehicular confusion
10. Tempe signage needs to inform drivers of the Garden
11. The Arizona Cross Cut Canal creates a barrier to the Garden's expansion
12. Service roads are visible from main entry drive
13. Existing capacity of Ullman Terrace is insufficient
14. Cottonwoods along the canal help screen power poles
15. Unsightly view of existing greenhouse
16. Confusing intersection of main loop trail
17. The amphitheater provides a cool, shady retreat
18. Disturbed area
19. The Arizona Cross Cut Canal acts as a definitive boundary to the Garden while linking it to other parts of the valley
20. Bike path has no clear connection to the Garden
21. Power lines interrupt view of east valley

site analysis map

DISTURBED AREA
NOISE
POWER LINES
VIEWS
MAJOR WASH
FENCE LINE
RUN-OFF
COLLECTION ZONE
EXISTING BLDGS

DIRECTOR'S NOTE
CONTENTS
FORWARD
CONTEXT
NATURAL PROCESSES
VEGETATION
UTILITIES
STRUCTURES
SITE AMENITIES
SITE ANALYSIS
PROGRAM
OPPORTUNITIES
NATURAL SETTING
THE EDGE PLAN
ENTRY FACILITIES
BUILDING STRUCTURES
WEBSTER DESERT LIVING
TRAILS
CIRCULATION A
CIRCULATION B
IMPLEMENTATION
APPENDIX

6

Desert Botanical Garden

VEGETATION

VEGETATION PATTERNS The natural vegetation at the Desert Botanical Garden is typical of the lower Sonoran Desert. Large Palo Verde and Ironwood trees and shrubs such as Wolfberry and Trixis delineate lush natural washes. The washes cut through the sparse Creosote flats – areas vegetated with Creosote, Bursage and occasional Foothills Palo Verde and Saguaro. Creigbaum Hill (the south butte) is fairly dense with vegetation because of the granite substrate. It is covered in Brittlebush, Bursage, Foothills Palo Verde Creosote and Saguaro. Although the same vegetation exists on Barnes Butte as on Creigbaum Hill, it is not nearly as dense because of the sedimentary rock that forms the Butte.

vegetation patterns

RESEARCH AREA
HILLSIDE AREA
CREOSOTE FLATS
MAIN WASHES
CULTIVATED AREA
FENCE LINE

McDOWELL ROAD

Desert Botanical Garden. Hand-drawn analysis over a topographic map printed on mylar. The map is scanned and imported into Quark Express to be composed with photos, text, legends, and titles.

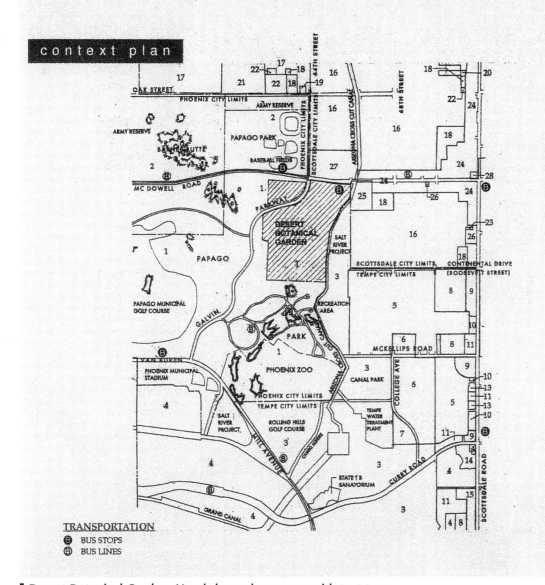

context plan

TRANSPORTATION
Ⓑ BUS STOPS
Ⓑ BUS LINES

Desert
Botanical
Garden

CONTEXT

legend

CITY OF PHOENIX

| 1 | R1-6 HP | Single Family Residential Historic Preservation |
| 2 | R1-6 | Single Family Residential |

CITY OF TEMPE

3	AG	Agricultural
4	I-1	Light Industrial
5	R1-6	One Family Residential
6	R1-4	One Family Residential
7	C-2	General Commercial
8	R-3	Multi Family Limited
9	CCD	Central Commercial District
10	R1-PAD	One Family Residential
11	R-4	Multi Family General
12	R-2	Multi Family Residential
13	CCR	Convenience Commercial Restricted
14	PCC-1	Planned Commercial Center
15	I-2	General Industrial

CITY OF SCOTTSDALE

16	R1-7	Single Family Residential
17	R1-10	Single Family Residential
18	R-5	Multifamily Residential
19	R-5 (C)	Multifamily Residential
20	R-3	Medium Density Residential
21	R-4	Townhouse Residential
22	S-R	Service Residential
23	C-1	Neighborhood Commercial
24	C-3	Highway Commercial
25	C-3 (C)	Highway Commercial
26	C-4	General Commercial
27	C-4 (C)	General Commercial
28	C-S	Regional Shopping Center
(C)		(See Zoning Ordinance for Open Space Requirements)

2

Desert Botanical Garden. Hand-drawn base map with text type added on a mylar base. The map is scanned and imported into Quark Express to be composed with text, legends, and titles.

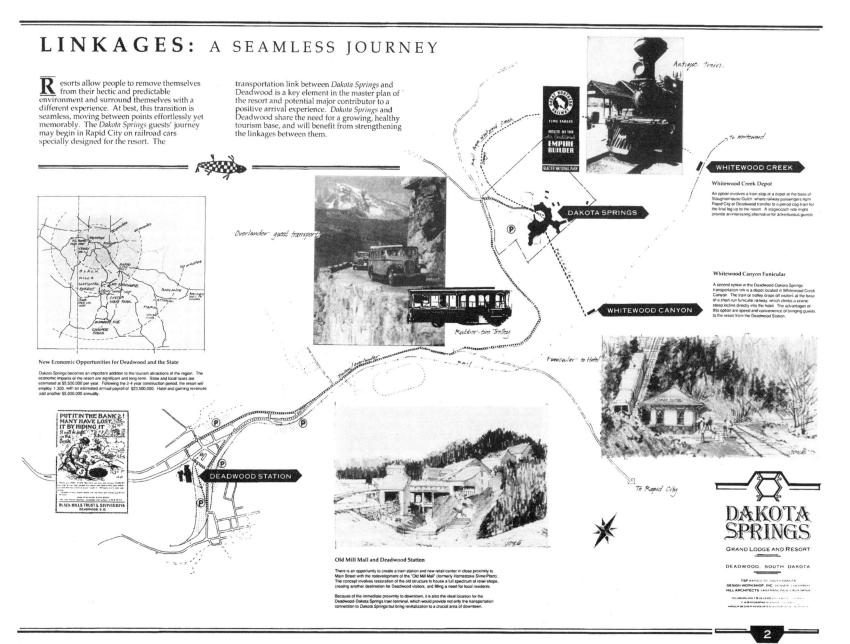

Dakota Springs. Color renderings and photographs superimposed on a context map and printed on brownline paper.

INFLUENCES OF THE LAND: SITE ANALYSIS

The development philosophy for *Dakota Springs* grows out of utmost respect for the land -- making an effort to fit the manmade environment into the existing natural environment. To that end, the land's natural systems are important to analyze and understand. If ignored, their influences on architecture and site development can significantly increase the cost of development, which in turn adversely effect the aesthetic impact on the land.

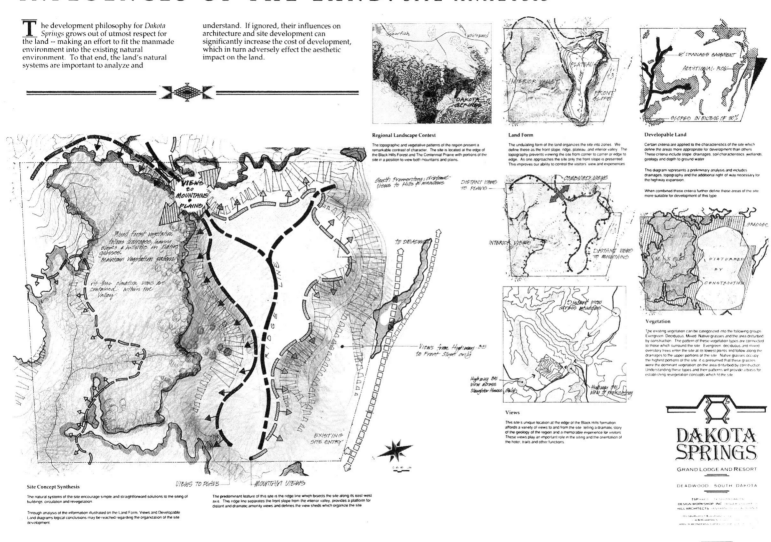

Regional Landscape Context

The topographic and vegetative patterns of the region present a remarkable contrast of character. The site is located at the edge of the Black Hills Forest and The Centennial Prairie with portions of the site in a position to view both mountains and plains.

Land Form

The undulating form of the land organizes the site into zones. We define these as the front slope, ridge, plateau, and interior valley. The topography prevents viewing the site from corner to corner or edge to edge. As one approaches the site only the front slope is presented. This improves our ability to control the visitors' view and experiences.

Developable Land

Certain criteria are applied to the characteristics of the site which define the areas more appropriate for development than others. These criteria include slope, drainages, soil characteristics, wetlands, geology and depth to ground water.

This diagram represents a preliminary analysis and includes drainages, topography and the additional right of way necessary for the highway expansion.

When combined these criteria further define those areas of the site more suitable for development of this type.

Vegetation

The existing vegetation can be categorized into the following groups: Evergreen, Deciduous, Mixed, Native grasses and the area disturbed by construction. The pattern of these vegetation types are connected to those which surround the site. Evergreen, deciduous and mixed overstory trees enter the site at its lowest points and follow along the drainages to the upper portions of the site. Native grasses occupy the highest portions of the site. It is presumed that these grasses were the dominant vegetation on the area disturbed by construction. Understanding these types and their patterns will provide a basis for establishing revegetation concepts which fit the site.

Views

This site's unique location at the edge of the Black Hills formation affords a variety of views to and from the site, telling a dramatic story of the geology of the region and a memorable experience for visitors. These views play an important role in the siting and the orientation of the hotel, trails and other functions.

Site Concept Synthesis

The natural systems of the site encourage simple and straightforward solutions to the siting of buildings, circulation and revegetation.

Through analysis of the information illustrated on the Land Form, Views and Developable Land diagrams logical conclusions may be reached regarding the organization of the site development.

The predominant feature of this site is the ridge line which bisects the site along its east-west axis. This ridge line separates the front slope from the interior valley, provides a platform for distant and dramatic amenity views and defines the view sheds which organize the site.

3

Dakota Springs. Color pencil on freehand vignettes that are organized in collage format with computer-generated text and title block. The title block and text are plotted on mylar. The vignettes are added on the mylar plot with ink. The brownline prints are rendered with color pencils and black markers.

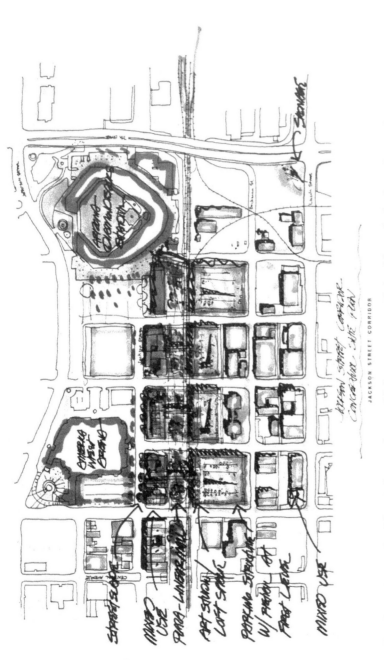

JACKSON STREET CORRIDOR

■ Jackson Street Corridor. Color marker and ink on 11" × 17" bristol board. The base image is pre-printed, with title block, on hand-held site cards to be used to record analysis during on-site reviews.

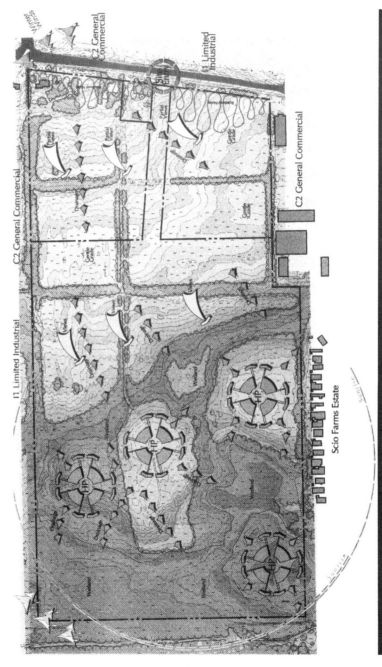

Site Analysis Summary	Hometown Village
April, 1998	of Scio
	JJR Incorporated

■ Hometown Village. Computer-generated rendering from Microstation. Printed on bond.

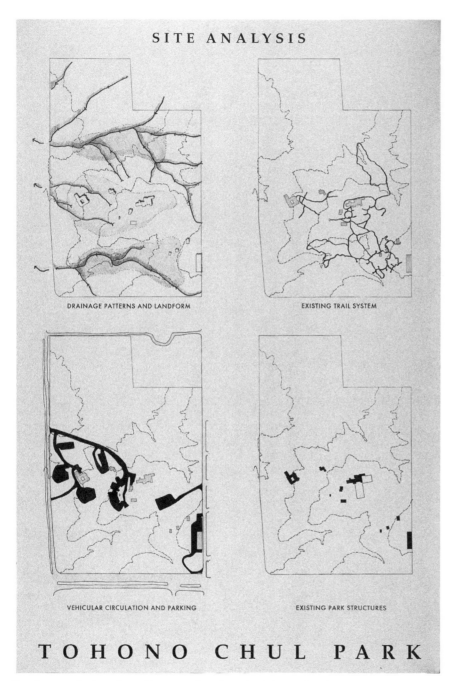

SITE ANALYSIS

DRAINAGE PATTERNS AND LANDFORM

EXISTING TRAIL SYSTEM

VEHICULAR CIRCULATION AND PARKING

EXISTING PARK STRUCTURES

TOHONO CHUL PARK

Tohono Chul Park. Color pencil on bond with freehand base drawing.

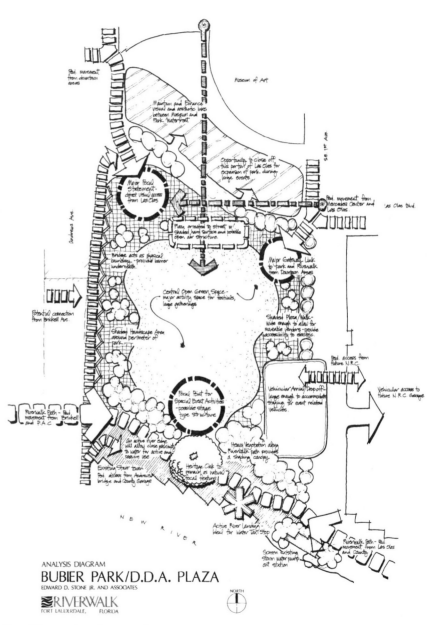

ANALYSIS DIAGRAM
BUBIER PARK/D.D.A. PLAZA
EDWARD D. STONE JR. AND ASSOCIATES

RIVERWALK
FORT LAUDERDALE, FLORIDA

Bubier Park. Ink on mylar.

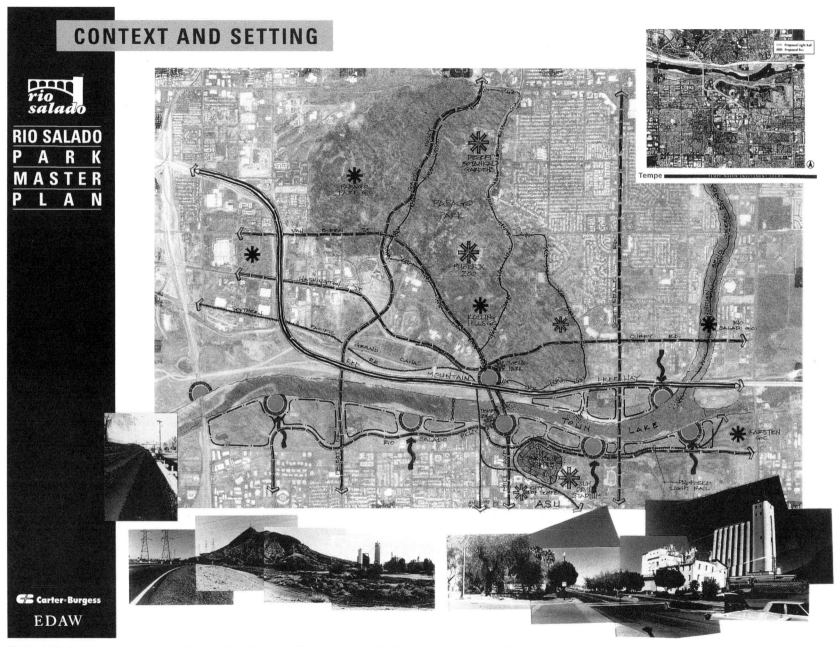

Rio Salado Park. Freehand in ink with color pencil vignettes; color images are cropped and mounted directly onto a color plot with title block from AutoCADD.

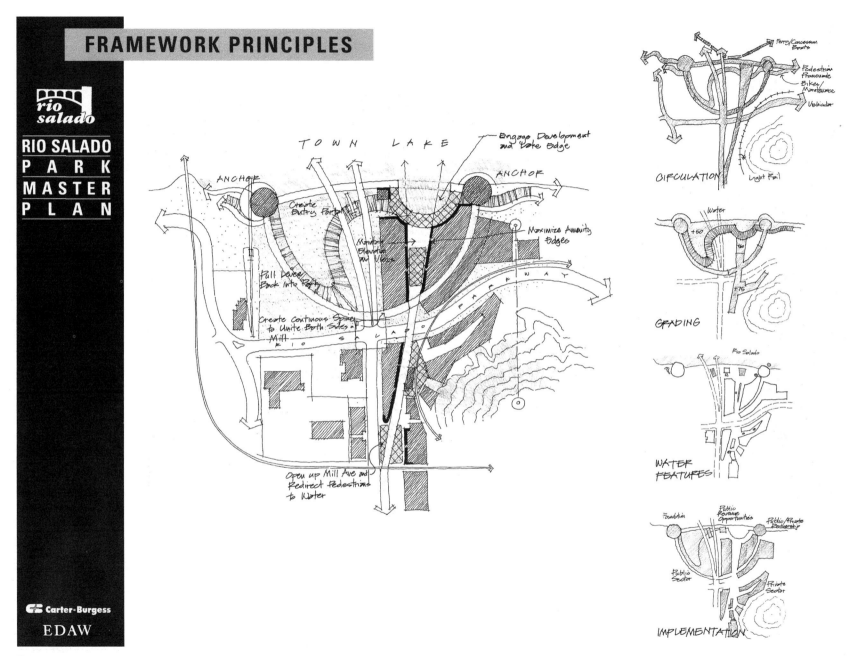

rio
salado

RIO SALADO
P A R K
M A S T E R
P L A N

Carter-Burgess

EDAW

Rio Salado Park. Freehand in ink with color pencil vignettes; color images are cropped and mounted directly onto a color plot with title block from AutoCADD.

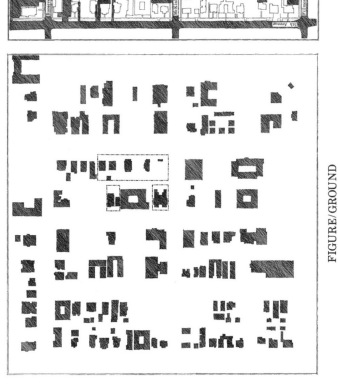

FIGURE/GROUND

ASPHALT/PARKING

Scale: 1"=100'

L A S   A N T I G U A S

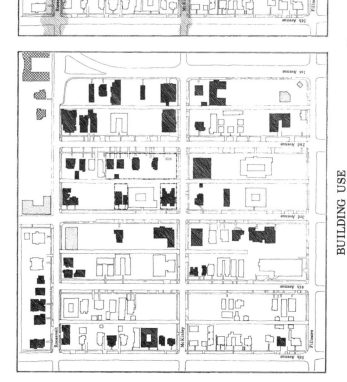

NEIGHBORHOOD CHARACTER

Scale: 1"=100'

BUILDING USE

☐ RESIDENTIAL
■ OFFICE
■ COMMERCIAL
▨ INSTITUTIONAL

L A S   A N T I G U A S

Las Antiguas. Freehand ink drawing on mylar. The base mylar is overlayed onto an aerial of existing conditions.

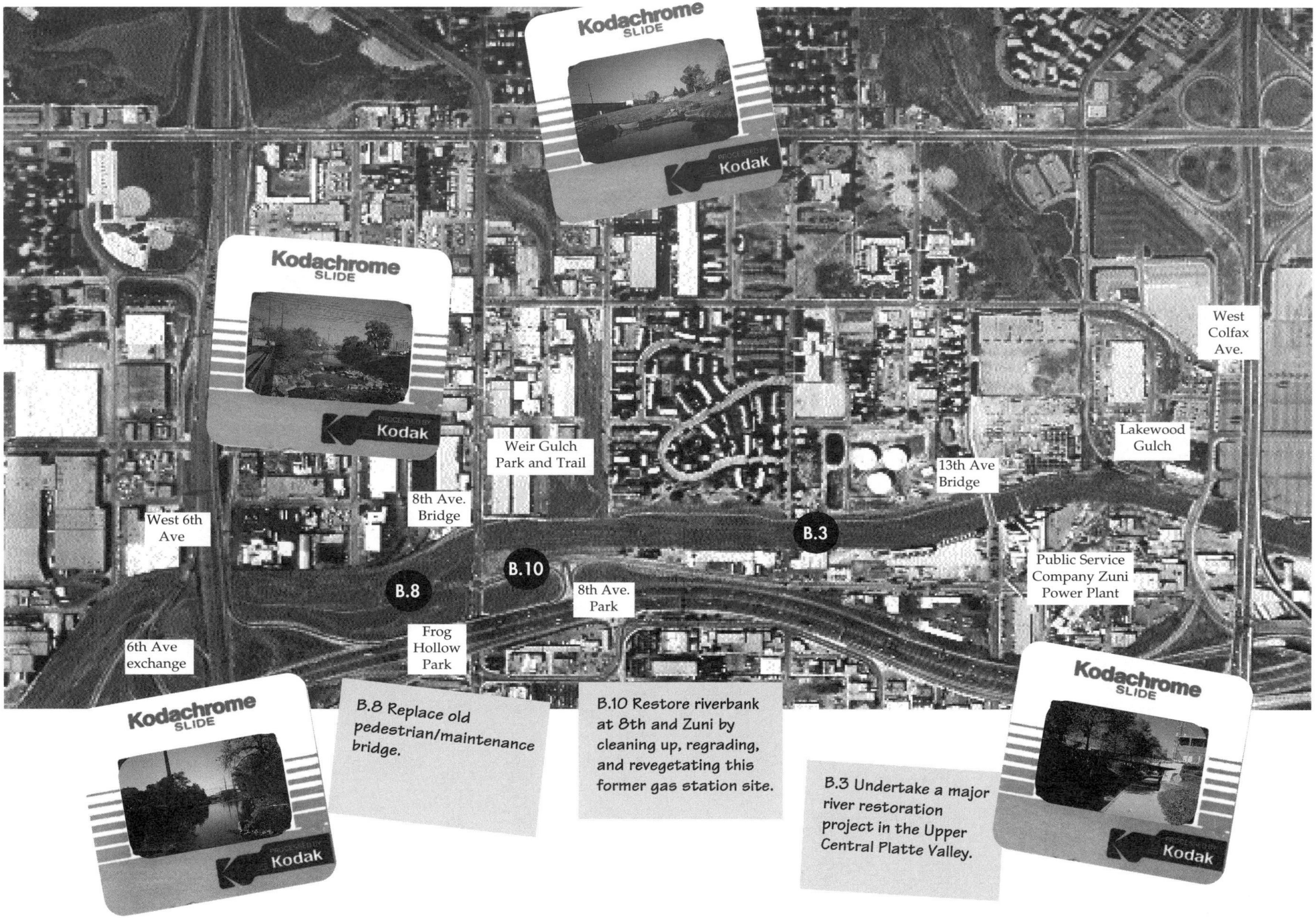

Kodachrome SLIDE
Kodak
Kodachrome SLIDE
Kodak
West Colfax Ave.
Weir Gulch Park and Trail
Lakewood Gulch
13th Ave Bridge
8th Ave. Bridge
West 6th Ave
B.3
B.10
B.8
Public Service Company Zuni Power Plant
8th Ave. Park
Frog Hollow Park
6th Ave exchange
Kodachrome SLIDE
Kodak
B.8 Replace old pedestrian/maintenance bridge.
B.10 Restore riverbank at 8th and Zuni by cleaning up, regrading, and revegetating this former gas station site.
B.3 Undertake a major river restoration project in the Upper Central Platte Valley.
Kodachrome SLIDE
Kodak

South Platte Redevelopment. Color slides and clipped text superimposed on aerial photograph.

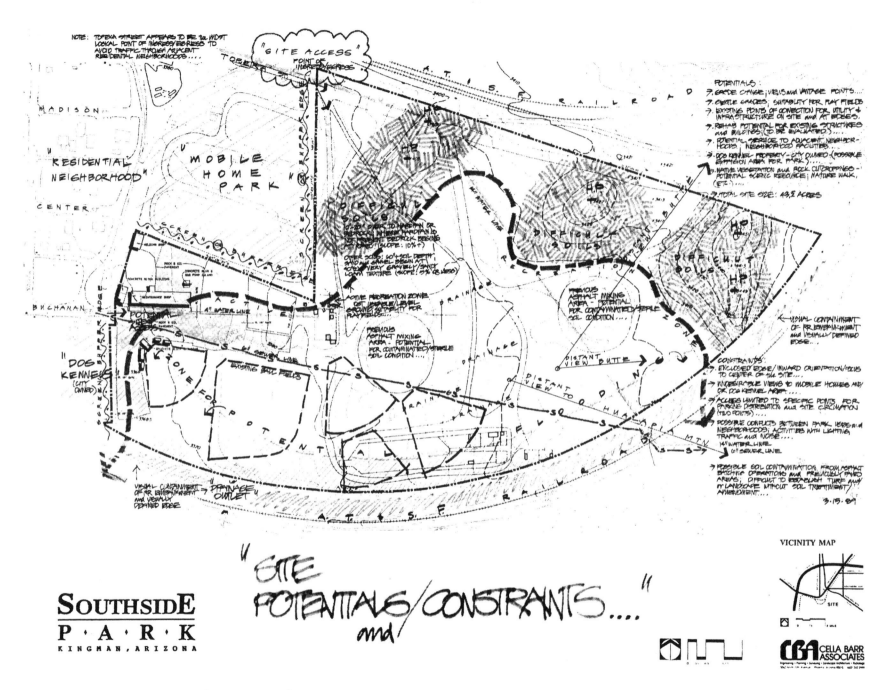

Southside Park. Freehand ink drawing on mylar.

NATIVE TREE SALVAGE PLAN

MARRIOTT SUITES at the T.P.C.

DEVELOPED BY

WALTON STREET CAPITAL L.L.C.

7373 EAST DOUBLETREE RANCH ROAD, SUITE 200
SCOTTSDALE, ARIZONA 85258

CORNOYER HEDRICK ARCHITECTS AND PLANNERS INC.

Marriott Suites. Computer-generated composite of proposed site plan over photographic aerial. The aerial is used to inventory existing native plant material that must be salvaged or removed. The aerial is scanned and x-referenced into title block and legends in AutoCADD.

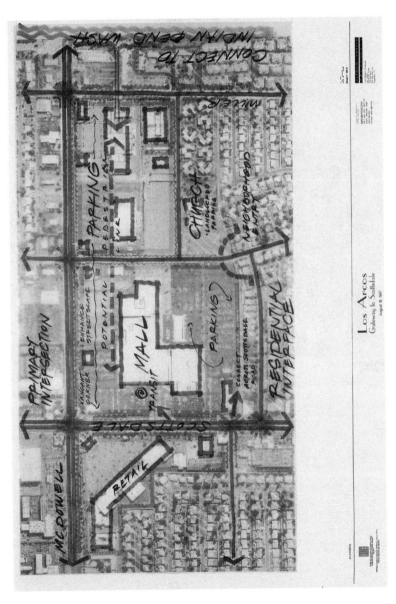

Los Arcos. Color marker on tracing paper over aerial photograph.

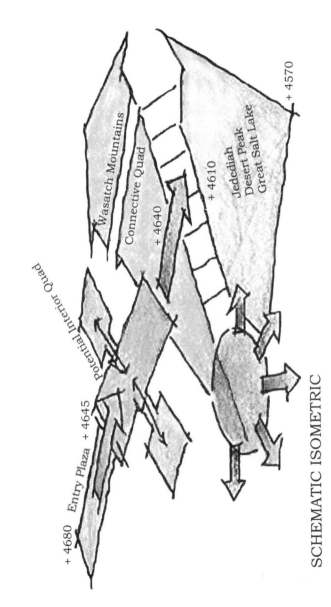

SCHEMATIC ISOMETRIC

Weber State. Color pencil on vellum with typed text manually
applied with sticky-back material.

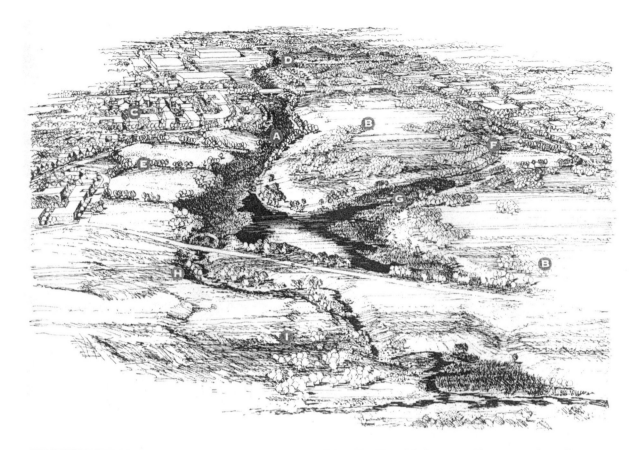

WESTERLY CREEK CORRIDOR AND SURROUNDINGS:

A birds-eye view looking south along a 1¹/₂ mile length of Westerly Creek between Sand Creek and Montview Boulevard. This segment of the corridor contains the following elements:

A) Excavation and restoration of the natural stream corridor where aircraft runways previously constricted local and regional storm flows;

B) major urban park adjacent to the District II employment neighborhood;

C) District III residential neighborhood;

D) learning golf course adjacent to Westerly Creek and the District I residential neighborhood;

E) tree-lined local drainage corridor connecting adjacent urban neighborhood flows through to Westerly Creek;

F) hierarchy of surface channels and canals convey stormwater from larger urbanized basins to water quality treatment areas;

G) ponds and wetlands where stormwater is temporarily detained allowing for biological uptake and sedimentation of pollutants and nutrients;

H) a series of grade control drop structures stabilize the stream bed, preventing further erosion; and

I) wetlands at the edge of Sand Creek valley provide wildlife habitat and improve Westerly Creek stormwater quality before entering Sand Creek.

❚ Stapleton Redevelopment. The base drawing of this analysis perspective is created with ink on vellum, then scanned and imported into graphics software for insertion of keys and notes. Note that the use of key callouts reduces the amount of text that might cover important information in the drawing.

Trails & Connections

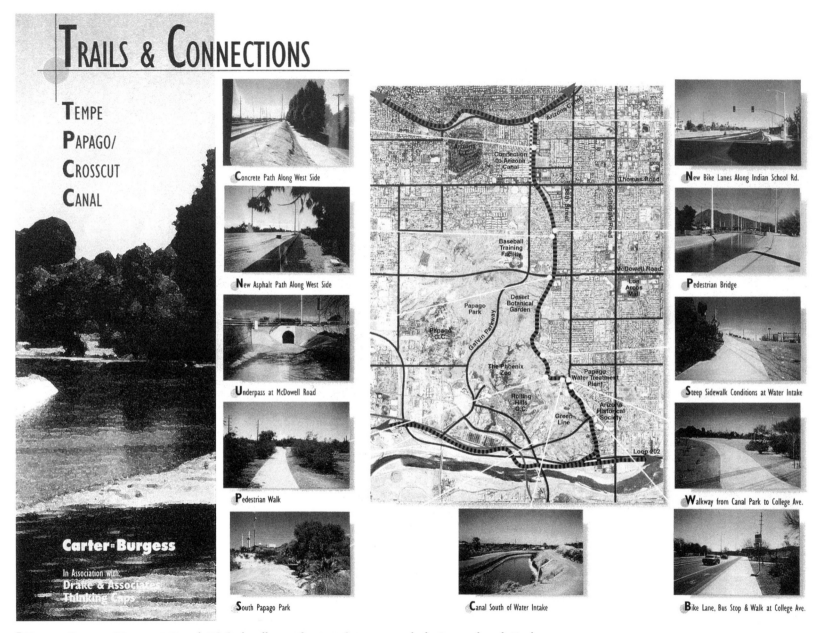

Tempe Papago/ Crosscut Canal

Carter-Burgess

In Association with:
Drake & Associates
Thinking Caps

Concrete Path Along West Side

New Asphalt Path Along West Side

Underpass at McDowell Road

Pedestrian Walk

South Papago Park

Connection to Arizona Canal

Baseball Training Facility

Papago Park

Papago G.C.

Desert Botanical Garden

Galvin Parkway

The Phoenix Zoo

Rolling Hills G.C.

Green Line

Papago Water Treatment Plant

Arizona Historical Society

Loop 202

Arizona Canal

Thomas Road

McDowell Road

Los Arcos Mall

Scottsdale Road

Canal South of Water Intake

New Bike Lanes Along Indian School Rd.

Pedestrian Bridge

Steep Sidewalk Conditions at Water Intake

Walkway from Canal Park to College Ave.

Bike Lane, Bus Stop & Walk at College Ave.

Tempe Papago/Crosscut Canal. Digital collage of maps, images, and photographs plotted on special paper. The images are scanned and imported into AutoCADD and composed around text and titles.

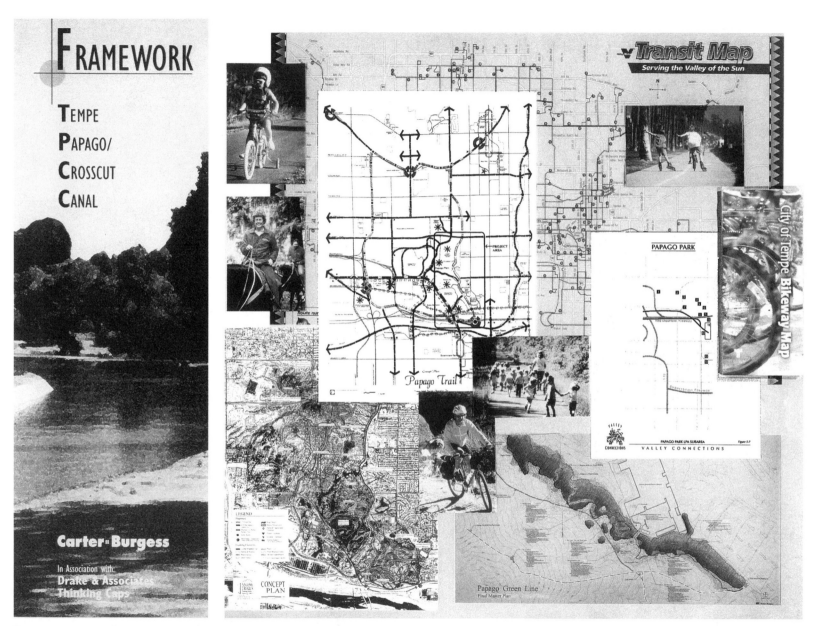

FRAMEWORK

TEMPE PAPAGO/ CROSSCUT CANAL

Carter=Burgess

In Association with:
Drake & Associates
Thinking Caps

Tempe Papago/Crosscut Canal. Digital collage of maps, images, and photographs plotted on special paper. The images are scanned and imported into AutoCADD and composed around text and titles.

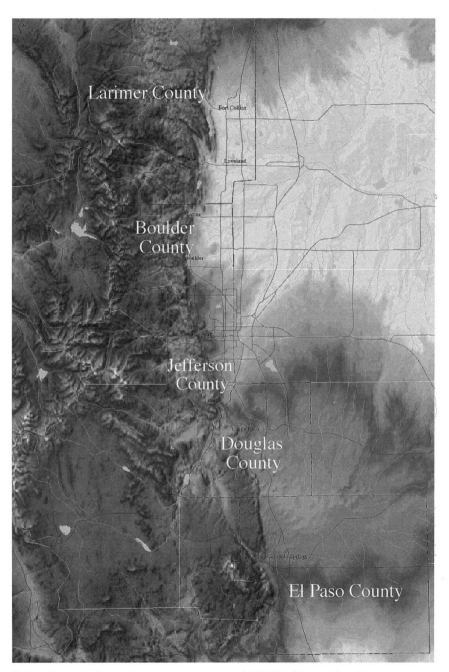

Five County Map. Computer-generated MiniCad base drawing of roadway network superimposed on satellite image.

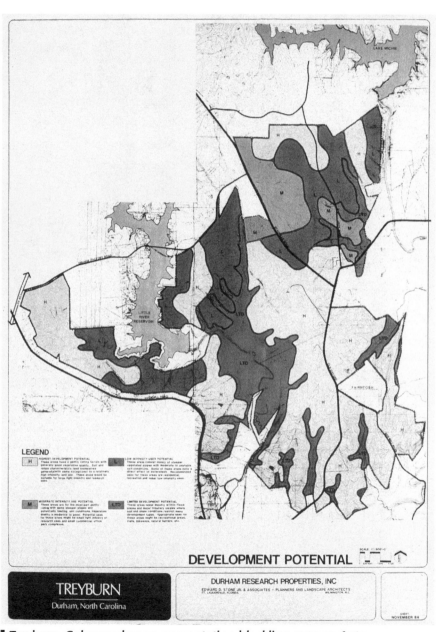

Treyburn. Color marker on presentation blackline over an Auto-CADD base.

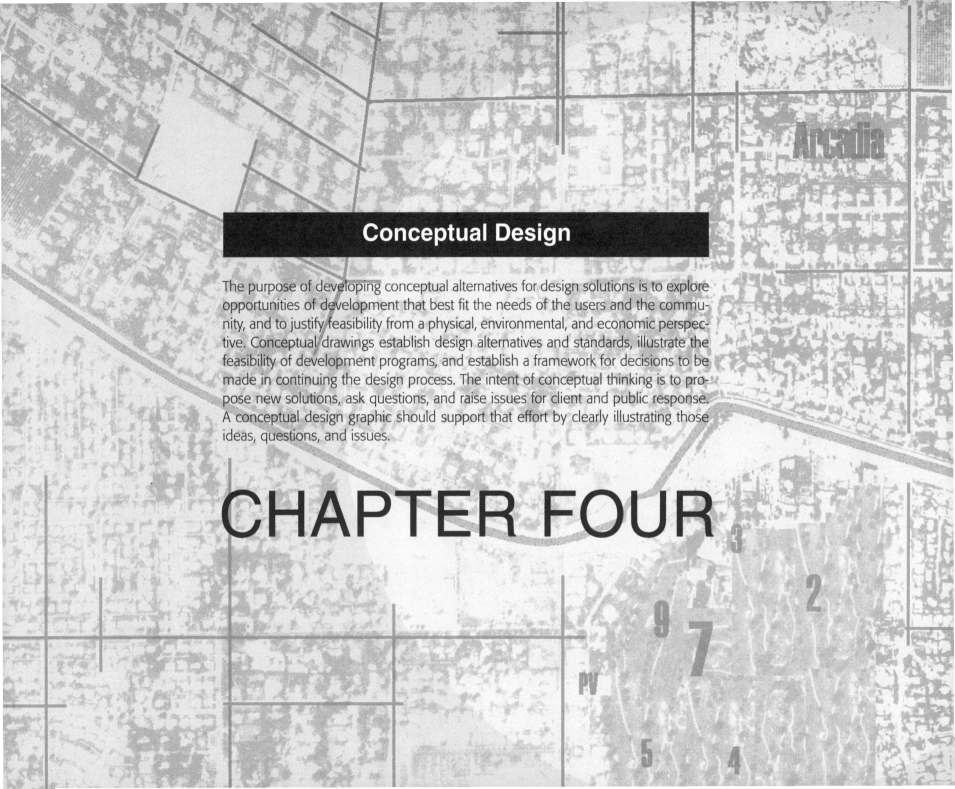

Conceptual Design

The purpose of developing conceptual alternatives for design solutions is to explore opportunities of development that best fit the needs of the users and the community, and to justify feasibility from a physical, environmental, and economic perspective. Conceptual drawings establish design alternatives and standards, illustrate the feasibility of development programs, and establish a framework for decisions to be made in continuing the design process. The intent of conceptual thinking is to propose new solutions, ask questions, and raise issues for client and public response. A conceptual design graphic should support that effort by clearly illustrating those ideas, questions, and issues.

CHAPTER FOUR

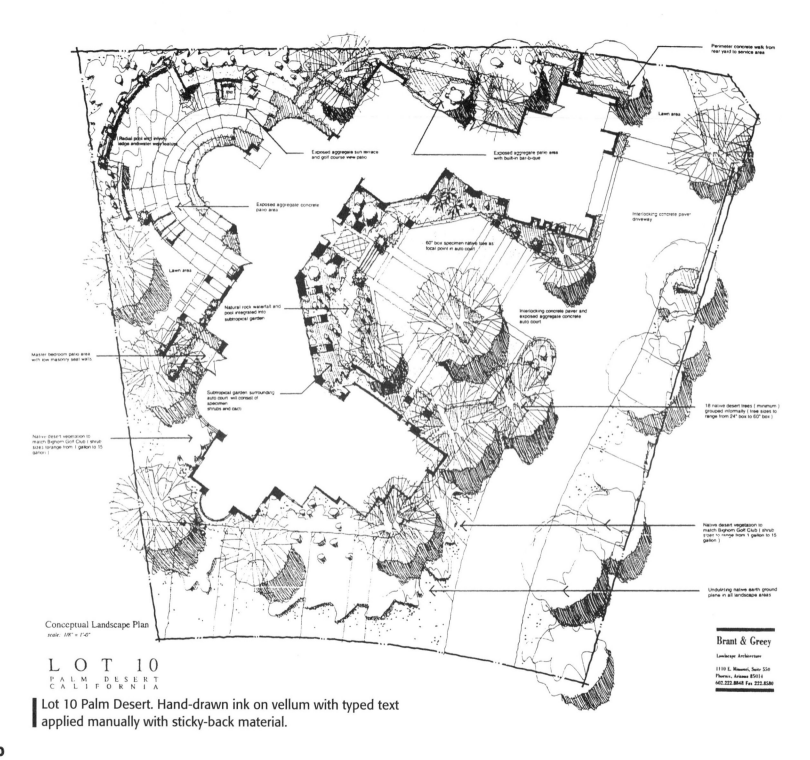

Perimeter concrete walk from rear yard to service area

Lawn area

Radial pool with infinity edge and water weir feature

Exposed aggregate sun terrace and golf course view patio

Exposed aggregate patio area with built-in bar-b-que

Exposed aggregate concrete patio area

Interlocking concrete paver driveway

60" box specimen native tree as focal point in auto court

Interlocking concrete paver and exposed aggregate concrete auto court

Natural rock waterfall and pool integrated into subtropical garden

Master bedroom patio area with low masonry seat walls

Subtropical garden surrounding auto court will consist of specimen shrubs and cacti

18 native desert trees (minimum) grouped informally (tree sizes to range from 24" box to 60" box)

Native desert vegetation to match Bighorn Golf Club (shrub sizes to range from 1 gallon to 15 gallon)

Native desert vegetation to match Bighorn Golf Club (shrub sizes to range from 1 gallon to 15 gallon)

Undulating native earth ground plane in all landscape areas

Conceptual Landscape Plan
scale: 1/8" = 1'-0"

LOT 10
PALM DESERT
CALIFORNIA

Brant & Greey

Landscape Architecture

1110 E. Missouri, Suite 550
Phoenix, Arizona 85014
602.222.8848 Fax 222.8580

| Lot 10 Palm Desert. Hand-drawn ink on vellum with typed text
| applied manually with sticky-back material.

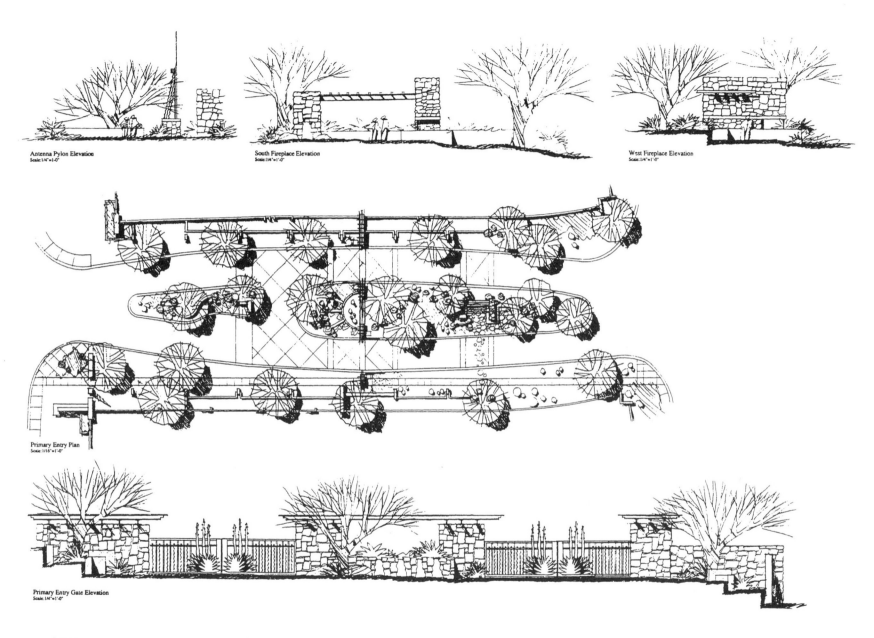

Antenna Pylon Elevation
Scale:1/4"=1'-0"

South Fireplace Elevation
Scale:1/4"=1'-0"

West Fireplace Elevation
Scale:1/4"=1'-0"

Primary Entry Plan
Scale:1/16"=1'-0"

Primary Entry Gate Elevation
Scale:1/4"=1'-0"

TROVA'S

▌ Trova's. Hand-drawn ink on vellum.

Brant & Green
Landscape Architecture

4.13.95

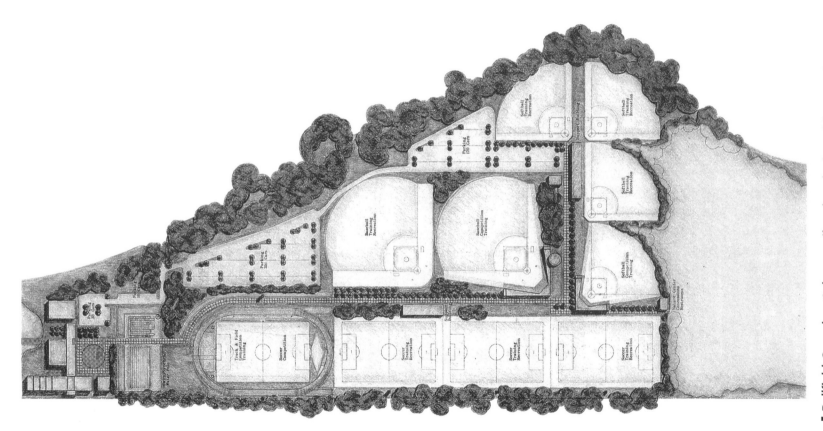

Ballfield Complex. Color pencil on bond, plotted from an Auto-CADD base drawing file.

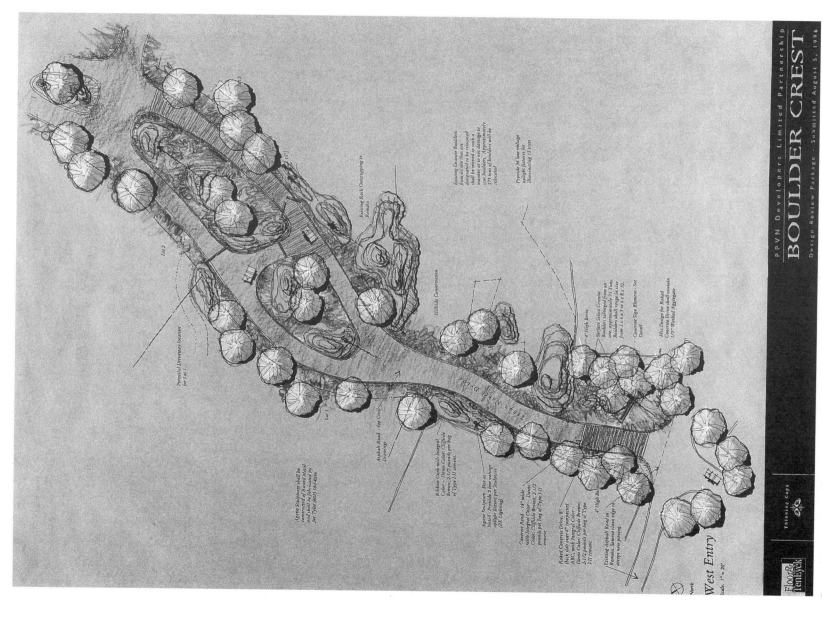

Boulder Crest. Color pencil on kraft paper with hand-drawn design over AutoCADD base.

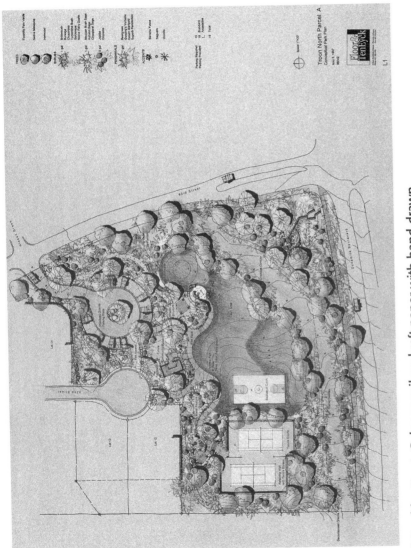

Boulder Crest. Color pencil on kraft paper with hand-drawn design over AutoCADD base.

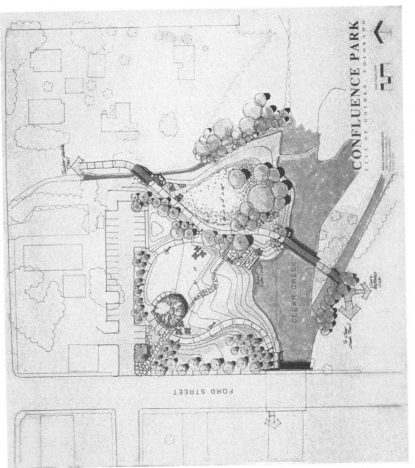

Confluence Park. Color marker on tracing paper over hand-drawn base.

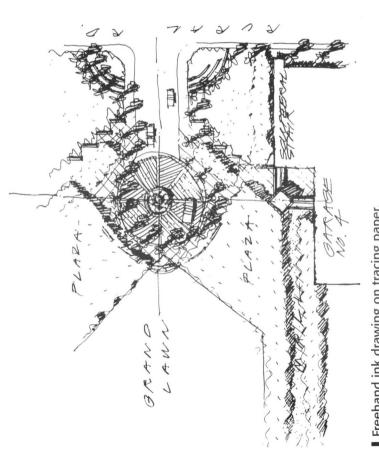

| Freehand ink drawing on tracing paper.

PLAZA

PLAZA

GRAND LAWN

GATAGE NO. 1

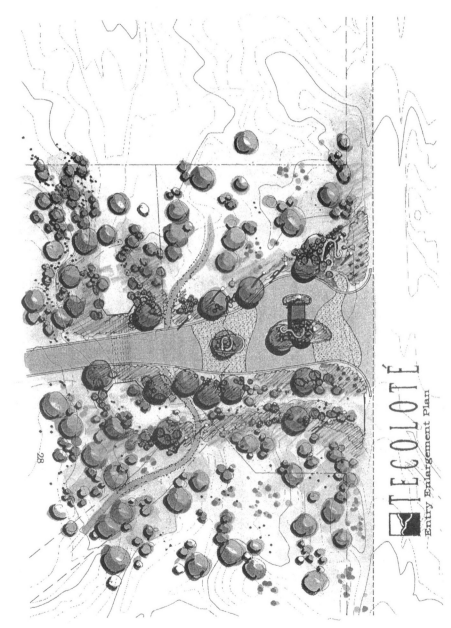

TECOLOTÉ
Entry Enlargement Plan

| Telecoté. Color marker and color pencil on presentation black-line. The base drawing is created in AutoCADD, with the land-scape design in freehand with ink.

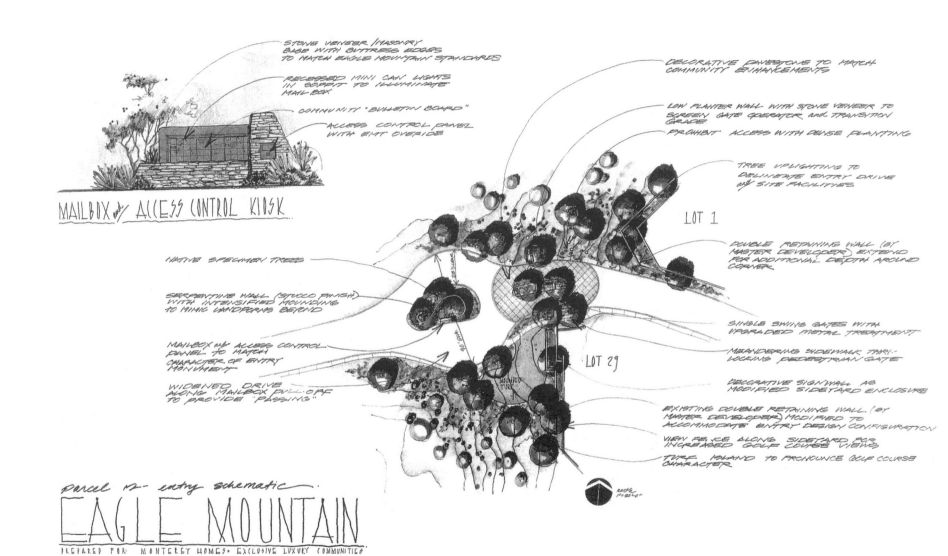

STONE VENEER/MASONRY BASE WITH BUTTRESS EDGES TO MATCH EAGLE MOUNTAIN STANDARDS

RECESSED MINI CAN LIGHTS IN SOFFIT TO ILLUMINATE MAIL BOX

COMMUNITY "BULLETIN BOARD"

ACCESS CONTROL PANEL WITH EMT OVERRIDE

MAILBOX and ACCESS CONTROL KIOSK

DECORATIVE PAVESTONE TO MATCH COMMUNITY ENHANCEMENTS

LOW PLANTER WALL WITH STONE VENEER TO SCREEN GATE OPERATOR AND TRANSITION GRADE

PROHIBIT ACCESS WITH DENSE PLANTING

TREE UPLIGHTING TO DELINEATE ENTRY DRIVE AND SITE FACILITIES

LOT 1

DOUBLE RETAINING WALL (BY MASTER DEVELOPER) EXTEND FOR ADDITIONAL DEPTH AROUND CORNER

NATIVE SPECIMEN TREES

SERPENTINE WALL (STUCCO FINISH) WITH INTENSIFIED MOUNDING TO MIMIC LANDFORMS BEYOND

MAILBOX and ACCESS CONTROL PANEL TO MATCH CHARACTER OF ENTRY MONUMENT

WIDENED DRIVE ALONG MAILBOX PULL-OFF TO PROVIDE "PASSING"

SINGLE SWING GATES WITH UPGRADED METAL TREATMENT

MEANDERING SIDEWALK THRU LOCKING PEDESTRIAN GATE

LOT 29

DECORATIVE SIGNWALL AS MODIFIED SIDEYARD ENCLOSURE

EXISTING DOUBLE RETAINING WALL (BY MASTER DEVELOPER) MODIFIED TO ACCOMMODATE ENTRY DESIGN CONFIGURATION

VIEW FENCE ALONG SIDEYARD FOR INCREASED GOLF COURSE VIEWS

TURF ISLAND TO PRONOUNCE GOLF COURSE CHARACTER

parcel 12 entry schematic

EAGLE MOUNTAIN

PREPARED FOR MONTEREY HOMES • EXCLUSIVE LUXURY COMMUNITIES

vollmer & associates

Eagle Mountain. Freehand in ink on vellum with color marker applied to presentation blackline print.

Las Hualtatas. Color marker on presentation blackline over hand-drawn base drawing.

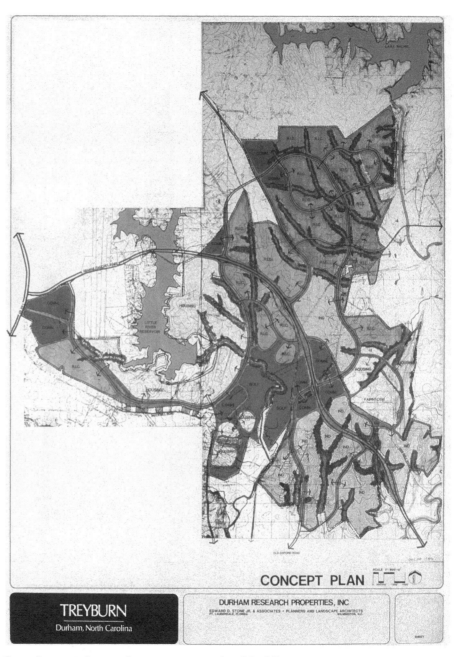

Treyburn. Color marker on presentation blackline over Auto-CADD base drawing.

OPPORTUNITIES & CONSTRAINTS

DOUGLAS ARCHITECTURE AND PLANNING

TOHONO CHUL PARK

▌Tohono Chul Park. Color pencil on bond with freehand base drawing.

CONCEPTUAL SITE PLAN

DOUGLAS ARCHITECTURE AND PLANNING

TOHONO CHUL PARK

▌Tohono Chul Park. Color pencil on bond with freehand base drawing.

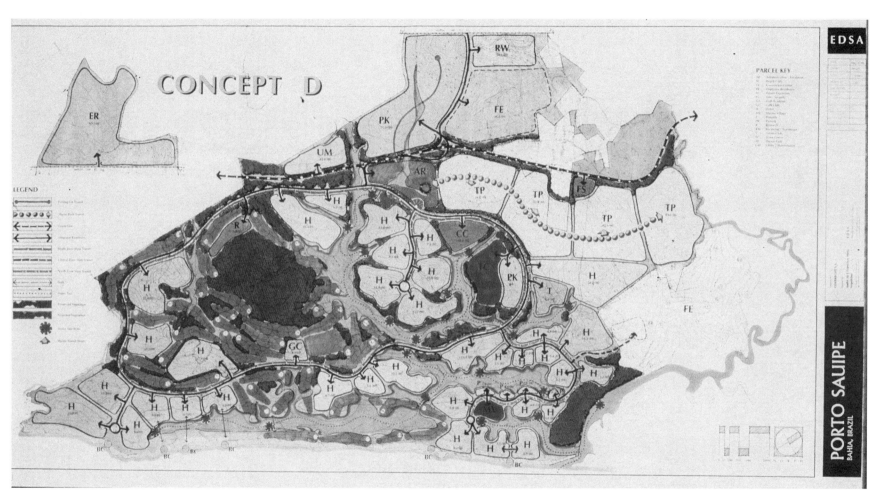

Porto Sauipe Color marker on presentation blackline over
AutoCADD base drawing.

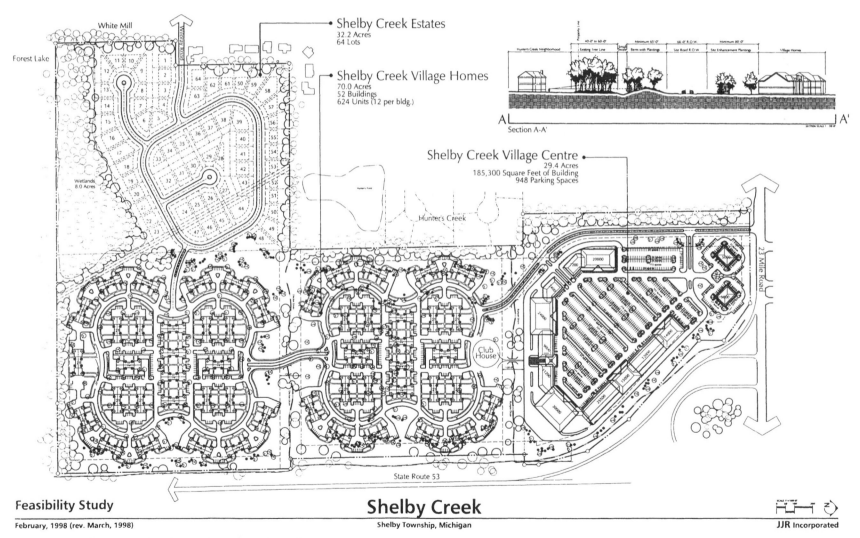

Shelby Creek Estates
32.2 Acres
64 Lots

Shelby Creek Village Homes
70.0 Acres
52 Buildings
624 Units (12 per bldg.)

Shelby Creek Village Centre
29.4 Acres
185,300 Square Feet of Building
948 Parking Spaces

Section A-A'

White Mill

Forest Lake

Wetlands
8.0 Acres

Hunter's Creek

Club House

State Route 53

23 Mile Road

Feasibility Study

February, 1998 (rev. March, 1998)

Shelby Creek

Shelby Township, Michigan

JJR Incorporated

▌ Shelby Creek. CADD drawing and section plotted on bond.

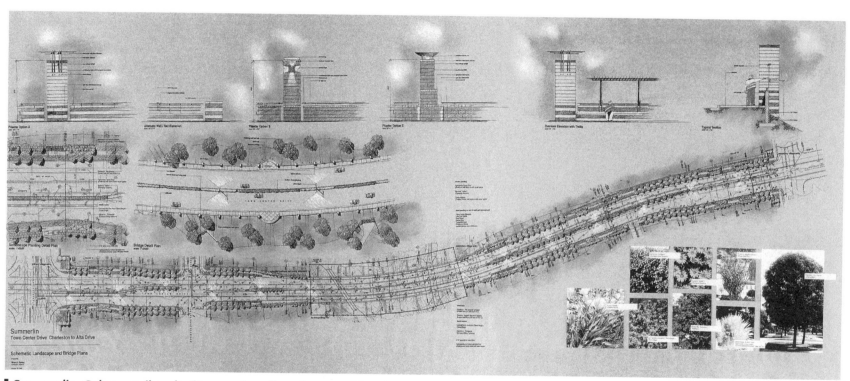

Summerlin. Color pencil on kraft paper in collage format with color photographs. The elevation drawings and photographs are organized in a simple fashion for clarity and compositional balance.

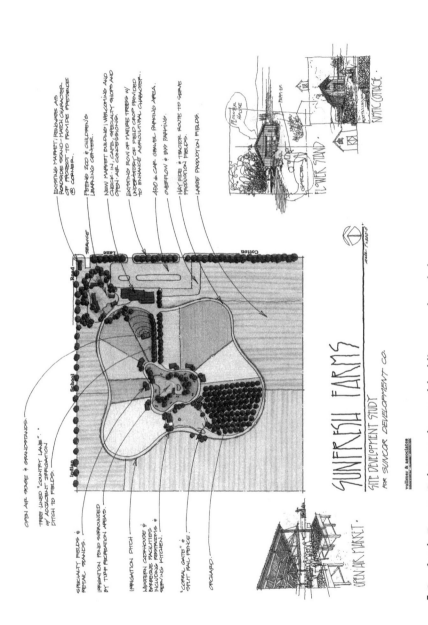

SUNFRESH FARMS

SITE DEVELOPMENT STUDY
FOR SUNCOR DEVELOPMENT CO.

vollmer & associates

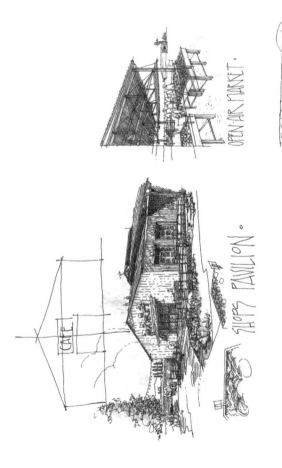

OPEN AIR MARKET

SHOPS PAVILION

CAFE

FLOWER STAND

RUSTIC COTTAGE

SUNFRESH FARMS

SITE FACILITY SKETCHES
FOR SUNCOR DEVELOPMENT CO.

vollmer & associates

Sunfresh Farms. Color marker on blackline over hand-drawn base. This land plan is loose and cartoonlike, yet conveys a rather conceptual idea at the beginning of the design process.

Sunfresh Farms. Freehand in ink on vellum.

Gary Waterfront. Hardlined hand drawing in ink and color pencil on tracing paper.

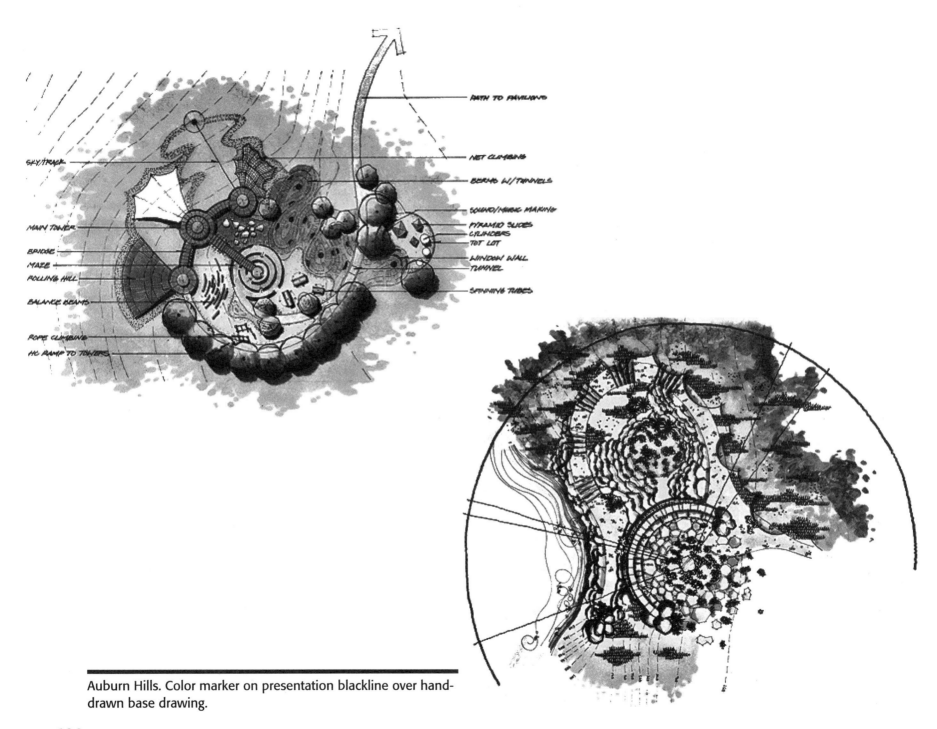

SKY/TRACK

MAIN TOWER

BRIDGE
MAZE
ROLLING HILL

BALANCE BEAMS

ROPE CLIMBING
HC RAMP TO TOWERS

PATH TO PAVILIONS

NET CLIMBING

BERMS W/TUNNELS

SOUND/MUSIC MAKING
PYRAMID SLIDES
CYLINDERS
TOT LOT
WINDOW WALL
TUNNEL

SPINNING TUBES

Auburn Hills. Color marker on presentation blackline over hand-drawn base drawing.

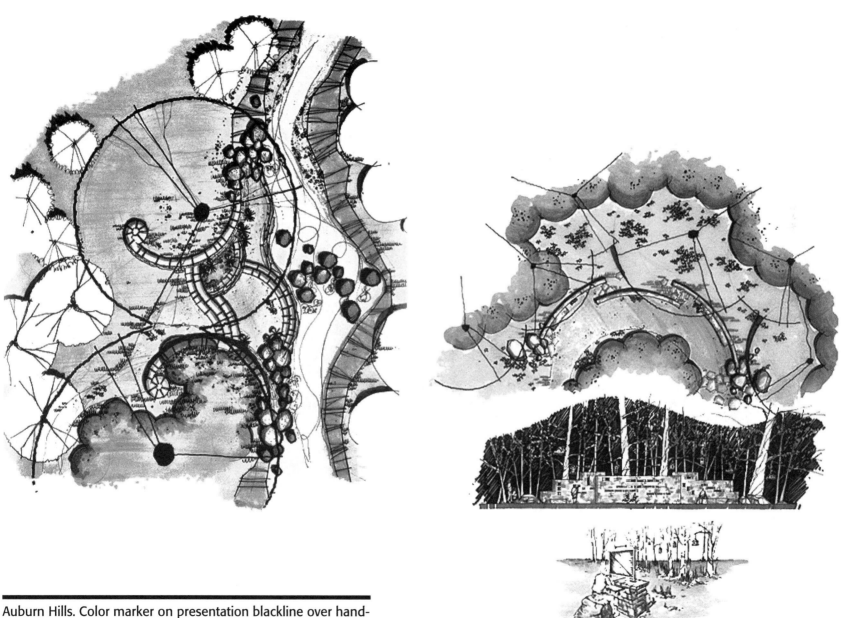

Auburn Hills. Color marker on presentation blackline over hand-drawn base drawing.

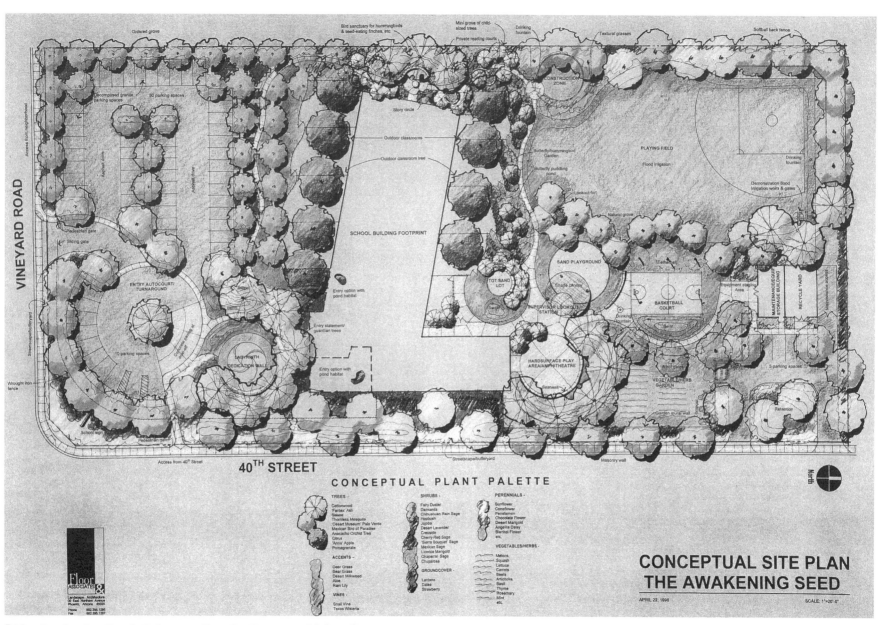

The Awakening Seed. Color pencil on kraft paper with hand-drawn design over AutoCADD base.

106

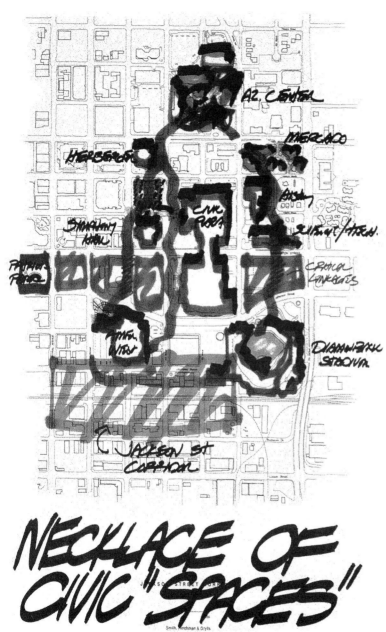

NECKLACE OF CIVIC "SPACES"

Jackson Street. Color marker and ink on 11″ × 17″ bristol board.

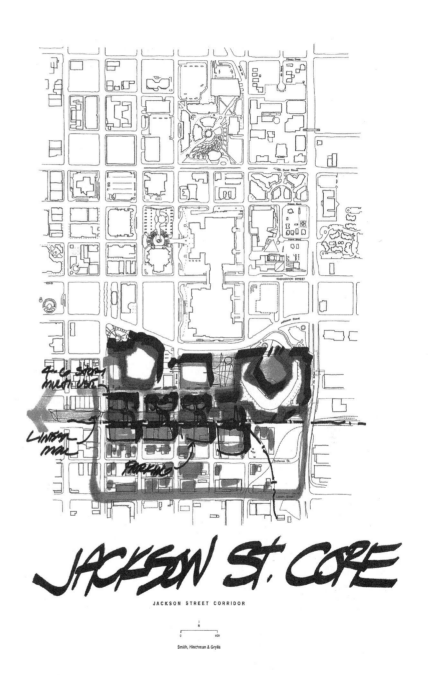

JACKSON ST. CORE

JACKSON STREET CORRIDOR

N
0   400

Smith, Hinchman & Grylls

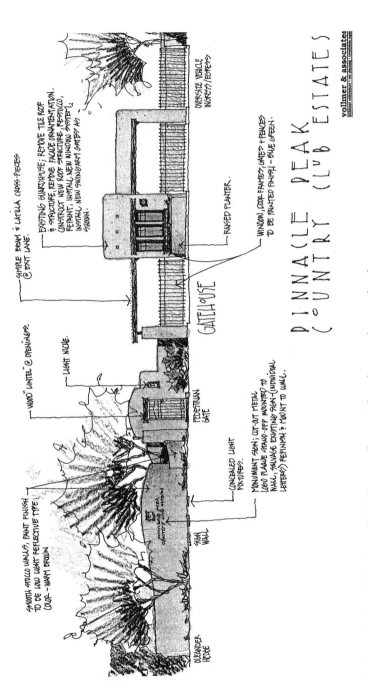

Pinnacle Peak. Freehand in ink on vellum with color marker on back.

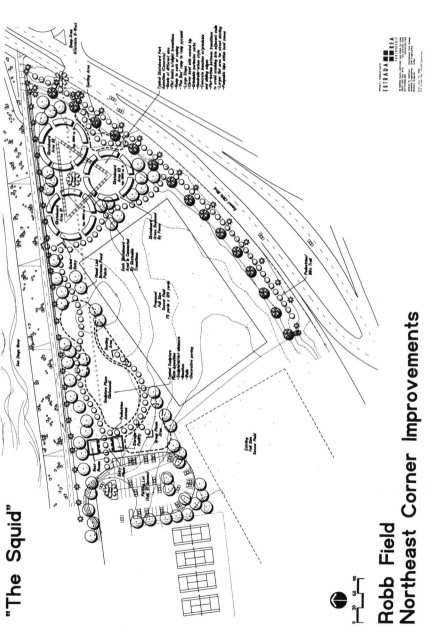

"The Squid"

Robb Field
Northeast Corner Improvements

Robb Field. Ink jet plot of AutoCADD drawing.

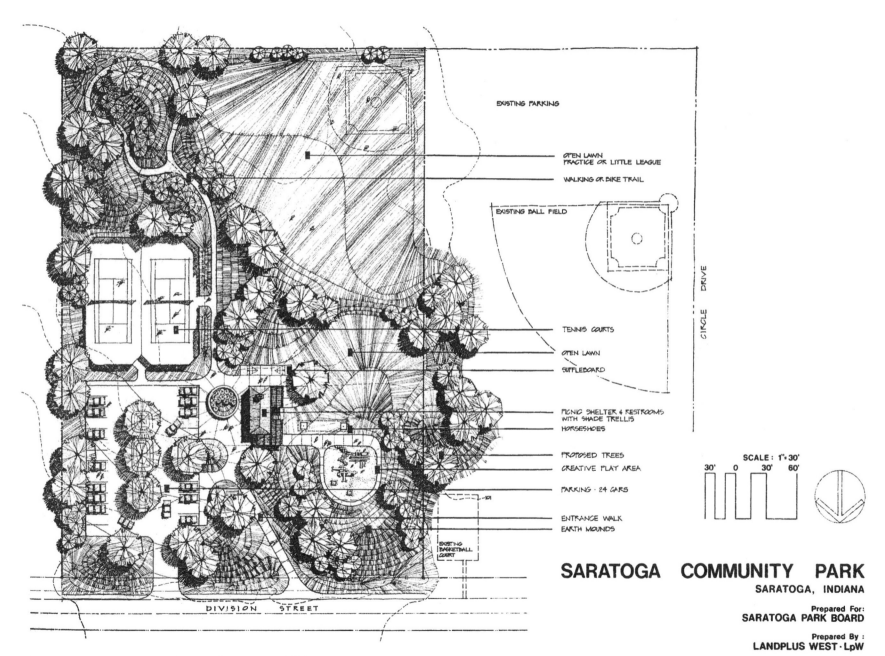

EXISTING PARKING

OPEN LAWN
PRACTICE OR LITTLE LEAGUE

WALKING OR BIKE TRAIL

EXISTING BALL FIELD

CIRCLE DRIVE

TENNIS COURTS

OPEN LAWN

SHUFFLEBOARD

PICNIC SHELTER & RESTROOMS
WITH SHADE TRELLIS

HORSESHOES

PROPOSED TREES

CREATIVE PLAY AREA

PARKING · 24 CARS

ENTRANCE WALK

EARTH MOUNDS

EXISTING
BASKETBALL
COURT

DIVISION STREET

SCALE : 1"=30'

30'   0   30'   60'

SARATOGA COMMUNITY PARK
SARATOGA, INDIANA

Prepared For:
SARATOGA PARK BOARD

Prepared By :
LANDPLUS WEST · LpW

▌Saratoga Community Park. Hand-drawn with ink.

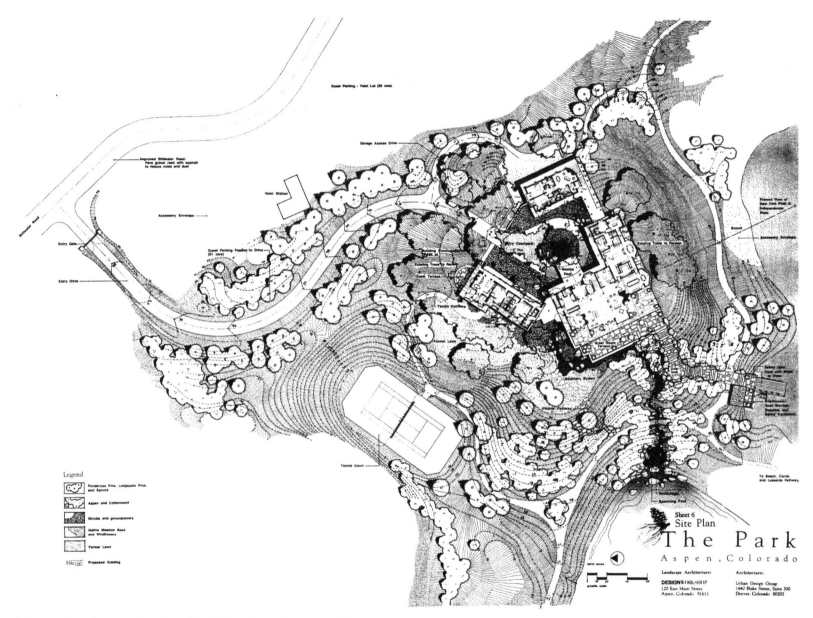

The Park. Ink on mylar plot of building footprint created in AutoCADD. The title block is created in AutoCADD and plotted with the building base drawing. The other text and legends are added, using sticky-back material. All the textures and patterns are done with ink in freehand.

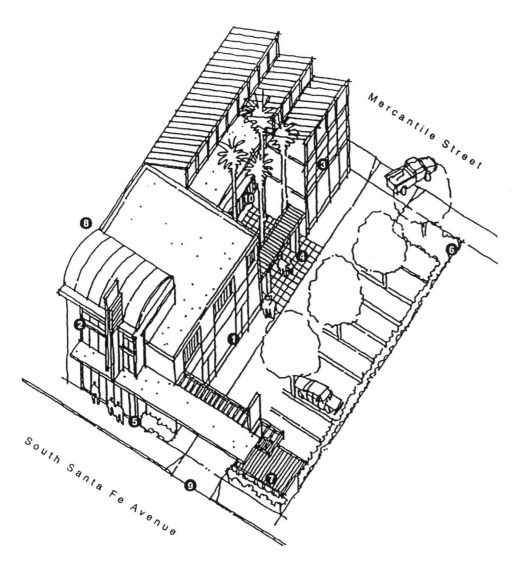

Development Concept

The drawing at left illustrates the development of a 100 x 140 foot parcel between South Santa Fe Avenue and Mercantile Street for a mix of commercial and artisan live/work space.

Uses

1. Restaurant/retail at 1st Floor.

2. Offices at 2nd Floor.

3. Artisan studios (live/work space) on two stories.

4. Access to 2nd Floor from courtyard.

Site Requirements

5. Five-foot maximum setback from street-fronting property lines allowed for 50% of frontage.

6. Required landscaped setback at Mercantile Street frontage.

Building Massing/Bulk

7. Mandatory architectural element at South Santa Fe Avenue property line

8. Maximum height three stories. Building massing shall follow topography.

Parking

9. Maximum of one curb cut per 100 feet of South Santa Fe Avenue frontage. No curb cuts allowed on parcels narrower than 100 feet.

Residential Guidelines

10. Provide usable exterior space (balcony or yard space) for each unit.

PROTOTYPE SITE B • SOUTH SANTA FE / MIXED ARTISAN RETAIL
Vista Village Specific Plan

CITY OF VISTA
California
COTTON/BELAND/ASSOCIATES
Urban and Environmental Planning
ANDREW SPURLOCK MARTIN POIRIER
Landscape Architects

▌ Vista Village. Freehand in ink on mylar with typed text.

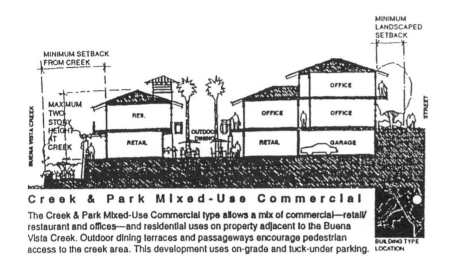

Creek & Park Mixed-Use Commercial

The Creek & Park Mixed-Use Commercial type allows a mix of commercial—retail/ restaurant and offices—and residential uses on property adjacent to the Buena Vista Creek. Outdoor dining terraces and passageways encourage pedestrian access to the creek area. This development uses on-grade and tuck-under parking.

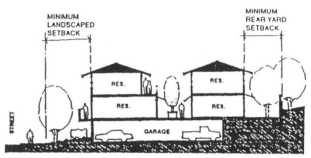

Large-Parcel Residential

This type of moderate-density residential development may occur where larger parcels are zoned to allow up to twenty dwelling units per acre.

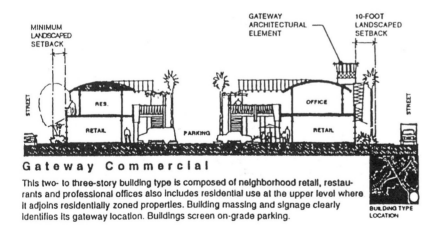

Gateway Commercial

This two- to three-story building type is composed of neighborhood retail, restaurants and professional offices also includes residential use at the upper level where it adjoins residentially zoned properties. Building massing and signage clearly identifies its gateway location. Buildings screen on-grade parking.

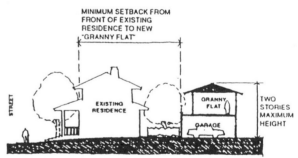

Granny Flat Addition

The "Granny Flat" type allows greater residential density without greatly affecting the visual character of existing single-family residential neighborhoods.

BUILDING TYPES
Vista Village Specific Plan

CITY OF VISTA
California
COTTON/BELAND/ASSOCIATES
Urban and Environmental Planning
ANDREW SPURLOCK MARTIN POIRIER
Landscape Architects

▌Vista Village. Freehand in ink on mylar with typed text.

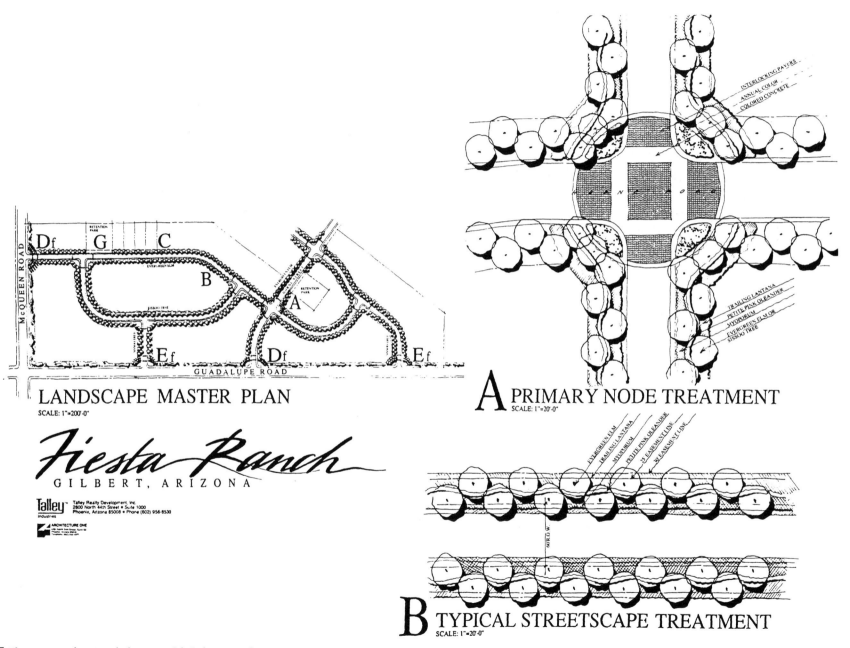

LANDSCAPE MASTER PLAN
SCALE: 1"=200'-0"

Fiesta Ranch
GILBERT, ARIZONA

Talley
Industries
Talley Realty Development, Inc.
2800 North 44th Street • Suite 1000
Phoenix, Arizona 85008 • Phone (602) 956-8530

ARCHITECTURE ONE

A PRIMARY NODE TREATMENT
SCALE: 1"=20'-0"

B TYPICAL STREETSCAPE TREATMENT
SCALE: 1"=20'-0"

▮ Fiesta Ranch. Hand-drawn with ink on mylar.

C TYPICAL STREETSCAPE
SCALE: 1"=20'-0"

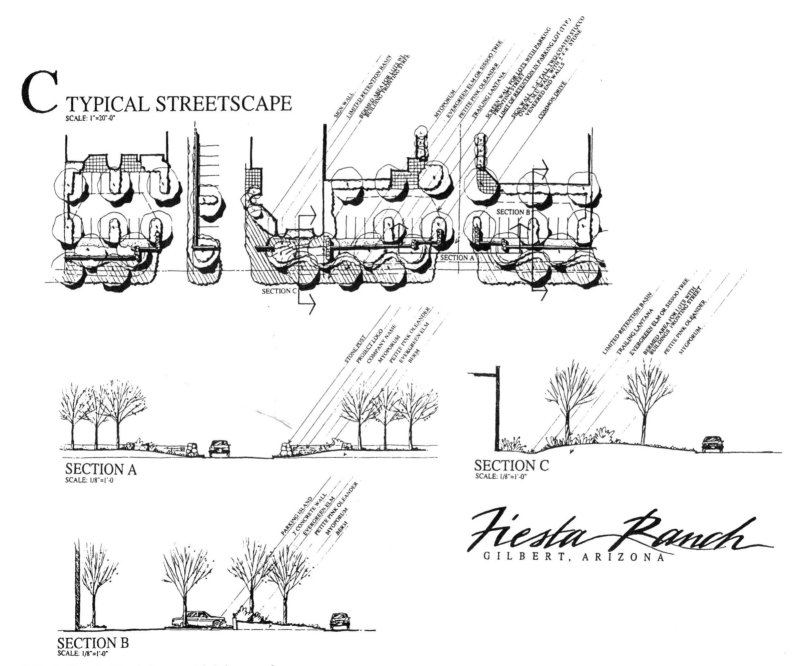

SECTION A
SCALE: 1/8"=1'-0

SECTION B
SCALE: 1/8"=1'-0"

SECTION C
SCALE: 1/8"=1'-0"

Fiesta Ranch
GILBERT, ARIZONA

■ Fiesta Ranch. Hand-drawn with ink on mylar.

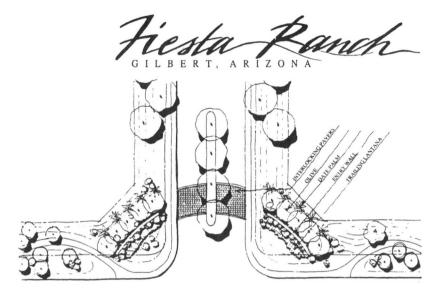

Fiesta Ranch

GILBERT, ARIZONA

INTERLOCKING PAVERS
OLIVE
DATE PALM
ENTRY WALL
TRAILING LANTANA

D PRIMARY ENTRY TREATMENT
SCALE: 1"=20'-0"

Fiesta Ranch

f ENTRY WALL

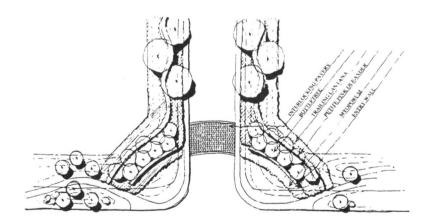

INTERLOCKING PAVERS
BOTTLETREE
TRAILING LANTANA
PETITE PINK OLEANDER
MYOPORUM
ENTRY WALL

E SECONDARY ENTRY TREATMENT
SCALE: 1"=20'-0"

❙ Fiesta Ranch. Hand-drawn with ink on mylar.

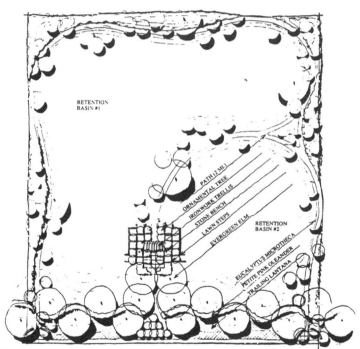

RETENTION BASIN #1

PATH (2 MI.)
ORNAMENTAL TREE
IRONWORK TRELLIS
STONE BENCH
LAWN STEPS
EVERGREEN ELM

RETENTION BASIN #2

EUCALYPTUS MICROTHECA
PETITE PINK OLEANDER
TRAILING LANTANA

G PARK DEVELOPMENT CONCEPT

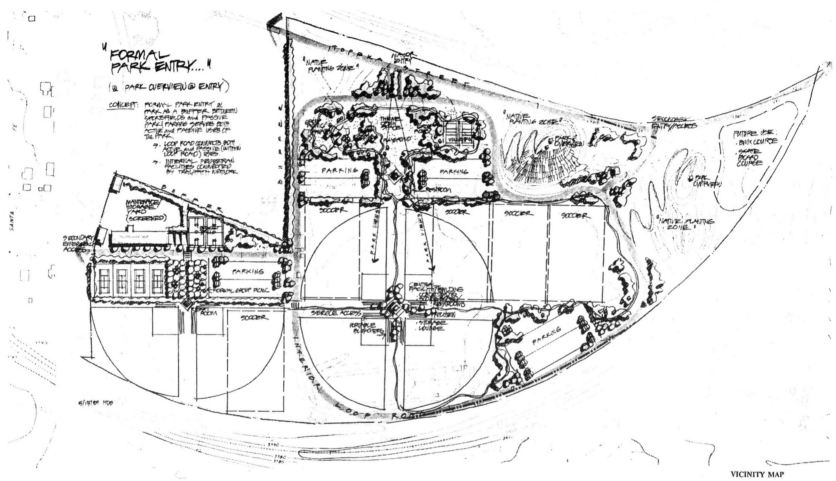

"FORMAL PARK ENTRY..."

(IN PARK OVERVIEW @ ENTRY)

CONCEPT: FORMAL PARK ENTRY IN PARK AS A BUFFER BETWEEN SPORTSFIELDS AND PASSIVE PARK / PARKING SERVES BOTH ACTIVE AND PASSIVE USES OF THE PARK.
→ LOOP ROAD CONNECTS BOTH ACTIVE AND PASSIVE (WITHIN LOOP ROAD) USES.
→ INTERNAL PEDESTRIAN FACILITIES CONNECTED BY TRAILPATH NETWORK.

SOUTHSIDE
P·A·R·K
KINGMAN, ARIZONA

Southside Park. Hand-drawn with ink on mylar over a topographic base created in Auto-CADD. Note that the base drawing is screened to minimize potential conflict with the illustrative information.

VICINITY MAP

CBA CELLA BARR ASSOCIATES

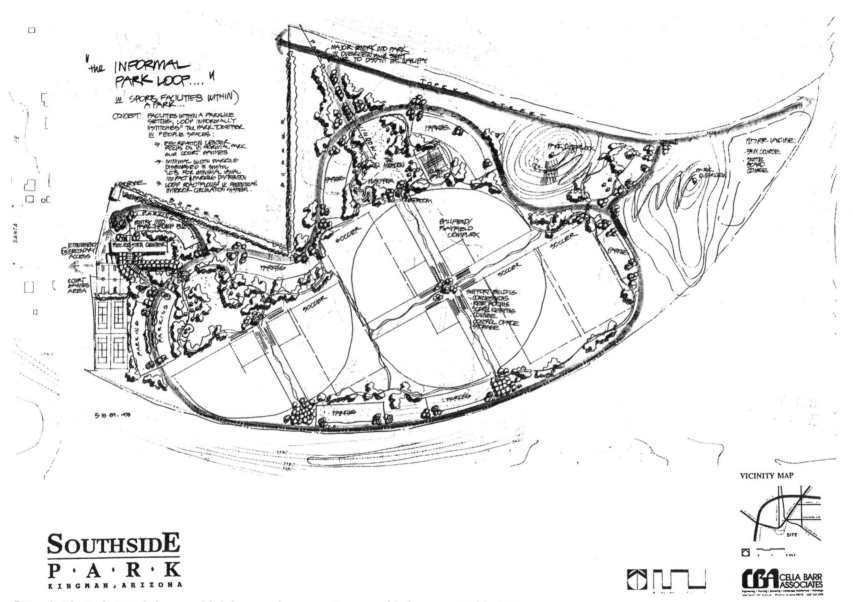

Southside Park. Hand-drawn with ink on mylar over a topographic base created in Auto-CADD. Note that the base drawing is screened to minimize potential conflict with the illustrative information.

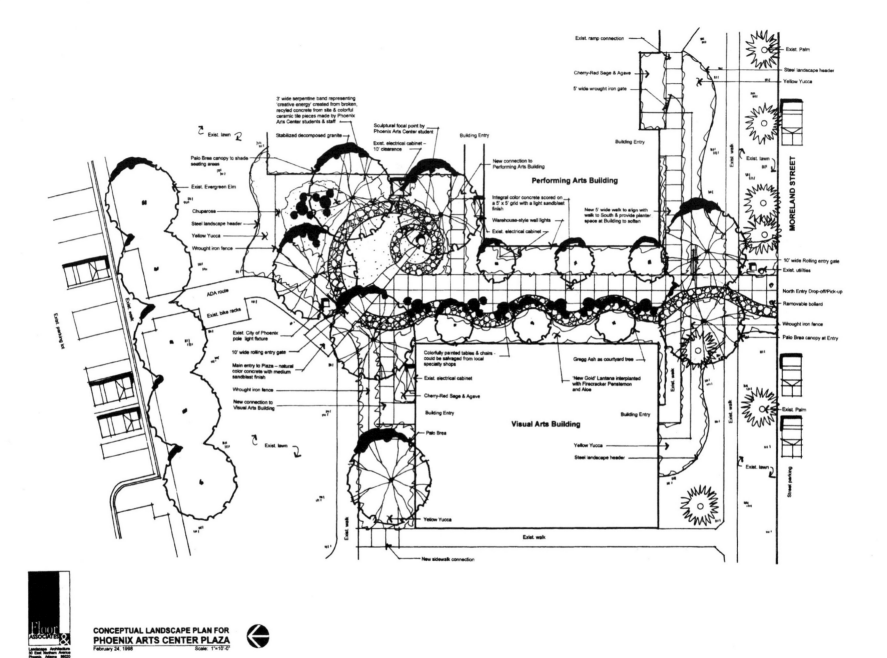

Exist. ramp connection

Exist. Palm

Steel landscape header

Cherry-Red Sage & Agave

Yellow Yucca

5' wide wrought iron gate

MORELAND STREET

Building Entry

Exist. lawn

3' wide serpentine band representing 'creative energy' created from broken, recyled concrete from site & colorful ceramic tile pieces made by Phoenix Arts Center students & staff

Sculptural focal point by Phoenix Arts Center student

Building Entry

Exist. lawn

Stabilized decomposed granite

Exist. electrical cabinet – 10' clearance

Performing Arts Building

Exist. walk

Palo Brea canopy to shade seating areas

New connection to Performing Arts Building

Exist. Evergreen Elm

Integral color concrete scored on a 5' x 5' grid with a light sandblast finish

New 5' wide walk to align with walk to South & provide planter space at Building to soften

Chuperosa

Warehouse-style wall lights

Steel landscape header

Exist. electrical cabinet

10' wide Rolling entry gate

Yellow Yucca

Exist. utilities

Wrought iron fence

North Entry Drop-off/Pick-up

ADA route

Removable bollard

Exist. bike racks

Wrought iron fence

Exist. City of Phoenix pole light fixture

Colorfully painted tables & chairs – could be salvaged from local specialty shops

Palo Brea canopy at Entry

Gregg Ash as courtyard tree

10' wide rolling entry gate

Main entry to Plaza – natural color concrete with medium sandblast finish

'New Gold' Lantana interplanted with Firecracker Penstemon and Aloe

Exist. electrical cabinet

Wrought iron fence

Cherry-Red Sage & Agave

New connection to Visual Arts Building

Building Entry

Building Entry

Exist. Palm

Exist. lawn

Visual Arts Building

Palo Brea

Yellow Yucca

Exist. lawn

Steel landscape header

Exist. walk

Exist. walk

Yellow Yucca

Street parking

Exist. walk

New sidewalk connection

CONCEPTUAL LANDSCAPE PLAN FOR
PHOENIX ARTS CENTER PLAZA
February 24, 1998   Scale: 1"=10'-0"

Floor & ASSOCIATES
Landscape Architecture
30 East Northern Avenue
Phoenix, Arizona 85020
Phone   602.386.1286
Fax   602.386.1307

Phoenix Arts Center Plaza. Hand-drawn with ink on base drawing generated in Auto-CADD. The text callouts and title block are created in AutoCADD on the base, with hand-drawn leader lines.

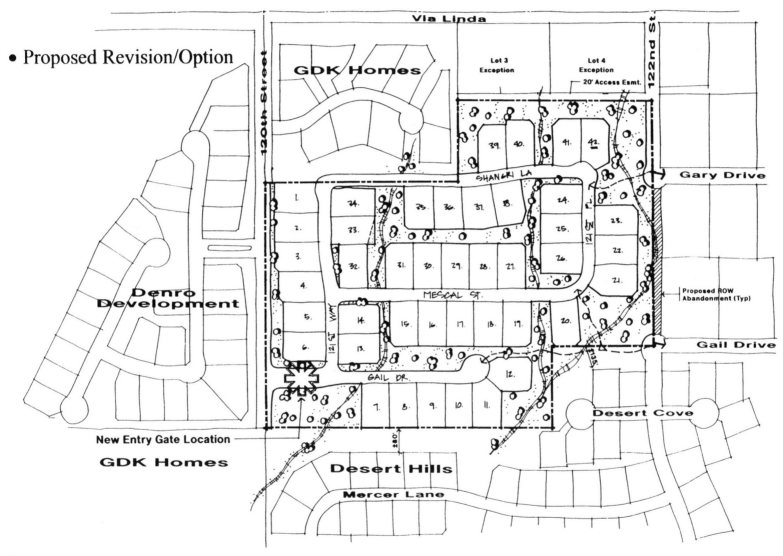

• Proposed Revision/Option

GDK Homes

Via Linda

120th Street

122nd St.

Lot 3 Exception

Lot 4 Exception

20' Access Esmt.

Gary Drive

SHANGRI LA

39. 40. 41. 42.

1. 34. 35. 36. 37. 38. 24. 23.

2. 33. 25.

12 ST PL.

Denro Development

3. 32. 31. 30. 29. 28. 27. 26. 22.

4. 21.

12 ST WAY

MESCAL ST.

Proposed ROW Abandonment (Typ)

5. 14. 15. 16. 17. 18. 19. 20.

6. 13.

Gail Drive

235'

GAIL DR. 12.

New Entry Gate Location

7. 8. 9. 10. 11.

Desert Cove

GDK Homes

±80'

Desert Hills

Mercer Lane

▌Freehand in ink on mylar.

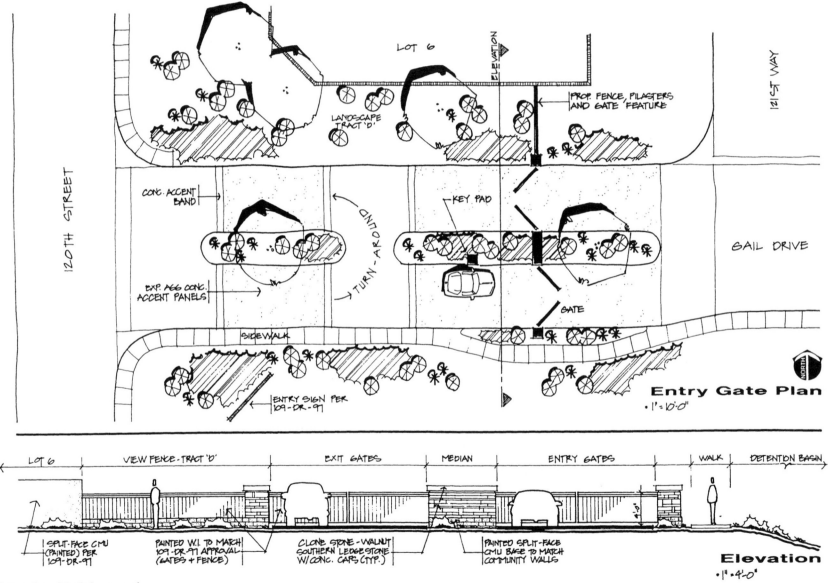

LOT 6

ELEVATION

121ST WAY

PROP. FENCE, PILASTERS AND GATE FEATURE

LANDSCAPE TRACT 'D'

120TH STREET

CONC. ACCENT BAND

KEY PAD

TURN-AROUND

GAIL DRIVE

EXP. AGG CONC. ACCENT PANELS

GATE

NORTH

SIDEWALK

ENTRY SIGN PER 109-DR-97

Entry Gate Plan
• 1" = 10'-0"

| LOT 6 | VIEW FENCE-TRACT 'D' | EXIT GATES | MEDIAN | ENTRY GATES | WALK | DETENTION BASIN |

SPLIT-FACE CMU (PAINTED) PER 109-DR-97

PAINTED W.I. TO MATCH 109-DR-97 APPROVAL (GATES + FENCE)

CLONE STONE - WALNUT SOUTHERN LEDGESTONE W/CONC. CAPS (TYP.)

PAINTED SPLIT-FACE CMU BASE TO MATCH COMMUNITY WALLS

4'-0"

Elevation
• 1" = 4'-0"

▌ Freehand in ink on mylar.

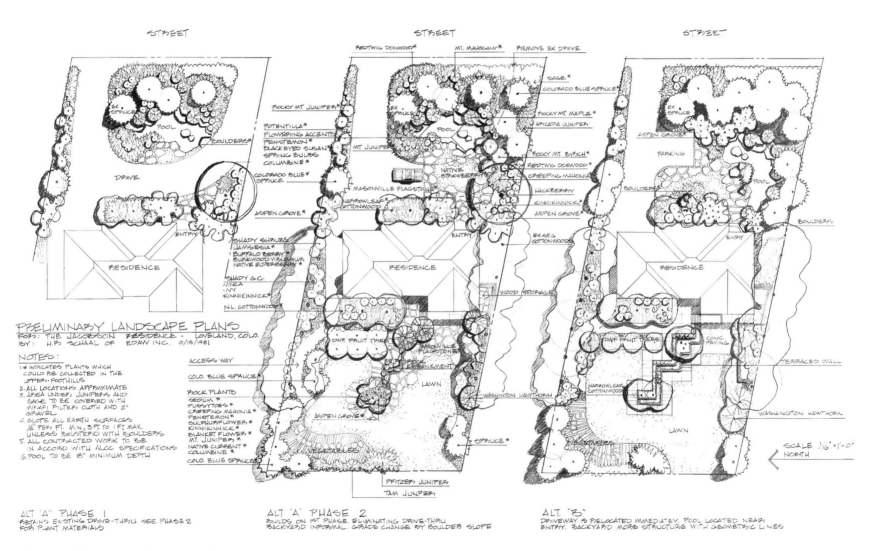

Jackson Residence. Graphite on mylar.

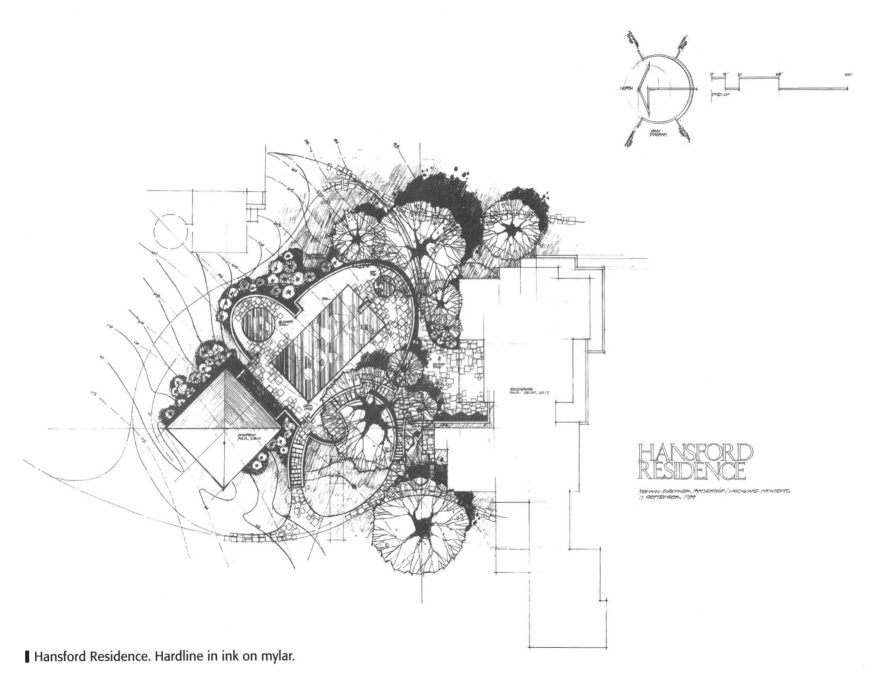

HANSFORD
RESIDENCE

REIMANN-BUECHNER PARTNERSHIP / LANDSCAPE ARCHITECTS
17 SEPTEMBER 1984

█ Hansford Residence. Hardline in ink on mylar.

GENERAL
INSTRUMENT
NOGALES, SONORA

General Instrument. Freehand in ink on tracing paper over AutoCADD base perspective. A presentation blackline is printed with a title block and rendered in color pencil and color marker.

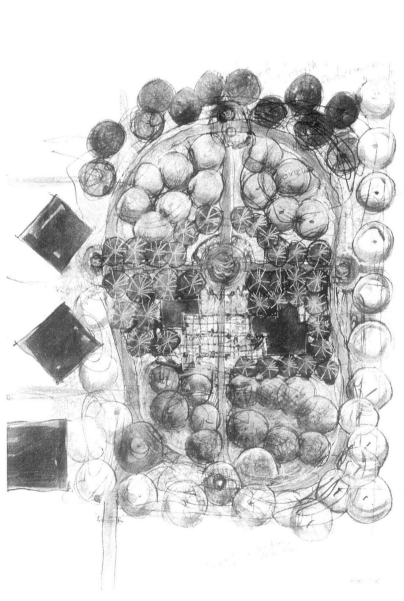

Elsie McCarthy Sensory Garden. Color marker on tracing paper.

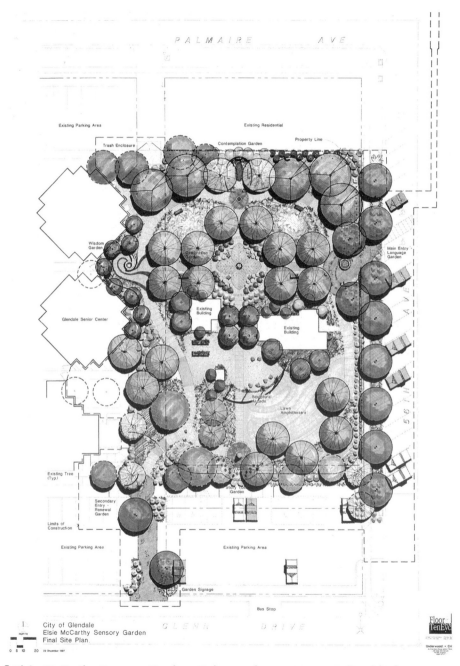

Elsie McCarthy Sensory Garden. Color marker on presentation black-line with hand-drawn design over AutoCADD base drawing.

124

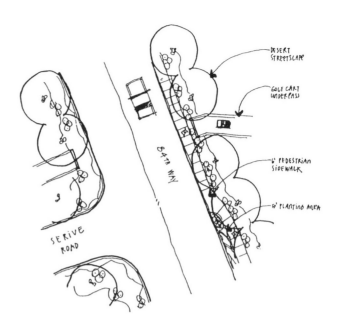

ENLARGED PLAN AT GOLF CART UNDERPASS

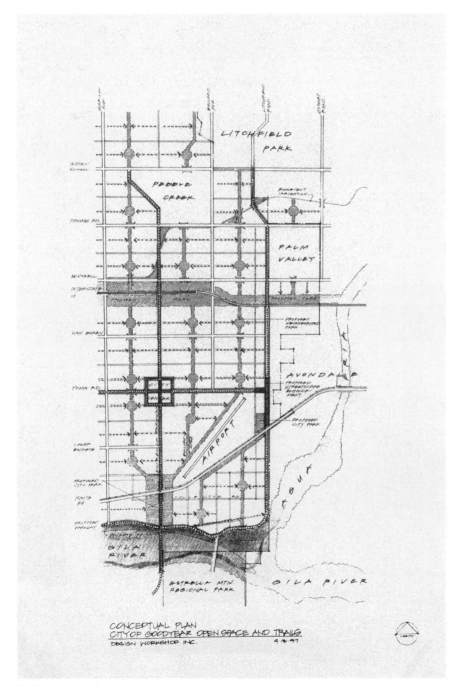

City of Goodyear. Hand-drawn with ink on tracing paper.

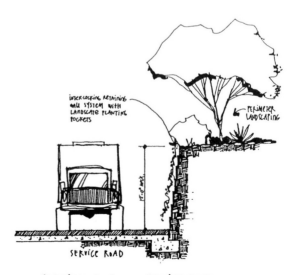

SECTION A-A AT SERVICE ROAD

Freehand ink drawing on vellum.

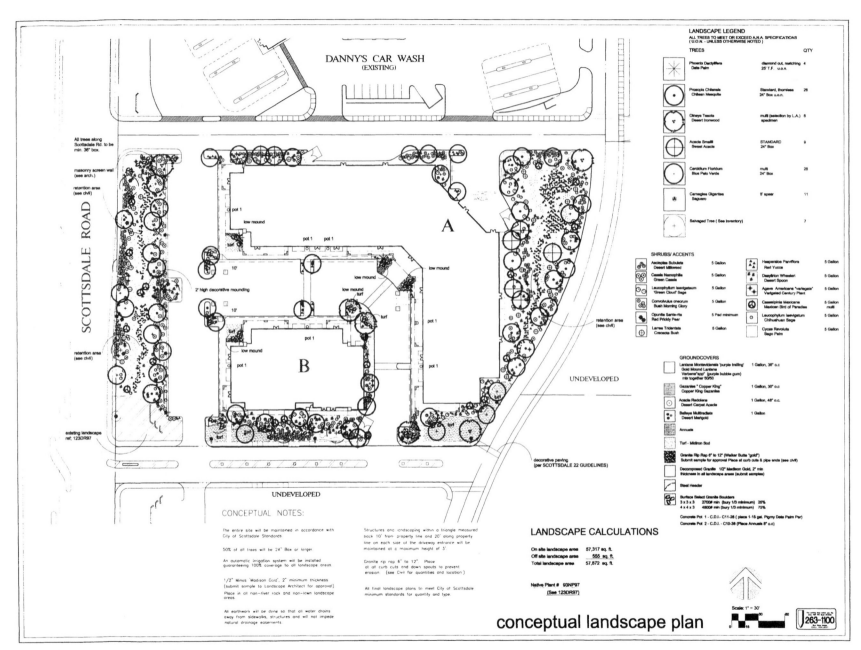

LANDSCAPE LEGEND

ALL TREES TO MEET OR EXCEED A.N.A. SPECIFICATIONS
(U.O.N. - UNLESS OTHERWISE NOTED)

DANNY'S CAR WASH
(EXISTING)

SCOTTSDALE ROAD

All trees along
Scottsdale Rd. to be
min. 36" box.

masonry screen wall
(see arch.)

retention area
(see civil)

2' high decorative mounding

retention area
(see civil)

existing landscape
ref; 123DR97

A

B

pot 1
low mound
pot 1   pot 1
turf
10'
low mound
10'
low mound
turf
low mound
pot 1
low mound
pot 1
turf

low mound
turf
low mound
turf
pot 1
pot 1
turf

retention area
(see civil)

UNDEVELOPED

decorative paving
(per SCOTTSDALE 22 GUIDELINES)

UNDEVELOPED

TREES   QTY

Phoenix Dactylifera   diamond cut, matching   4
Date Palm   25' T.F. u.o.n.

Prosopis Chilensis   Standard, thornless   26
Chilean Mesquite   24" Box u.o.n.

Olneya Tesota   multi (selection by L.A.) 6
Desert Ironwood   specimen

Acacia Smallii   STANDARD   9
Sweet Acacia   24" Box

Cercidium Floridum   multi   28
Blue Palo Verde   24" Box

Carnegiea Gigantea   5' spear   11
Saguaro

Salvaged Tree (See Inventory)   7

SHRUBS/ ACCENTS

Asclepias Subulata   5 Gallon   Hesperaloe Parviflora   5 Gallon
Desert Milkweed   Red Yucca

Cassia Nemophila   5 Gallon   Dasylirion Wheeleri   5 Gallon
Green Cassia   Desert Spoon

Leucophyllum laevigatum 5 Gallon   Agave Americana "variegata" 5 Gallon
'Green Cloud' Sage   Variegated Century Plant

Convolvulus cneorum   5 Gallon   Caesalpinia Mexicana   5 Gallon
Bush Morning Glory   Mexican Bird of Paradise multi

Opuntia Santa-rita   5 Pad minimum Leucophyllum laevigatum 5 Gallon
Red Prickly Pear   Chihuahuan Sage

Larrea Tridentata   5 Gallon   Cycas Revoluta   5 Gallon
Creosote Bush   Sago Palm

GROUNDCOVERS

Lantana Montevidensis 'purple trailing'   1 Gallon, 36" o.c.
Gold Mound Lantana
Verbena"app" (purple bubble gum)
mix together 50/50

Gazanias " Copper KIng"   1 Gallon, 30" o.c.
Copper King Gazanias

Acacia Redolens   1 Gallon, 48" o.c.
Desert Carpet Acacia

Baileya Multiradiata   1 Gallon
Desert Marigold

Annuals

Turf - Midiron Sod

Granite Rip Rap 6" to 12" (Walker Butte "gold")
Submit sample for approval Place at curb cuts & pipe ends (see civil)

Decomposed Granite 1/2" Madison Gold, 2" min
thickness in all landscape areas (submit samples)

Steel Header

Surface Select Granite Boulders
3 x 3 x 3   2700# min (bury 1/3 minimum)   25%
4 x 4 x 3   4500# min (bury 1/3 minimum)   75%

Concrete Pot 1 - C.D.I. - C11-28 (place 1-15 gal. Pigmy Date Palm Per)
Concrete Pot 2 - C.D.I. - C10-38 (Place Annuals 8" o.c)

CONCEPTUAL NOTES:

The entire site will be maintained in accordance with
City of Scottsdale Standards.

50% of all trees will be 24" Box or larger.

An automatic irrigation system will be installed
guaranteeing 100% coverage to all landscape areas.

1/2" Minus 'Madison Gold', 2" minimum thickness
(submit sample to Landscape Architect for approval).
Place in all non-river rock and non-lawn landscape
areas.

All earthwork will be done so that all water drains
away from sidewalks, structures and will not impede
natural drainage easements.

Structures and landscaping within a triangle measured
back 10' from property line and 20' along property
line on each side of the driveway entrance will be
maintained at a maximum height of 3'.

Granite rip rap 6" to 12". Place
at all curb cuts and down spouts to prevent
erosion. (see Civil for quantities and location)

All final landscape plans to meet City of Scottsdale
minimum standards for quantity and type.

LANDSCAPE CALCULATIONS

On site landscape area   57,317 sq. ft.
Off site landscape area   555 sq. ft.
Total landscape area   57,872 sq. ft.

Native Plant # 93NP97
(See 123DR97)

Scale: 1" = 30'

263-1100

conceptual landscape plan

▌Zocallo. Conceptual plan in AutoCADD.

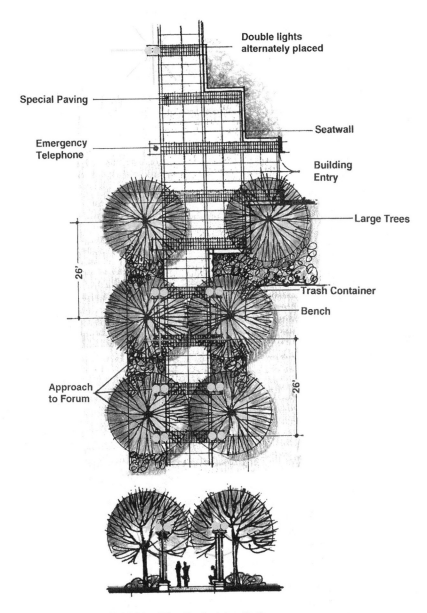

Double lights alternately placed

Special Paving

Emergency Telephone

Seatwall

Building Entry

Large Trees

26'

Trash Container

Bench

26'

Approach to Forum

Babbidge Way Pedestrian Path

UNIVERSITY OF CONNECTICUT CAMPUS MASTER PLAN

JOHNSON JOHNSON & ROY/INC • SVIGALS ASSOCIATES • CHANCE MANAGEMENT ADVISORS, INC. • SMITH, HINCHMAN & GRYLLS ASSOCIATES

University of Connecticut. Color pencil and ink on tracing paper with freehand base drawing.

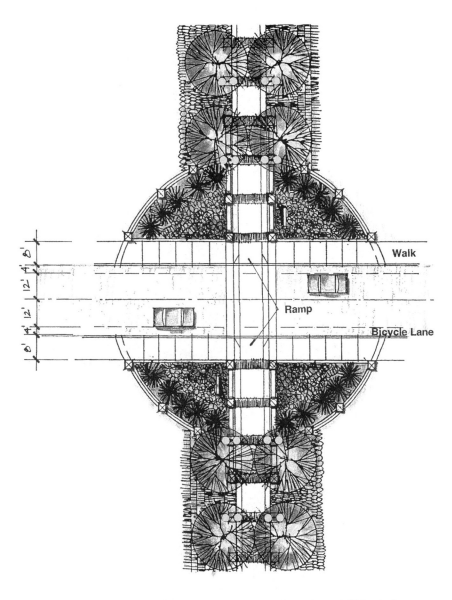

Walk

12'

4'

12'

Ramp

4'

6'

Bicycle Lane

Babbidge Way Pedestrian Crossing of Gilbert & Glenbrook Roads

UNIVERSITY OF CONNECTICUT CAMPUS MASTER PLAN

JOHNSON JOHNSON & ROY/INC • SVIGALS ASSOCIATES • CHANCE MANAGEMENT ADVISORS, INC. • SMITH, HINCHMAN & GRYLLS ASSOCIATES

University of Connecticut. Color pencil and ink on tracing paper with freehand base drawing.

127

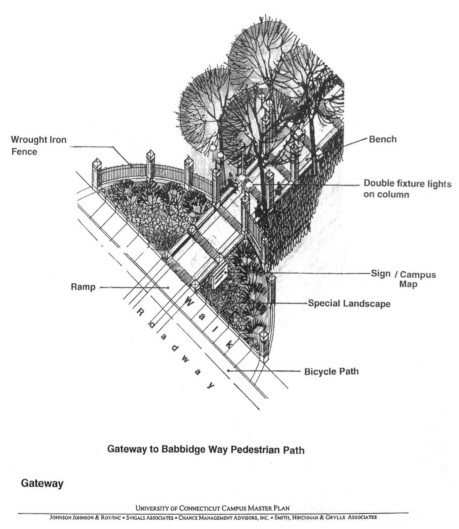

Wrought Iron Fence

Bench

Double fixture lights on column

Ramp

Sign / Campus Map

Special Landscape

Bicycle Path

R o a d w a y

W a l k

Gateway to Babbidge Way Pedestrian Path

Gateway

UNIVERSITY OF CONNECTICUT CAMPUS MASTER PLAN

JOHNSON JOHNSON & ROY/INC • SVIGALS ASSOCIATES • CHANCE MANAGEMENT ADVISORS, INC. • SMITH, HINCHMAN & GRYLLS ASSOCIATES

University of Connecticut. Color pencil and ink on tracing paper with freehand base drawing.

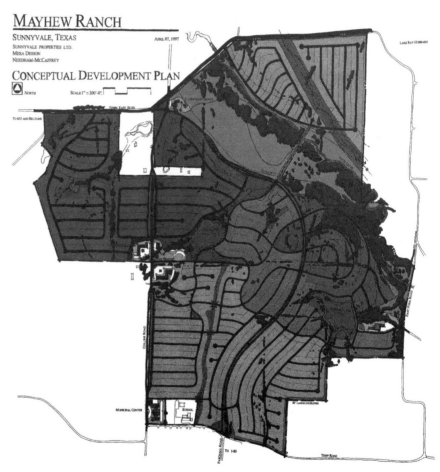

MAYHEW RANCH

SUNNYVALE, TEXAS   APRIL 07, 1997
SUNNYVALE PROPERTIES LTD.
MESA DESIGN
NEEDHAM-MCCAFFREY

CONCEPTUAL DEVELOPMENT PLAN

NORTH   SCALE 1" = 300'-0"

Mayhew Ranch. Color marker on presentation blackline over hand-drawn base drawing.

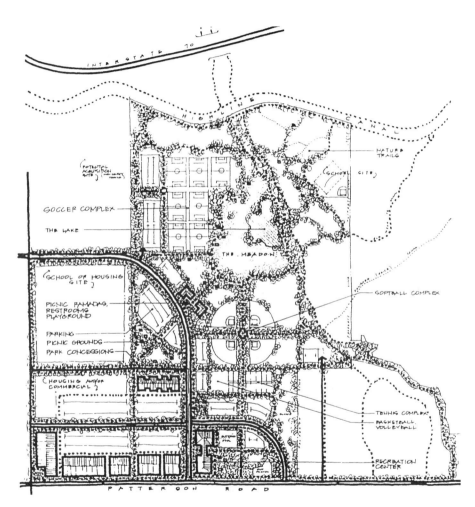

Grand Junction, Colorado. Freehand in ink on tracing paper.

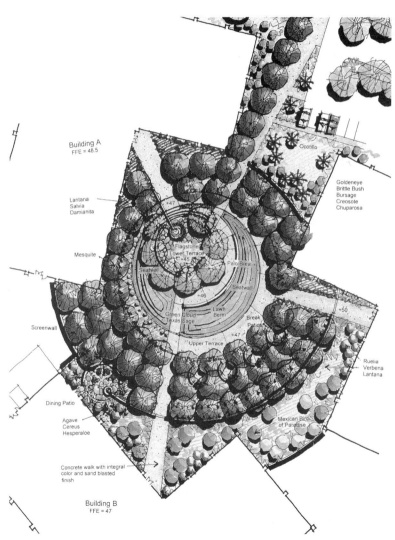

Color marker on presentation blackline with handdrawn design over AutoCADD base drawing.

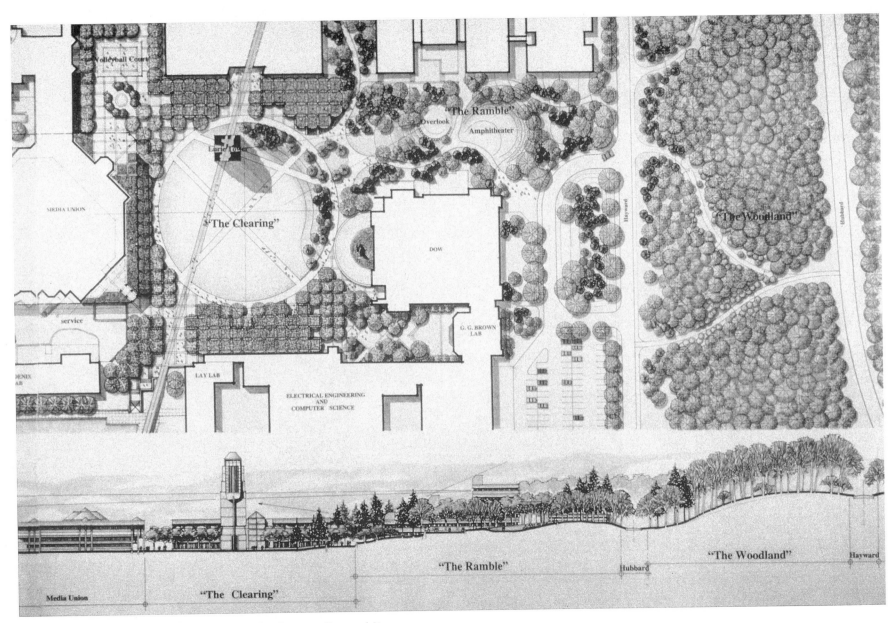

University of Michigan. Color marker and color pencil on white
trace paper over hand-drawn base.

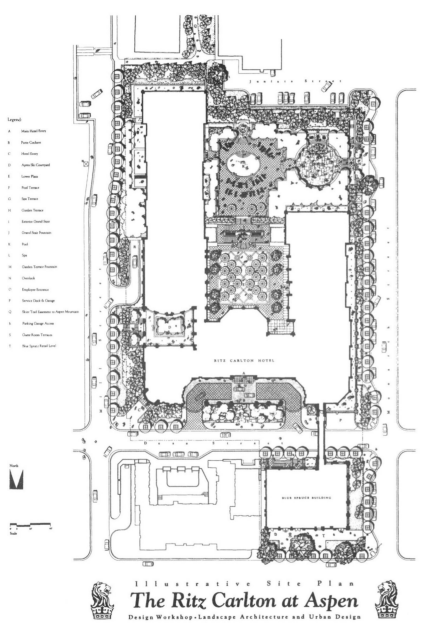

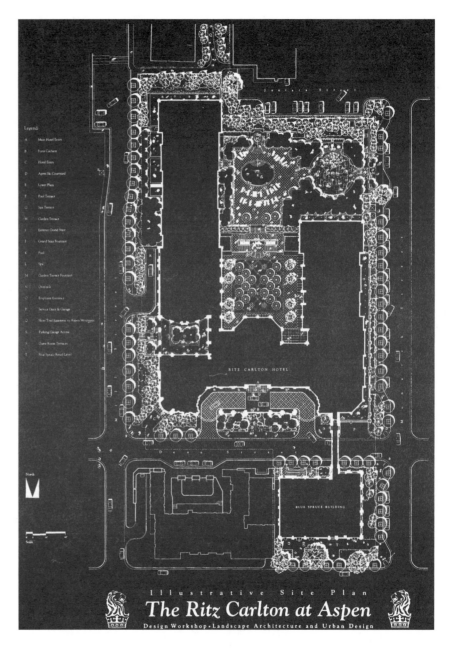

Ritz Carlton at Aspen. Hard-line in ink on mylar. The right side image is produced from a photographic negative.

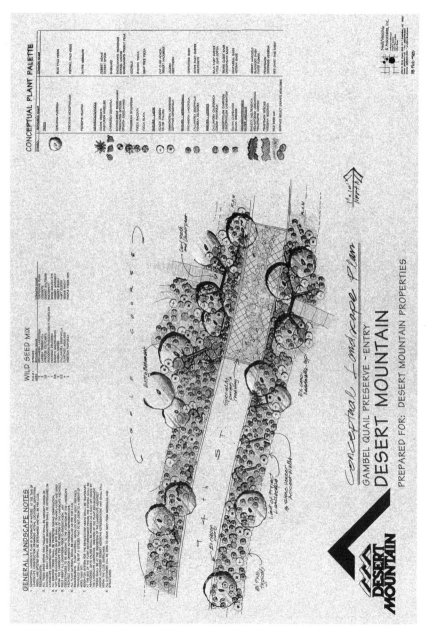

Desert Mountain. Color pencil on kraft paper with hand-drawn design over AutoCADD base.

Desert Mountain. Color pencil on kraft paper with hand-drawn vignettes.

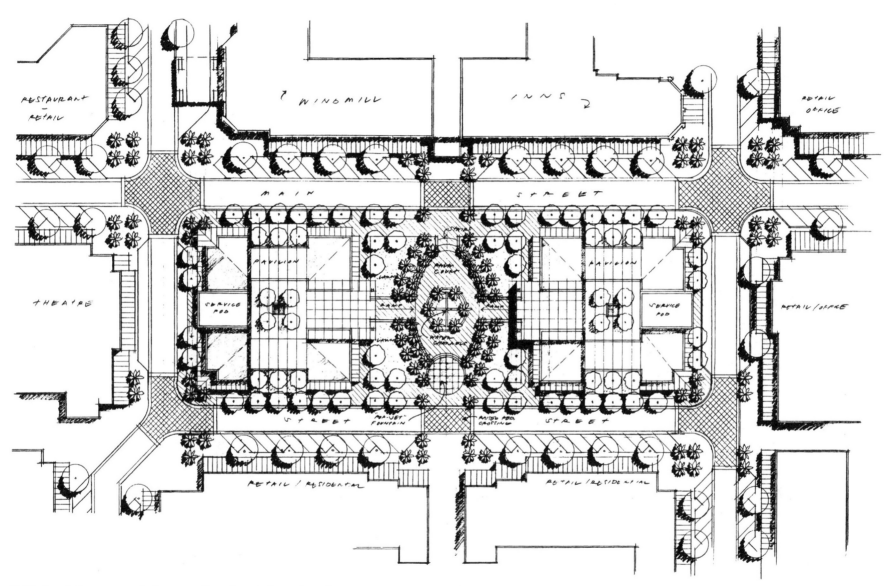

Kierland Commons. Color pencil and pastels on bond over a
hand drawn base drawing.

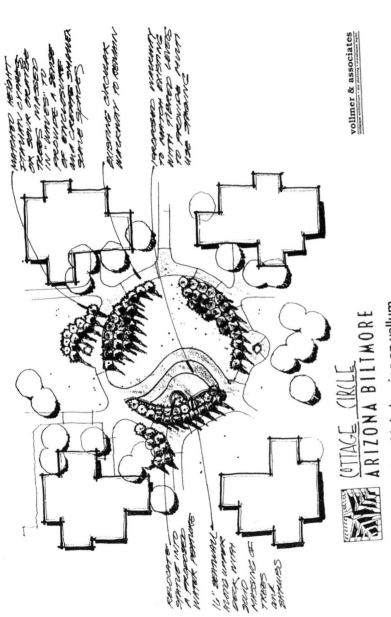

COTTAGE CIRCLE
ARIZONA BILTMORE

Arizona Biltmore. Freehand ink drawing on vellum.

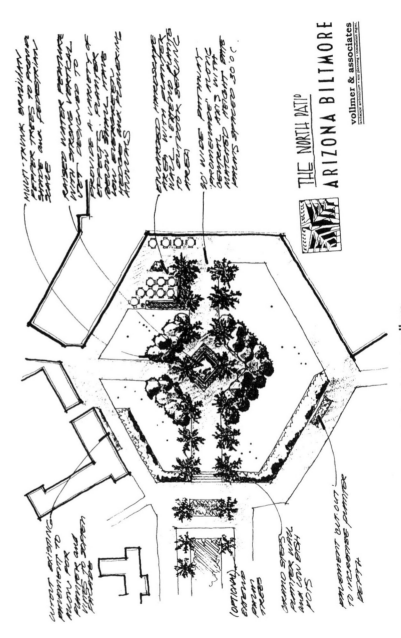

THE NORTH PATIO
ARIZONA BILTMORE

Arizona Biltmore. Freehand ink drawing on vellum.

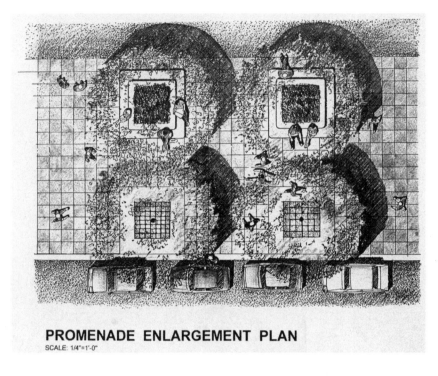

PROMENADE ENLARGEMENT PLAN

SCALE: 1/4"=1'-0"

Promenade. Color pencil on bond.

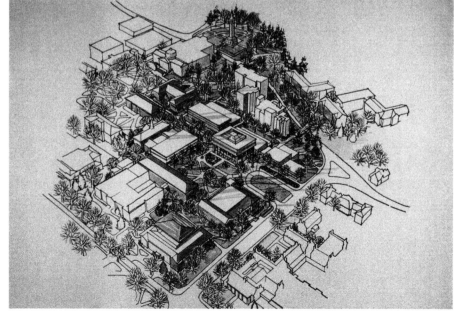

Urban center perspective. Color marker, ink, and color pencil on tracing paper over a computer-generated wire frame base. The wire frame base was created with AutoCADD.

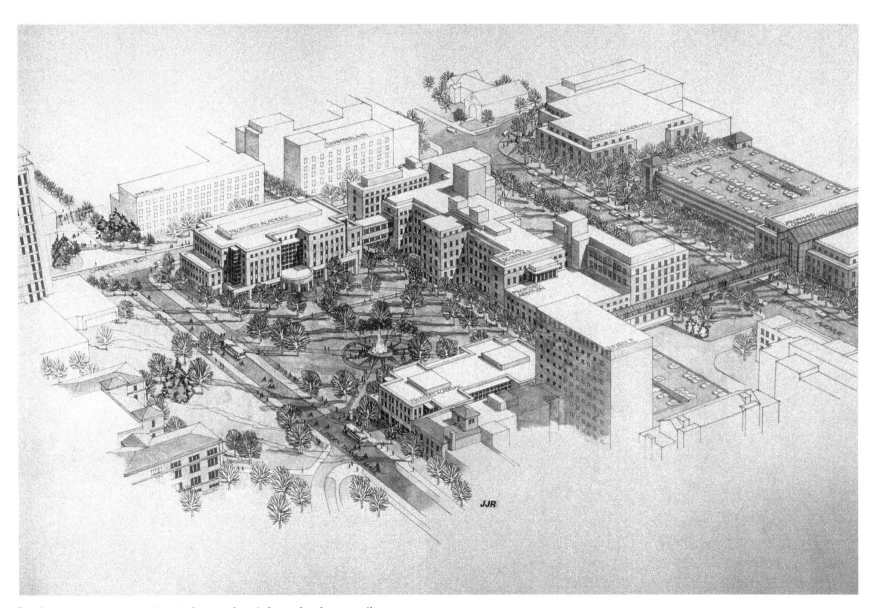

Urban center perspective. Color marker, ink, and color pencil
on tracing paper over a computer-generated wire frame base.
The wire frame base was created with AutoCADD.

136

5 MINUTE WALK DESIRABLE

TRAFFIC INTERSECTION

PARKING

PEDESTRIANIZED INTERSECTION

PARKING

SHOPS

MAIN STREET

SHOPS

PEDESTRIAN LINKAGE TO PARKING

PEDESTRIAN LINKAGE TO PARKING

WALKING DISTANCE
1/4 MILE GRID MAX.
(400 M)

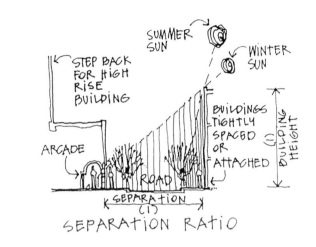

STEP BACK FOR HIGH RISE BUILDING

SUMMER SUN

WINTER SUN

ARCADE

BUILDINGS TIGHTLY SPACED OR ATTACHED

BUILDING HEIGHT (1)

ROAD

SEPARATION (1)

SEPARATION RATIO

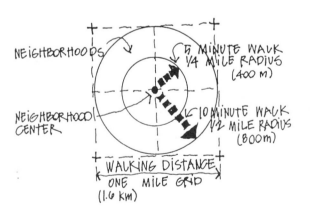

NEIGHBORHOODS

5 MINUTE WALK 1/4 MILE RADIUS (400 M)

NEIGHBORHOOD CENTER

10 MINUTE WALK 1/2 MILE RADIUS (800 M)

WALKING DISTANCE
ONE MILE GRID (1.6 KM)

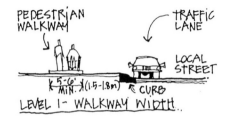

PEDESTRIAN WALKWAY

TRAFFIC LANE

LOCAL STREET

5'-6' MIN. (1.5-1.8 m)

CURB

LEVEL 1 - WALKWAY WIDTH

PEDESTRIAN WALKWAY

TRAFFIC LANE

LOCAL STREET

6'-8' MIN. (1.8-2.4m)

CURB

LEVEL 2 - WALKWAY WIDTH

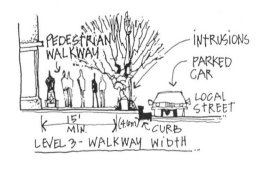

PEDESTRIAN WALKWAY

INTRUSIONS

PARKED CAR

LOCAL STREET

15' MIN. (4.6m)

CURB

LEVEL 3 - WALKWAY WIDTH

▌ MAG design guideline. Hand-drawn with ink.

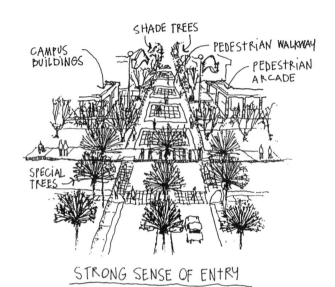

STRONG SENSE OF ENTRY

CAMPUS BUILDINGS
SHADE TREES
PEDESTRIAN WALKWAY
PEDESTRIAN ARCADE
SPECIAL TREES

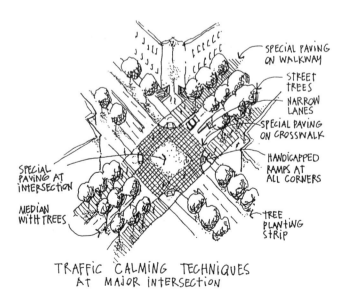

SPECIAL PAVING ON WALKWAY
STREET TREES
NARROW LANES
SPECIAL PAVING ON CROSSWALK
HANDICAPPED RAMPS AT ALL CORNERS
TREE PLANTING STRIP
SPECIAL PAVING AT INTERSECTION
MEDIAN WITH TREES

TRAFFIC CALMING TECHNIQUES
AT MAJOR INTERSECTION

▌MAG design guideline. Hand-drawn with ink.

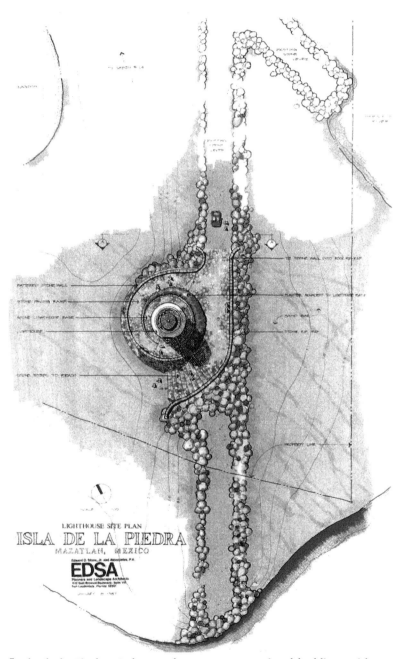

LIGHTHOUSE SITE PLAN
ISLA DE LA PIEDRA
MAZATLAN, MEXICO
Edward D. Stone, Jr. and Associates, P.A.

EDSA
Planners and Landscape Architects

▌Isla de la Piedra. Color marker on presentation blackline, with hand-drawn design over AutoCADD base drawing.

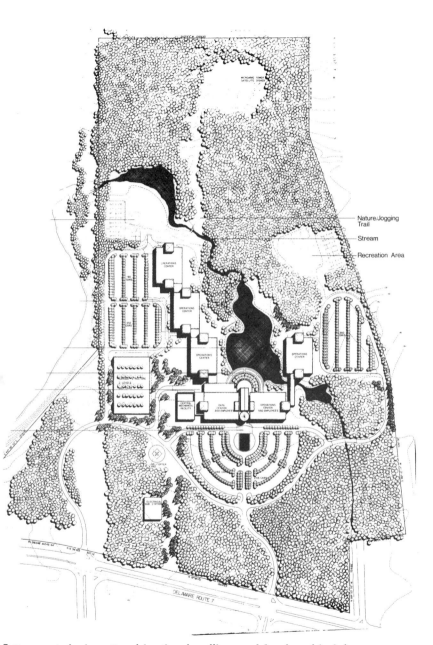

Concept design. Combination hardline and freehand in ink on mylar.

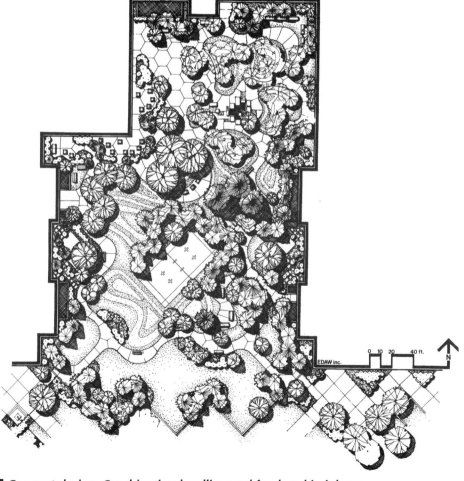

Concept design. Combination hardline and freehand in ink on mylar.

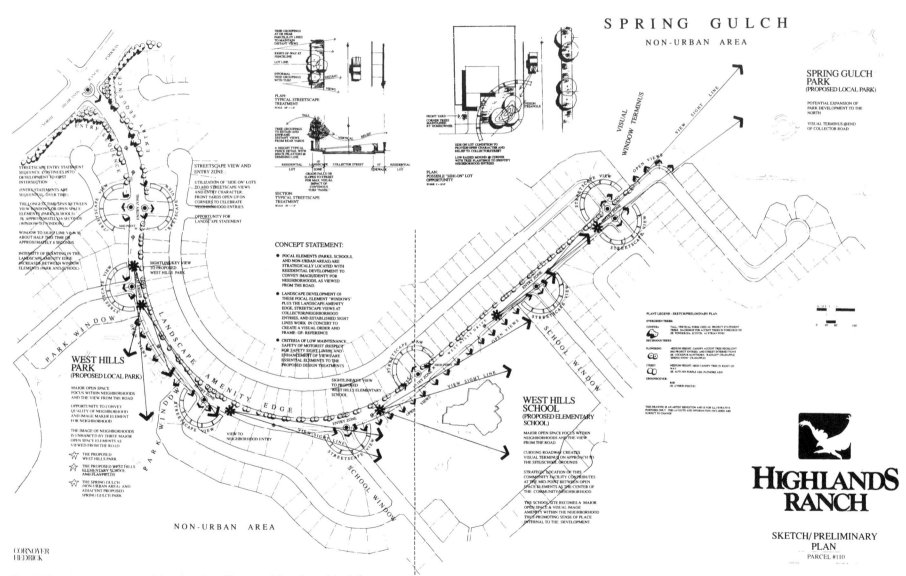

SPRING GULCH
NON-URBAN AREA

TREE GROUPINGS
AT OR NEAR
PARCEL/LOT LINES
TO MAINTAIN
DISTANT VIEWS

RIGHT-OF-WAY AT
FENCELINE

LOT LINE

INFORMAL
TREE GROUPINGS
WITH TURF

PLAN:
TYPICAL STREETSCAPE
TREATMENT
SCALE 1/8" = 1'-0"

TALL

VERTICAL RELIEF

TREE GROUPINGS
TO RETAIN AND
ENFRAME
DISTANT VIEWS
FROM REAR YARDS

6' HEIGHT TYPICAL
FENCE DETAIL WITH
BRICK PILASTERS @
DEMISING LINE

RESIDENTIAL LANDSCAPE COLLECTOR STREET RESIDENTIAL
LOT ZONE SIDEWALK LOT
GRADE FALLS OR
SLOPES TO STREET
FOR MAX. VISUAL
IMPACT OF
CONTINOUS
TURF "PANEL"

SECTION:
TYPICAL STREETSCAPE
TREATMENT
SCALE 1/8" = 1'-0"

FRONT YARD
CORNER TREES
MAINTAINED
BY HOMEOWNER

VISION
TRIANGLE

SIDE ON LOT CONDITION TO
PROVIDED OPEN CHARACTER AND
RELIEF TO COLLECTOR STREET

LOW RAISED MOUND @ CORNER
WITH TREE PLANTINGS TO IDENTIFY
NEIGHBORHOOD ENTRIES

PLAN:
POSSIBLE "SIDE-ON" LOT
OPPORTUNITY
SCALE 1" = 10'-0"

STREETSCAPE ENTRY STATEMENT
SEQUENCE CONTINUES INTO
DEVELOPMENT TO FIRST
INTERSECTION

(ENTRY STATEMENTS ARE
SEQUENTIAL OVER TIME)

THE LONGEST TIME SPAN BETWEEN
VIEW WINDOW (OR OPEN SPACE
ELEMENTS (PARKS SCHOOLS)
IS APPROXIMATELY 16 SECONDS
(WINDOW TO WINDOW)

WINDOW TO SIGHT LINE VIEW IS
ABOUT HALF THIS TIME OR
APPROXIMATELY 8 SECONDS

INTENSITY OF PLANTING IN THE
LANDSCAPE AMENITY EDGE
INCREASES BETWEEN WINDOW
ELEMENTS (PARK AND SCHOOL)

STREETSCAPE VIEW AND
ENTRY ZONE:

UTILIZATION OF "SIDE-ON" LOTS
TO ADD STREETSCAPE VIEWS
AND ENTRY CHARACTER.
FRONT YARDS OPEN UP ON
CORNERS TO CELEBRATE
NEIGHBORHOOD ENTRIES

OPPORTUNITY FOR
LANDSCAPE STATEMENT

SIGHTLINE/KEY VIEW
TO PROPOSED
WEST HILLS PARK

CONCEPT STATEMENT:

● FOCAL ELEMENTS (PARKS, SCHOOLS,
AND NON-URBAN AREAS) ARE
STRATEGICALLY LOCATED WITH
RESIDENTIAL DEVELOPMENT TO
CONVEY IMAGE/IDENTY FOR
NEIGHBORHOODS, AS VIEWED
FROM THE ROAD.

● LANDSCAPE DEVELOPMENT OF
THESE FOCAL ELEMENT "WINDOWS"
PLUS THE LANDSCAPE AMENITY
EDGE, STREETSCAPE VIEWS AT
COLLECTOR/NEIGHBORHOOD
ENTRIES, AND ESTABLISHED SIGHT
LINES WORK IN CONCERT TO
CREATE A VISUAL ORDER AND
FRAME- OF- REFERENCE

● CRITERIA OF LOW MAINTENANCE,
SAFETY OF MOTORIST (RESPECT
FOR SAFETY SIGHT LINES), AND
ENHANCEMENT OF VIEWS ARE
ESSENTIAL ELEMENTS TO THE
PROPOSED DESIGN TREATMENTS

SIGHTLINE/KEY VIEW
TO PROPOSED
WEST HILLS ELEMENTARY
SCHOOL

WEST HILLS
PARK
(PROPOSED LOCAL PARK)

MAJOR OPEN SPACE
FOCUS WITHIN NEIGHBORHOODS
AND THE VIEW FROM THE ROAD

OPPORTUNITY TO CONVEY
QUALITY OF NEIGHBORHOOD
AND IMAGE MAKER ELEMENT
FOR NEIGHBORHOOD

THE IMAGE OF NEIGHBORHOODS
IS ENHANCED BY THREE MAJOR
OPEN SPACE ELEMENTS AS
VIEWED FROM THE ROAD

☆ THE PROPOSED
WEST HILLS PARK

☆ THE PROPOSED WEST HILLS
ELEMENTARY SCHOOL
AND PLAYFIELDS

☆ THE SPRING GULCH
(NON-URBAN AREA) AND
ADJACENT PROPOSED
SPRING GULCH PARK

NON-URBAN AREA

WEST HILLS
SCHOOL
(PROPOSED ELEMENTARY
SCHOOL)

MAJOR OPEN SPACE FOCUS WITHIN
NEIGHBORHOODS AND THE VIEW
FROM THE ROAD

CURVING ROADWAY CREATES
VISUAL TERMINUS ON APPROACH TO
THE SITE/SCHOOL GROUNDS

STRATEGIC LOCATION OF THIS
COMMUNITY FACILITY CONTRIBUTES
AT THE MID-POINT BETWEEN OPEN
SPACE ELEMENTS AS THE CENTER OF
THE COMMUNITY/NEIGHBORHOOD

THE SCHOOL SITE BECOMES A MAJOR
OPEN SPACE & VISUAL IMAGE
AMENITY WITHIN THE NEIGHBORHOOD
THUS PROMOTING SENSE OF PLACE
INTERNAL TO THE DEVELOPMENT

VIEW TO
NEIGHBORHOOD ENTRY

SPRING GULCH
PARK
(PROPOSED LOCAL PARK)

POTENTIAL EXPANSION OF
PARK DEVELOPMENT TO THE
NORTH

VISUAL TERMINUS @ END
OF COLLECTOR ROAD

PLANT LEGEND - SKETCH/PRELIMINARY PLAN

EVERGREEN TREES:

CONIFER: TALL, VERTICAL FORM USED AS PROJECT STATEMENT
TREES. BACKDROP FOR ACCENT TREES IN FOREGROUND
(IE PONDEROSA, SCOTCH, AUSTRIAN PINE)

DECIDUOUS TREES:

FLOWERING: MEDIUM HEIGHT. CANOPY ACCENT TREE HIGHLIGHT
2ND PROJECT ENTRIES, AND STREET INTERSECTIONS
(IE COCKSPUR HAWTHORN, RADIANT CRABAPPLE,
SPRING SNOW CRABAPPLE)

STREET: MEDIUM HEIGHT, HIGH CANOPY TREE IN RIGHT OF
WAY
(IE AUTUMN PURPLE ASH, PATMORE ASH)

GROUNDCOVER: SOD
(IE HYBRID FESCUE)

THIS DRAWING IS AN ARTIST RENDITION AND IS FOR ILLUSTRATIVE
PURPOSES ONLY. THE LAYOUTS AND INFORMATION INCLUDED ARE
SUBJECT TO CHANGE.

HIGHLANDS
RANCH

SKETCH/ PRELIMINARY
PLAN
PARCEL #110

CORNOYER
HEDRICK

Highlands Ranch. Combination hardline and freehand in ink
on vellum.

140

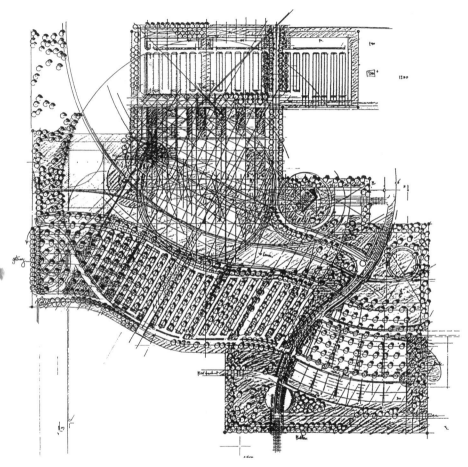

Weber State University. Hardline in ink on vellum. Color pencil is applied over the original, adding clarity to a busy concept plan.

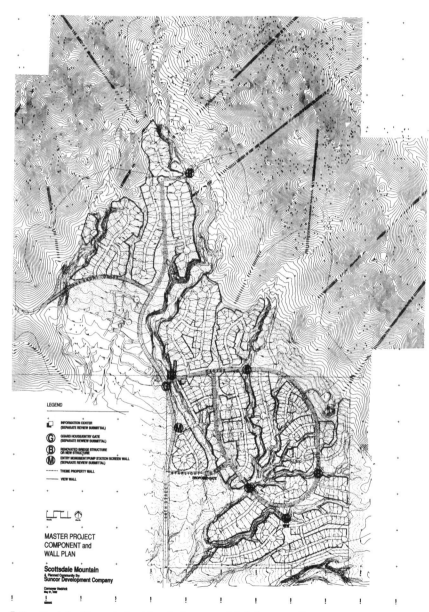

LEGEND

- INFORMATION CENTER (SEPARATE REVIEW SUBMITTAL)
- G GUARD HOUSE/ENTRY GATE (SEPARATE REVIEW SUBMITTAL)
- B RENOVATED BRIDGE STRUCTURE OR NEW STRUCTURE
- M ENTRY MONUMENT/PUMP STATION SCREEN WALL (SEPARATE REVIEW SUBMITTAL)
- — — — THEME PROPERTY WALL
- ——— VIEW WALL

MASTER PROJECT
COMPONENT and
WALL PLAN

Scottsdale Mountain
A Planned Community By:
Suncor Development Company

Conveyor Hedrick
May 31, 1995

Scottsdale Mountain. Hand-drawn with ink on vellum over an AutoCADD base drawing. The text and title block are computer generated and manually applied with sticky-back material.

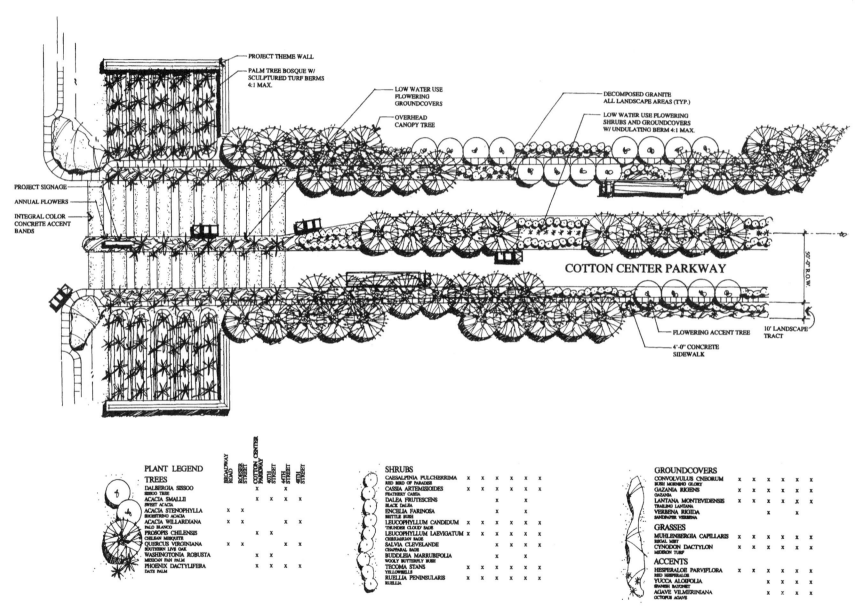

Cotton Center. Freehand ink on mylar, with computer-generated base, title block, and legends.

PLANT LEGEND

TREES

	Broadway Road	Rosser Street	Cotton Center Parkway	40th Street	44th Street	46th Street
DALBERGIA SISSOO — Sissoo Tree			X	X	X	X
ACACIA SMALLII — Sweet Acacia			X	X	X	X
ACACIA STENOPHYLLA — Shoestring Acacia	X	X				
ACACIA WILLARDIANA — Palo Blanco	X	X			X	X
PROSOPIS CHILENSIS — Chilean Mesquite			X	X		
QUERCUS VIRGINIANA — Southern Live Oak	X	X			X	X
WASHINGTONIA ROBUSTA — Mexican Fan Palm			X	X		
PHOENIX DACTYLIFERA — Date Palm			X	X	X	X

SHRUBS

	Broadway Road	Rosser Street	Cotton Center Parkway	40th Street	44th Street	46th Street
CAESALPINIA PULCHERRIMA — Red Bird of Paradise	X	X	X	X	X	X
CASSIA ARTEMISIOIDES — Feathery Cassia	X	X	X	X	X	X
DALEA FRUTESCENS — Black Dalea			X		X	
ENCELIA FARINOSA — Brittle Bush			X		X	
LEUCOPHYLLUM CANDIDUM — 'Thunder Cloud' Sage	X	X	X	X		
LEUCOPHYLLUM LAEVIGATUM — Chihuahuan Sage	X	X	X	X	X	
SALVIA CLEVELANDII — Chaparral Sage			X	X	X	
BUDDLEIA MARRUBIFOLIA — Wooly Butterfly Bush			X		X	
TECOMA STANS — Yellowbells	X	X	X	X	X	
RUELLIA PENINSULARIS — Ruellia	X	X	X	X	X	X

GROUNDCOVERS

	Broadway Road	Rosser Street	Cotton Center Parkway	40th Street	44th Street	46th Street
CONVOLVULUS CNEORUM — Bush Morning Glory	X	X	X	X	X	X
GAZANIA RIGENS — Gazania	X	X	X	X	X	X
LANTANA MONTEVIDENSIS — Trailing Lantana	X	X	X	X	X	X
VERBENA RIGIDA — Sandpaper Verbena			X		X	

GRASSES

	Broadway Road	Rosser Street	Cotton Center Parkway	40th Street	44th Street	46th Street
MUHLENBERGIA CAPILLARIS — Regal Mist	X	X	X	X	X	X
CYNODON DACTYLON — Midiron Turf	X	X	X	X	X	X

ACCENTS

	Broadway Road	Rosser Street	Cotton Center Parkway	40th Street	44th Street	46th Street
HESPERALOE PARVIFLORA — Red Hesperaloe	X	X	X	X	X	X
YUCCA ALOIFOLIA — Spanish Bayonet			X	X	X	X
AGAVE VILMERINIANA — Octopus Agave			X	X	X	X

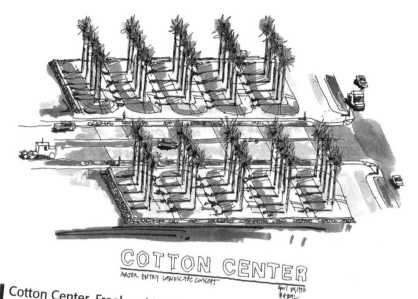

COTTON CENTER
MAJOR ENTRY LANDSCAPE CONCEPT
April 29, 1998
#97109L

Cotton Center. Freehand in ink on tracing paper with color marker on original.

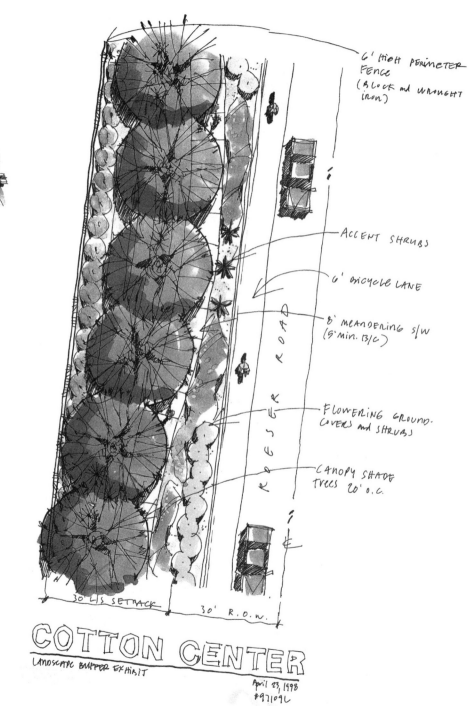

6' HIGH PERIMETER FENCE
(BLOCK and WROUGHT IRON)

ACCENT SHRUBS

6' BICYCLE LANE

8' MEANDERING S/W
(5' MIN. B/C)

FLOWERING GROUND-COVERS and SHRUBS

CANOPY SHADE TREES 20' O.C.

KOGER ROAD

30' L/S SETBACK

30' R.O.W.

COTTON CENTER
LANDSCAPE BUFFER EXHIBIT
April 23, 1998
#97109L

153

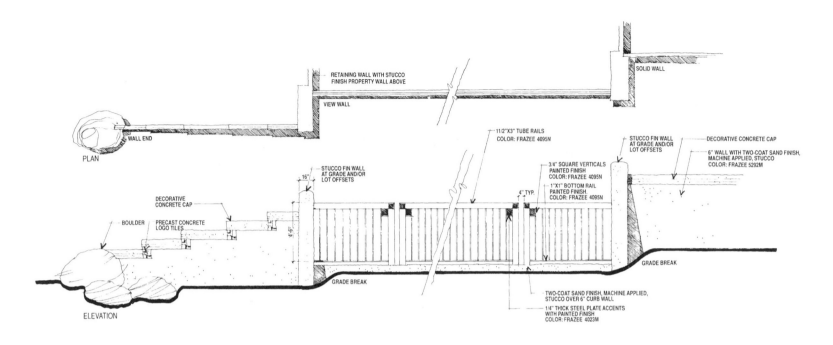

PLAN

WALL END

RETAINING WALL WITH STUCCO
FINISH PROPERTY WALL ABOVE

VIEW WALL

SOLID WALL

11/2"X3" TUBE RAILS
COLOR: FRAZEE 4095N

STUCCO FIN WALL
AT GRADE AND/OR
LOT OFFSETS

DECORATIVE CONCRETE CAP

3/4" SQUARE VERTICALS
PAINTED FINISH
COLOR: FRAZEE 4095N

6" WALL WITH TWO-COAT SAND FINISH,
MACHINE APPLIED, STUCCO
COLOR: FRAZEE 5292M

DECORATIVE
CONCRETE CAP

STUCCO FIN WALL
AT GRADE AND/OR
LOT OFFSETS

16"

4" TYP.

1"X1" BOTTOM RAIL
PAINTED FINISH.
COLOR: FRAZEE 4095N

BOULDER

PRECAST CONCRETE
LOGO TILES

3'-6"

GRADE BREAK

GRADE BREAK

ELEVATION

GRADE BREAK

TWO-COAT SAND FINISH, MACHINE APPLIED,
STUCCO OVER 6" CURB WALL

1/4" THICK STEEL PLATE ACCENTS
WITH PAINTED FINISH
COLOR: FRAZEE 4023M

PROPERTY WALL   1/2"=1'-0"

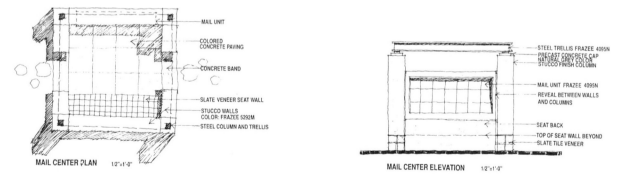

MAIL UNIT

COLORED
CONCRETE PAVING

CONCRETE BAND

SLATE VENEER SEAT WALL

STUCCO WALLS
COLOR: FRAZEE 5292M

STEEL COLUMN AND TRELLIS

MAIL CENTER PLAN   1/2"=1'-0"

STEEL TRELLIS FRAZEE 4095N
PRECAST CONCRETE CAP
NATURAL GREY COLOR
STUCCO FINISH COLUMN

MAIL UNIT FRAZEE 4095N

REVEAL BETWEEN WALLS
AND COLUMNS

SEAT BACK

TOP OF SEAT WALL BEYOND

SLATE TILE VENEER

MAIL CENTER ELEVATION   1/2"=1'-0"

Scottsdale Mountain
A Planned Community By:
Suncor Development Company

Cornoyer Hedrick
May 21, 1992
92055G

| Scottsdale Mountain. Hand-drawn with ink on vellum. The text
and title block are computer generated and manually applied
with sticky-back material.

Construction Documents

Construction documents are developed as graphic and written instructions for contractors to use as a guide for implementation. The technical plans, when combined with specifications and contractor agreements, represent the full set of contract documents. Construction documents are highly accurate and detailed. The graphic composition should be clear, concise, and efficient in its use of space. Duplication of information is not desirable, because it wastes time and resources and the risk of creating errors is greater. Construction documents are prepared in stages—typically referred to as Schematic Design (30% complete), Design Development (60% complete), and Construction Documents (100% complete). The Schematic Design package contains accurate base information and establishes all the design elements in the location and elevations proposed. The Design Development package is a preliminary set of construction documents with plan refinements, details, sections, and draft specifications. The Construction Documents are fully completed, typically sealed by a design professional, and require submission to the appropriate public agencies for review and approval. This chapter is dedicated to illustrating examples of construction documents that share a successful blend of style, accuracy, and composition. All of the examples illustrated are, in some form or another, created in AutoCADD or Microstation and represent 100% design packages. The following examples are exerpted from complete design packages.

CHAPTER FIVE

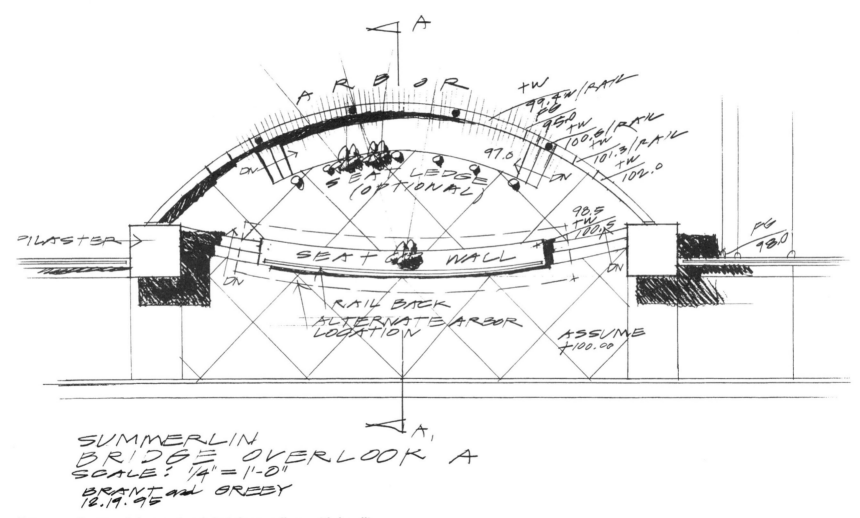

ARBOR

+W
99.4 W/RAIL
TW
95.0
+W
100.6/RAIL
+W
101.3/RAIL
+W
102.0

97.0

SEAT LEDGE
(OPTIONAL)

98.5
TW
100.5

PILASTER

SEAT ⊕ WALL

FG
98.0

RAIL BACK
ALTERNATE ARBOR
LOCATION

ASSUME
+100.00

DN

DN

DN

DN

SUMMERLIN
BRIDGE OVERLOOK A
SCALE: 1/4" = 1'-0"
BRANT and GREEY
12.19.95

Summerlin. Hand-drawn sketch in ink on vellum with hardline
base.

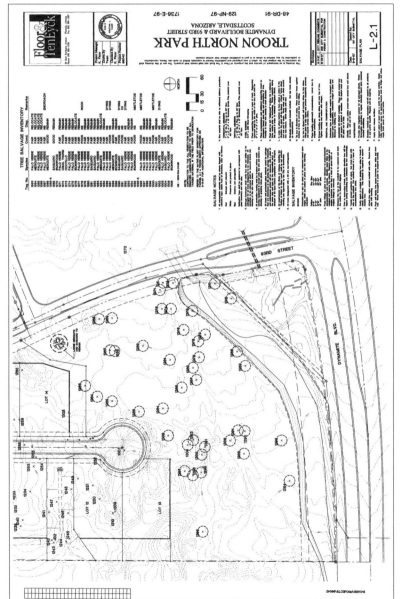

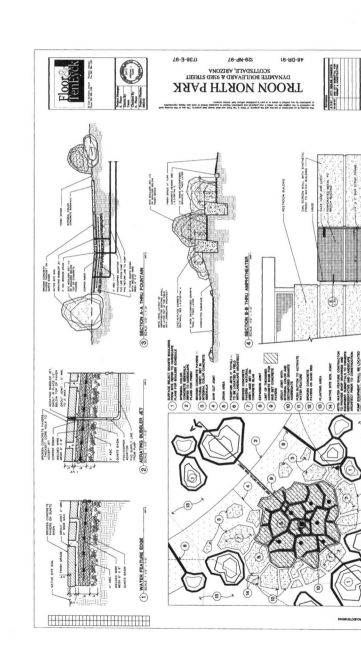

Troon North

Troon North

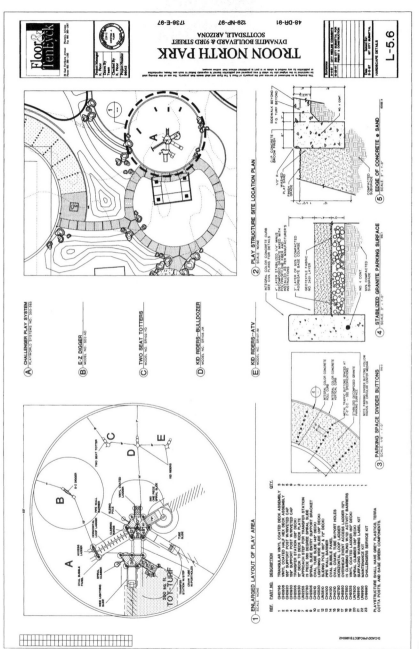

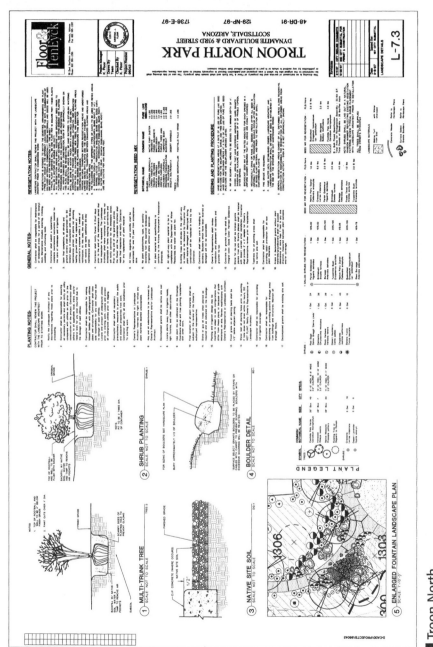

Troon North

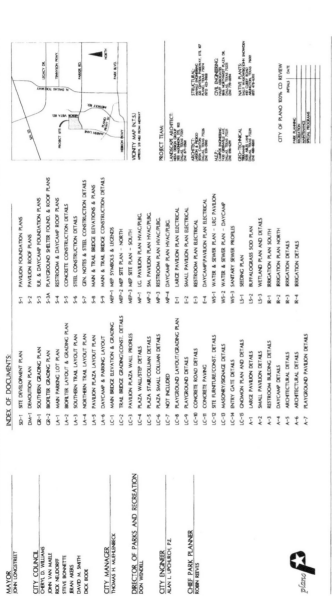

Arbor Hills Cover Sheet

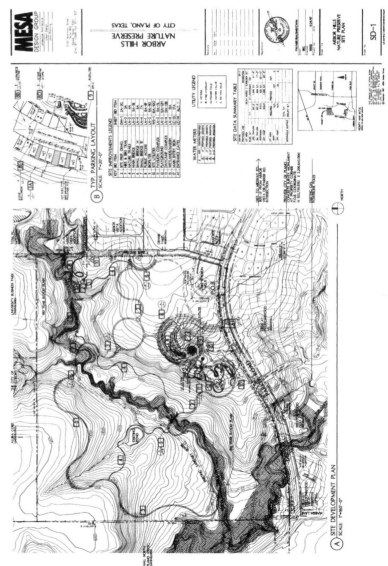

Arbor Hills

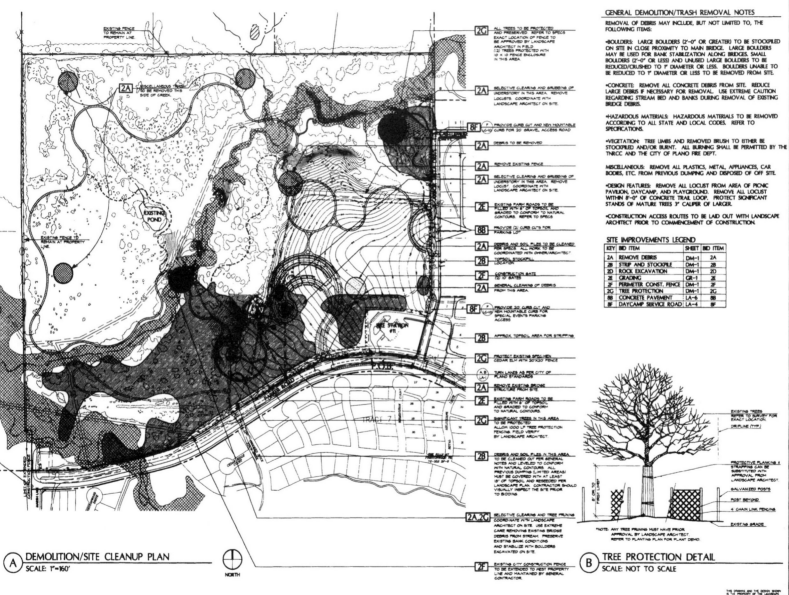

REMOVAL OF DEBRIS MAY INCLUDE, BUT NOT LIMITED TO, THE FOLLOWING ITEMS:

•BOULDERS: LARGE BOULDERS (2'-0" OR GREATER) TO BE STOCKPILED ON SITE IN CLOSE PROXIMITY TO MAIN BRIDGE. LARGE BOULDERS MAY BE USED FOR BANK STABILIZATION ALONG BRIDGES. SMALL BOULDERS (2'-0" OR LESS) AND UNUSED LARGE BOULDERS TO BE REDUCED/CRUSHED TO 1" DIAMETER OR LESS. BOULDERS UNABLE TO BE REDUCED TO 1" DIAMETER OR LESS TO BE REMOVED FROM SITE.

•CONCRETE: REMOVE ALL CONCRETE DEBRIS FROM SITE. REDUCE LARGE DEBRIS IF NECESSARY FOR REMOVAL. USE EXTREME CAUTION REGARDING STREAM BED AND BANKS DURING REMOVAL OF EXISTING BRIDGE DEBRIS.

•HAZARDOUS MATERIALS: HAZARDOUS MATERIALS TO BE REMOVED ACCORDING TO ALL STATE AND LOCAL CODES. REFER TO SPECIFICATIONS.

•VEGETATION: TREE LIMBS AND REMOVED BRUSH TO EITHER BE STOCKPILED AND/OR BURNT. ALL BURNING SHALL BE PERMITTED BY THE TNRCC AND THE CITY OF PLANO FIRE DEPT.

MISCELLANEOUS: REMOVE ALL PLASTICS, METAL, APPLIANCES, CAR BODIES, ETC. FROM PREVIOUS DUMPING AND DISPOSED OF OFF SITE.

•DESIGN FEATURES: REMOVE ALL LOCUST FROM AREA OF PICNIC PAVILION, DAYCAMP, AND PLAYGROUND. REMOVE ALL LOCUST WITHIN 8'-0" OF CONCRETE TRAIL LOOP. PROTECT SIGNIFICANT STANDS OF MATURE TREES 3" CALIPER OR LARGER.

•CONSTRUCTION ACCESS ROUTES TO BE LAID OUT WITH LANDSCAPE ARCHITECT PRIOR TO COMMENCEMENT OF CONSTRUCTION.

SITE IMPROVEMENTS LEGEND

KEY	BID ITEM	SHEET	BID ITEM
2A	REMOVE DEBRIS	DM-1	2A
2B	STRIP AND STOCKPILE	DM-1	2B
2D	ROCK EXCAVATION	DM-1	2D
2E	GRADING	GR-1	2E
2F	PERIMETER CONST. FENCE	DM-1	2F
2G	TREE PROTECTION	DM-1	2G
8B	CONCRETE PAVEMENT	LA-6	8B
8F	DAYCAMP SERVICE ROAD	LA-4	8F

A DEMOLITION/SITE CLEANUP PLAN
SCALE: 1"=160'

NORTH

B TREE PROTECTION DETAIL
SCALE: NOT TO SCALE

MESA
DESIGN GROUP

Landscape Architecture
Urban Design
Land Planning

3100 McKinnon Street
Suite 905
Dallas, Texas 75201
(214) 871-0568 Fax: 871-1507

ARBOR HILLS
NATURE PRESERVE
CITY OF PLANO, TEXAS

Revisions
No. Date Item

Registration

Drawn RLW/PH/CWM
BRC
Checked 95102 4/24/97
Project No. Date

Sheet Title
DEMOLITION/SITE
CLEANUP PLAN

BID ITEM 2, 8

Sheet No.
DM-1

Arbor Hills

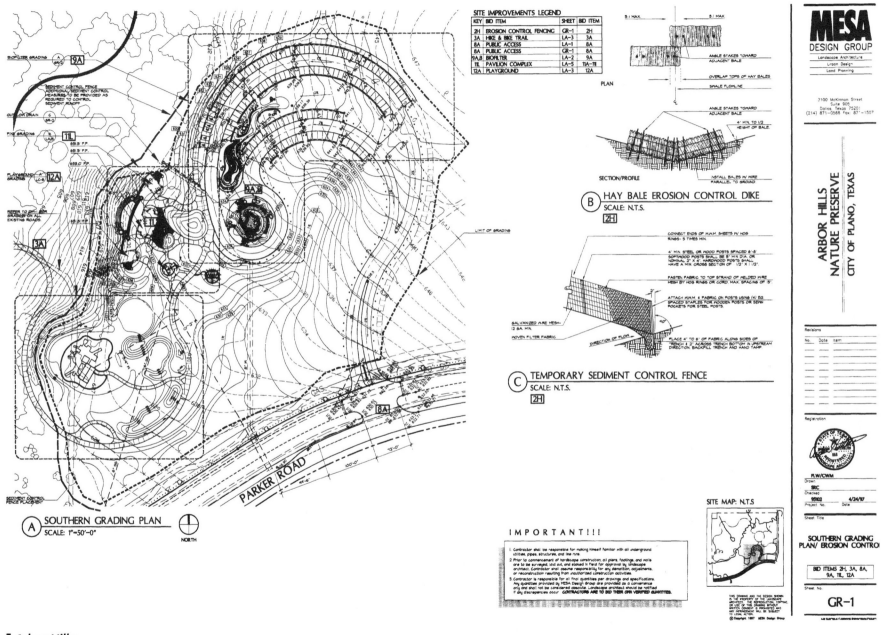

SITE IMPROVEMENTS LEGEND

KEY	BID ITEM	SHEET	BID ITEM
2H	EROSION CONTROL FENCING	GR-1	2H
3A	HIKE & BIKE TRAIL	LA-3	3A
8A	PUBLIC ACCESS	LA-1	8A
8A	PUBLIC ACCESS	GR-1	8A
9A,B	BIOFILTER	LA-2	9A
11L	PAVILION COMPLEX	LA-5	11A-11L
12A	PLAYGROUND	LA-3	12A

PLAN

(B) HAY BALE EROSION CONTROL DIKE
SCALE: N.T.S.
2H

(C) TEMPORARY SEDIMENT CONTROL FENCE
SCALE: N.T.S.
2H

(A) SOUTHERN GRADING PLAN
SCALE: 1"=50'-0"
NORTH

PARKER ROAD

MESA
DESIGN GROUP
Landscape Architecture
Urban Design
Land Planning

3100 McKinnon Street
Suite 905
Dallas, Texas 75201
(214) 871-0568 Fax: 87-1507

ARBOR HILLS
NATURE PRESERVE
CITY OF PLANO, TEXAS

Revisions
No. Date Item

Registration

PLW/CWM
Drawn
SRC
Checked
95122   4/24/97
Project No.   Date

Sheet Title

SOUTHERN GRADING
PLAN/ EROSION CONTROL

BID ITEMS 2H, 3A, 8A,
9A, 11L, 12A

Sheet No.
GR-1

IMPORTANT!!!

1. Contractor shall be responsible for making himself familiar with all underground utilities, pipes, structures, and line runs.

2. Prior to commencement of hardscape construction, all piers, footings, and walls are to be surveyed, laid out, and staked in field for approval by landscape architect. Contractor shall assume responsibility for any demolition, adjustments, or reconstruction resulting from unauthorized construction activities.

3. Contractor is responsible for all final quantities per drawings and specifications. Any quantities provided by MESA Design Group are provided as a convenience only and shall not be considered absolute. Landscape architect should be notified if any discrepancies occur. CONTRACTORS ARE TO BID THEIR OWN VERIFIED QUANTITIES.

SITE MAP: N.T.S

Arbor Hills

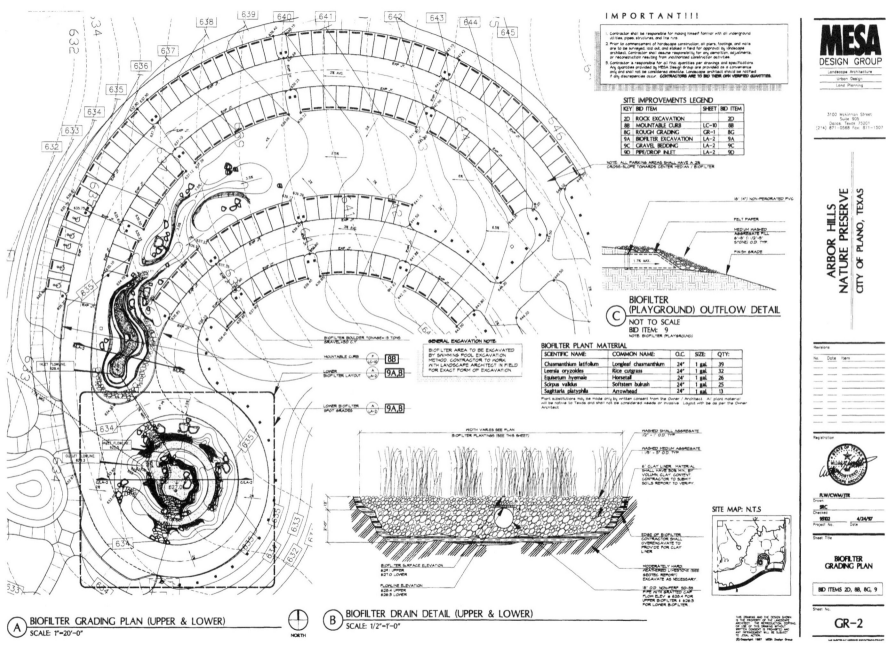

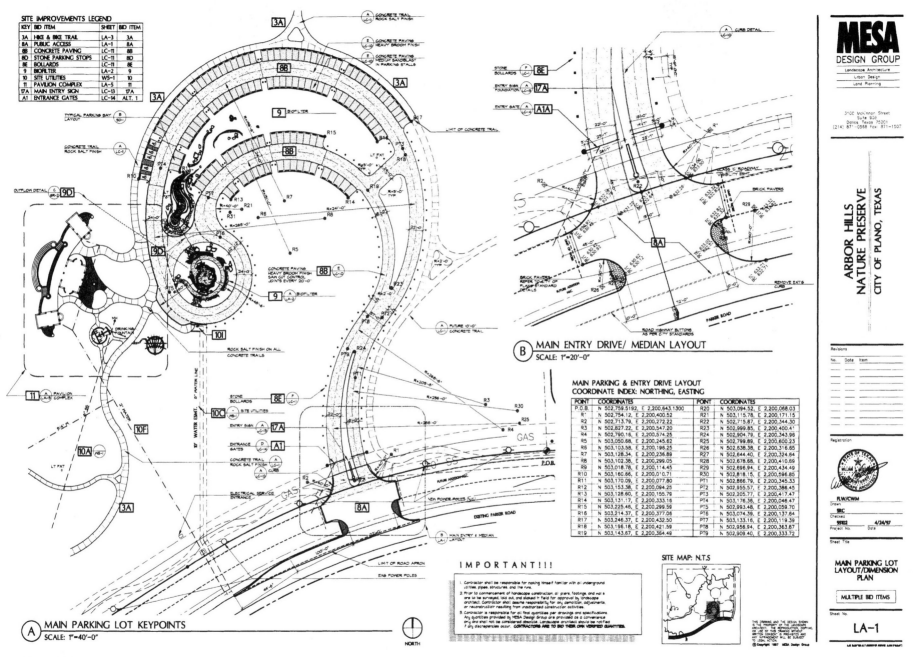

A MAIN PARKING LOT KEYPOINTS
SCALE: 1"=40'-0"

B MAIN ENTRY DRIVE/ MEDIAN LAYOUT
SCALE: 1"=20'-0"

SITE IMPROVEMENTS LEGEND

KEY	BID ITEM	SHEET	BID ITEM
3A	HIKE & BIKE TRAIL	LA-3	3A
8A	PUBLIC ACCESS	LA-1	8A
8B	CONCRETE PAVING	LC-11	8B
8D	STONE PARKING STOPS	LC-11	8D
8E	BOLLARDS	LC-11	8E
9	BIOFILTER	LA-2	9
10	SITE UTILITIES	WS-1	10
11	PAVILION COMPLEX	LA-5	11
17A	MAIN ENTRY SIGN	LC-13	17A
A1	ENTRANCE GATES	LC-14	ALT. 1

MAIN PARKING & ENTRY DRIVE LAYOUT
COORDINATE INDEX: NORTHING, EASTING

POINT	COORDINATES	POINT	COORDINATES
P.O.B.	N 502,759.5192, E 2,200,643.1300	R20	N 503,094.52, E 2,200,068.03
R1	N 502,754.12, E 2,200,400.52	R21	N 503,115.78, E 2,200,171.15
R2	N 502,713.79, E 2,200,272.22	R22	N 502,719.87, E 2,200,344.30
R3	N 502,827.22, E 2,200,547.20	R23	N 502,999.85, E 2,200,400.41
R4	N 502,790.16, E 2,200,574.25	R24	N 502,904.79, E 2,200,343.96
R5	N 503,050.68, E 2,200,245.62	R25	N 502,799.89, E 2,200,600.23
R6	N 503,103.58, E 2,200,198.25	R26	N 502,638.38, E 2,200,316.65
R7	N 503,128.34, E 2,200,236.89	R27	N 502,644.40, E 2,200,324.64
R8	N 503,102.38, E 2,200,299.05	R28	N 502,678.68, E 2,200,410.89
R9	N 503,018.78, E 2,200,114.45	R29	N 502,696.94, E 2,200,434.49
R10	N 503,160.66, E 2,200,0'0.71	R30	N 502,818.15, E 2,200,596.85
R11	N 503,170.09, E 2,200,077.80	PT1	N 502,866.79, E 2,200,345.33
R12	N 503,153.38, E 2,200,094.25	PT2	N 502,955.57, E 2,200,386.45
R13	N 503,128.60, E 2,200,155.79	PT3	N 502,205.77, E 2,200,417.47
R14	N 503,131.17, E 2,200,333.16	PT4	N 503,176.36, E 2,200,046.47
R15	N 503,225.46, E 2,200,299.59	PT5	N 502,993.48, E 2,200,059.70
R16	N 503,214.37, E 2,200,377.06	PT6	N 503,074.39, E 2,200,137.64
R17	N 503,246.37, E 2,200,432.50	PT7	N 503,133.16, E 2,200,119.39
R18	N 503,196.18, E 2,200,421.59	PT8	N 502,956.94, E 2,200,363.87
R19	N 503,143.67, E 2,200,364.49	PT9	N 502,908.40, E 2,200,333.72

IMPORTANT!!!

1. Contractor shall be responsible for making himself familiar with all underground utilities, pipes, structures, and line runs.

2. Prior to commencement of landscape construction, all piers, footings, and wall are to be surveyed, laid out, and staked in field for approval by landscape architect. Contractor shall assume responsibility for any demolition, adjustments, or reconstruction resulting from unauthorized construction activities.

3. Contractor is responsible for all final quantities per drawings and specifications. Any quantities provided by MESA Design Group are provided as a convenience only and shall not be considered absolute. Landscape architect should be notified if any discrepancies occur. **CONTRACTORS ARE TO BID THEIR OWN VERIFIED QUANTITIES.**

SITE MAP: N.T.S

MESA
DESIGN GROUP
Landscape Architecture
Urban Design
Land Planning

3100 McKinnon Street
Suite 905
Dallas, Texas 75201
(214) 871-0568 Fax: 871-1507

ARBOR HILLS
NATURE PRESERVE
CITY OF PLANO, TEXAS

Revisions		
No.	Date	Item

Registration

Drawn: RLW/CWM
Checked: SRC
Project No. 95102
Date: 4/24/97

Sheet Title:
MAIN PARKING LOT
LAYOUT/DIMENSION
PLAN

MULTIPLE BID ITEMS

Sheet No.
LA-1

NORTH

■ Arbor Hills

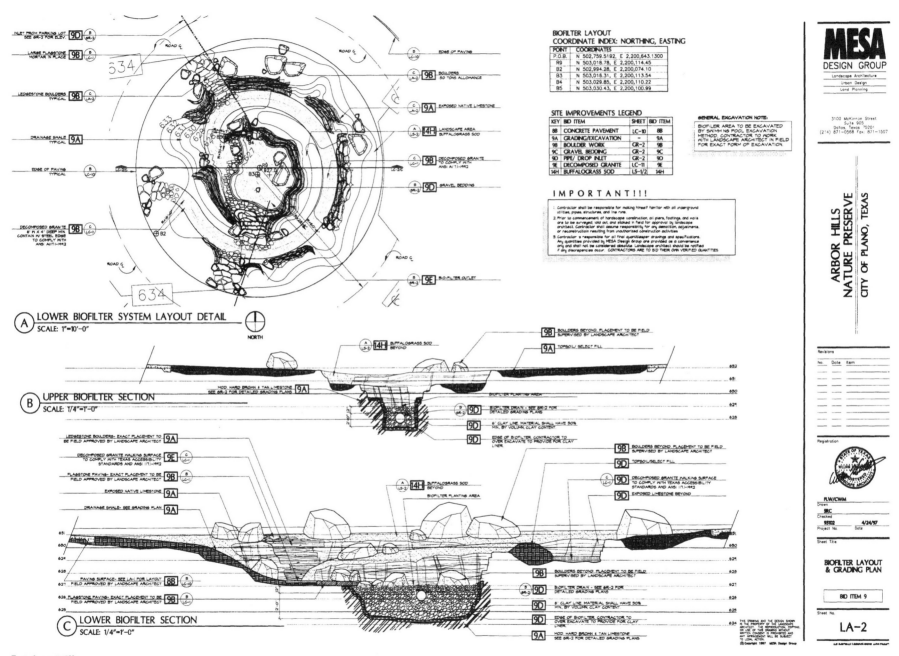

BIOFILTER LAYOUT
COORDINATE INDEX: NORTHING, EASTING

POINT	COORDINATES
P.O.B.	N 502,759.5192, E 2,200,643.1300
R9	N 503,018.78, E 2,200,114.45
B2	N 502,994.28, E 2,200,074.10
B3	N 503,018.31, E 2,200,113.54
B4	N 503,029.85, E 2,200,110.22
B5	N 503,030.43, E 2,200,100.99

SITE IMPROVEMENTS LEGEND

KEY	BID ITEM	SHEET	BID ITEM
8B	CONCRETE PAVEMENT	LC-10	8B
9A	GRADING/EXCAVATION		9A
9B	BOULDER WORK	GR-2	9B
9C	GRAVEL BEDDING	GR-2	9C
9D	PIPE/ DROP INLET	GR-2	9D
9E	DECOMPOSED GRANITE	LC-11	9E
14H	BUFFALOGRASS SOD	LS-1/2	14H

GENERAL EXCAVATION NOTE:
BIOFILTER AREA TO BE EXCAVATED BY SWIMMING POOL EXCAVATION METHOD. CONTRACTOR TO WORK WITH LANDSCAPE ARCHITECT IN FIELD FOR EXACT FORM OF EXCAVATION.

IMPORTANT!!!

1. Contractor shall be responsible for making himself familiar with all underground utilities, pipes, structures, and line runs.

2. Prior to commencement of hardscape construction, all piers, footings, and walls are to be surveyed, and laid out, and staked in field for approval by landscape architect. Contractor shall assume responsibility for any demolition, adjustments, or reconstruction resulting from unauthorized construction activities.

3. Contractor is responsible for all final quant.takeoff drawings and specifications. Any quantities provided by MESA Design Group are provided as a convenience only and shall not be considered absolute. Landscape architect should be notified if any discrepancies occur. CONTRACTORS ARE TO BID THEIR OWN VERIFIED QUANTITIES.

(A) LOWER BIOFILTER SYSTEM LAYOUT DETAIL
SCALE: 1"=10'-0"

(B) UPPER BIOFILTER SECTION
SCALE: 1/4"=1'-0"

(C) LOWER BIOFILTER SECTION
SCALE: 1/4"=1'-0"

MESA
DESIGN GROUP
Landscape Architecture
Urban Design
Land Planning

3100 McKinnon Street
Suite 905
Dallas, Texas 75201
(214) 871-0568 Fax: 871-1507

ARBOR HILLS
NATURE PRESERVE
CITY OF PLANO, TEXAS

Revisions
No. Date Item

Registration

FLW/CWM
Drawn
SRC
Checked
93102   4/24/97
Project No.   Date

Sheet Title

BIOFILTER LAYOUT
& GRADING PLAN

BID ITEM 9

Sheet No.

LA-2

■ Arbor Hills

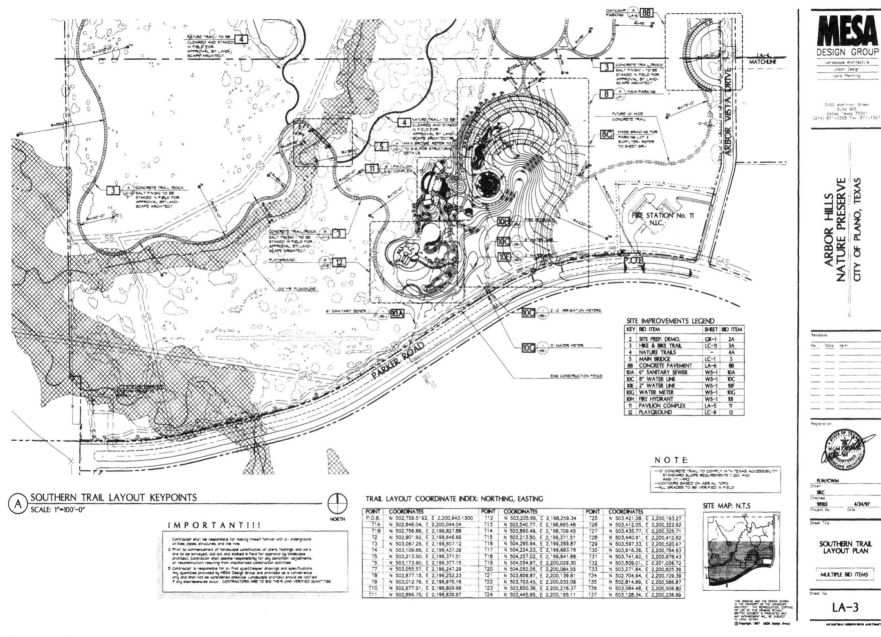

Arbor Hills

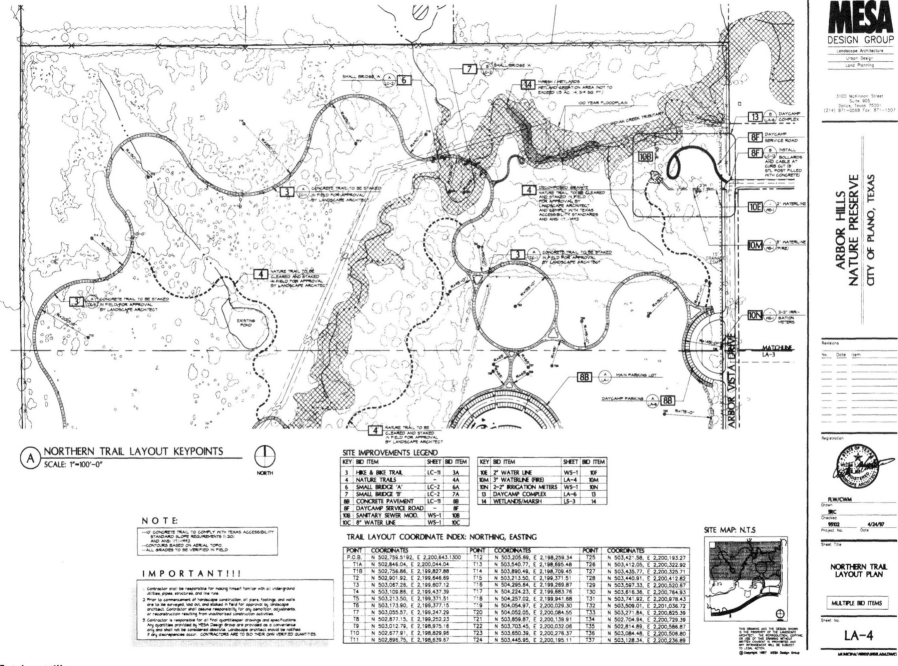

NORTHERN TRAIL LAYOUT KEYPOINTS
A SCALE: 1"=100'-0"

NORTH

NOTE:
- --10' CONCRETE TRAIL TO COMPLY WITH TEXAS ACCESSIBILITY STANDARD SLOPE REQUIREMENTS (1:20) AND ANSI 117.1-1992
- --CONTOURS BASED ON AERIAL TOPO.
- --ALL GRADES TO BE VERIFIED IN FIELD

IMPORTANT!!!
1. Contractor shall be responsible for making himself familiar with all underground utilities, pipes, structures, and the runs.
2. Prior to commencement of landscape construction, all piers, footings, and walls are to be surveyed, laid out, and staked in field for approval by landscape architect. Contractor shall assume responsibility for any demolition, adjustments, or reconstruction resulting from unauthorized construction activities.
3. Contractor is responsible for all final quantities per drawings and specifications. Any quantities provided by MESA Design Group are provided as a convenience only and shall not be considered absolute. Landscape architect should be notified if any discrepancies occur. CONTRACTORS ARE TO BID THEIR OWN VERIFIED QUANTITIES.

SITE IMPROVEMENTS LEGEND

KEY	BID ITEM	SHEET	BID ITEM
3	HIKE & BIKE TRAIL	LC-11	3A
4	NATURE TRAILS	–	4A
6	SMALL BRIDGE 'A'	LC-2	6A
7	SMALL BRIDGE 'B'	LC-2	7A
8B	CONCRETE PAVEMENT	LC-11	8B
8F	DAYCAMP SERVICE ROAD	–	8F
10B	SANITARY SEWER MOD.	WS-1	10B
10C	8" WATER LINE	WS-1	10C

KEY	BID ITEM	SHEET	BID ITEM
10E	2" WATER LINE	WS-1	10F
10M	3" WATERLINE (FIRE)	LA-4	10M
10N	2-2" IRRIGATION METERS	WS-1	10N
13	DAYCAMP COMPLEX	LA-6	13
14	WETLANDS/MARSH	LS-3	14

TRAIL LAYOUT COORDINATE INDEX: NORTHING, EASTING

POINT	COORDINATES	POINT	COORDINATES	POINT	COORDINATES
P.O.B.	N 502,759.5192, E 2,200,643.1300	T12	N 503,205.69, E 2,198,259.34	T25	N 503,421.58, E 2,200,193.27
T1A	N 502,846.04, E 2,200,044.04	T13	N 503,540.77, E 2,198,695.48	T26	N 503,412.05, E 2,200,322.92
T1B	N 502,756.86, E 2,199,827.88	T14	N 503,890.49, E 2,198,709.45	T27	N 503,435.77, E 2,200,325.71
T2	N 502,901.92, E 2,199,646.69	T15	N 503,213.50, E 2,199,371.51	T28	N 503,440.91, E 2,200,412.82
T3	N 503,067.26, E 2,199,607.12	T16	N 504,295.64, E 2,199,269.87	T29	N 503,597.33, E 2,200,520.67
T4	N 503,109.86, E 2,199,437.39	T17	N 504,224.23, E 2,199,683.76	T30	N 503,616.36, E 2,200,764.93
T5	N 503,213.50, E 2,199,371.51	T18	N 504,257.02, E 2,199,941.68	T31	N 503,741.92, E 2,200,978.43
T6	N 503,173.90, E 2,199,377.15	T19	N 504,054.97, E 2,200,029.30	T32	N 503,509.01, E 2,201,036.72
T7	N 503,055.57, E 2,199,247.29	T20	N 504,052.05, E 2,200,084.55	T33	N 503,271.84, E 2,200,825.39
T8	N 502,877.15, E 2,199,252.23	T21	N 503,859.87, E 2,200,139.91	T34	N 502,704.94, E 2,200,729.39
T9	N 502,012.79, E 2,198,975.16	T22	N 503,703.45, E 2,200,032.06	T35	N 502,814.89, E 2,200,586.87
T10	N 502,677.91, E 2,198,829.96	T23	N 503,650.39, E 2,200,276.37	T36	N 503,084.48, E 2,200,506.80
T11	N 502,896.75, E 2,198,639.67	T24	N 503,445.95, E 2,200,195.11	T37	N 503,128.34, E 2,200,236.89

MESA
DESIGN GROUP

Landscape Architecture
Urban Design
Land Planning

3100 McKinnon Street
Suite 905
Dallas, Texas 75201
(214) 871-0568 Fax. 871-1507

ARBOR HILLS NATURE PRESERVE
CITY OF PLANO, TEXAS

Revisions

No.	Date	Item

Registration

RLW/CWM
Drawn
SRC
Checked
95102   4/24/97
Project No.   Date

Sheet Title

NORTHERN TRAIL LAYOUT PLAN

MULTIPLE BID ITEMS

Sheet No.

LA-4

SITE MAP: N.T.S

THIS DRAWING AND THE DESIGN SHOWN IS THE PROPERTY OF THE LANDSCAPE ARCHITECT. THE REPRODUCTION, COPYING OR USE OF THIS DRAWING WITHOUT WRITTEN CONSENT IS PROHIBITED AND ANY INFRINGEMENT WILL BE SUBJECT TO LEGAL ACTION.

© Copyright 1997 MESA Design Group

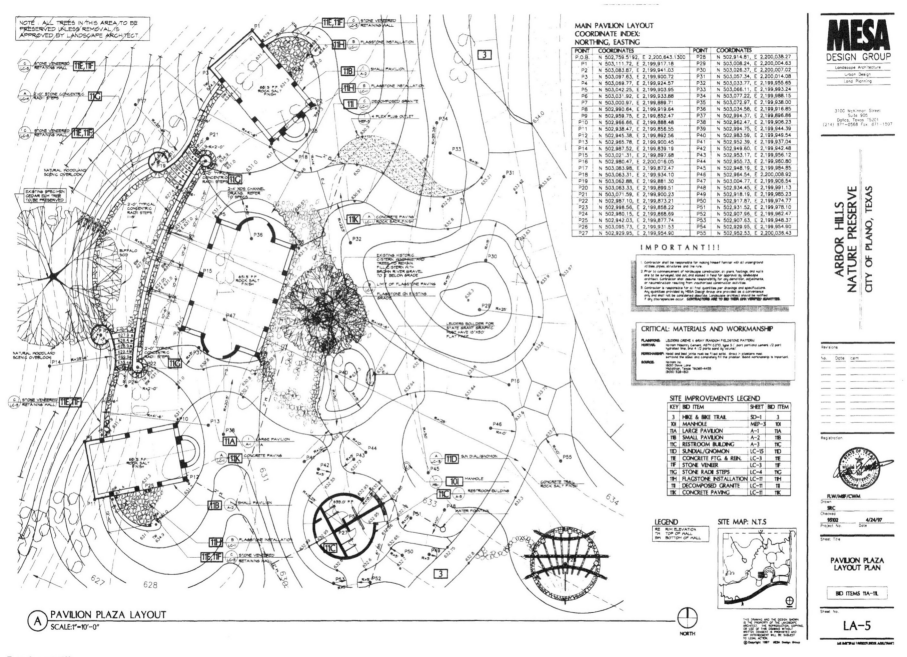

MAIN PAVILION LAYOUT
COORDINATE INDEX:
NORTHING, EASTING

POINT	COORDINATES		POINT	COORDINATES
P.O.B.	N 502,759.5192, E 2,200,643.1300		P28	N 502,914.81, E 2,200,038.27
P2	N 503,111.72, E 2,199,917.18		P29	N 503,008.24, E 2,200,004.63
P3	N 503,083.87, E 2,199,941.03		P30	N 503,026.37, E 2,200,007.02
P4	N 503,097.63, E 2,199,900.72		P31	N 503,057.34, E 2,200,014.08
P5	N 503,089.77, E 2,199,924.57		P32	N 503,033.77, E 2,199,955.65
P6	N 503,042.25, E 2,199,903.95		P33	N 503,066.11, E 2,199,993.24
P7	N 503,031.92, E 2,199,933.88		P34	N 503,077.22, E 2,199,988.15
P8	N 503,000.97, E 2,199,889.71		P35	N 503,072.97, E 2,199,938.00
P9	N 502,990.64, E 2,199,919.64		P36	N 503,034.58, E 2,199,916.85
P10	N 502,959.75, E 2,199,852.47		P37	N 502,994.37, E 2,199,896.86
P11	N 502,966.66, E 2,199,888.48		P38	N 502,962.47, E 2,199,906.23
P12	N 502,938.47, E 2,199,856.55		P39	N 502,994.75, E 2,199,944.39
P13	N 502,945.38, E 2,199,892.56		P40	N 502,983.59, E 2,199,949.54
P14	N 502,965.78, E 2,199,900.45		P41	N 502,952.39, E 2,199,937.04
P15	N 502,987.52, E 2,199,839.19		P42	N 502,949.60, E 2,199,942.48
P16	N 503,021.31, E 2,199,897.68		P43	N 502,953.17, E 2,199,956.12
P17	N 502,980.47, E 2,200,016.05		P44	N 502,955.73, E 2,199,950.80
P18	N 503,083.98, E 2,199,872.47		P45	N 502,948.19, E 2,199,984.85
P19	N 503,063.31, E 2,199,934.10		P46	N 502,964.54, E 2,200,008.92
P20	N 503,062.88, E 2,199,881.30		P47	N 503,004.77, E 2,199,906.54
P21	N 503,063.33, E 2,199,899.51		P48	N 502,934.45, E 2,199,991.13
P22	N 503,071.59, E 2,199,900.23		P49	N 502,918.19, E 2,199,985.23
P23	N 502,987.10, E 2,199,873.21		P50	N 502,917.87, E 2,199,974.77
P24	N 502,998.56, E 2,199,858.22		P51	N 502,931.52, E 2,199,978.10
P25	N 502,980.15, E 2,199,868.69		P52	N 502,907.96, E 2,199,962.47
P26	N 502,942.03, E 2,199,877.74		P53	N 502,907.63, E 2,199,948.37
P27	N 503,095.73, E 2,199,931.53		P54	N 502,929.95, E 2,199,954.90
	N 502,929.95, E 2,199,954.90		P55	N 502,952.53, E 2,200,036.43

IMPORTANT!!!

1. Contractor shall be responsible for making himself familiar with all underground utilities, pipes, structures and the runs.

2. Prior to commencement of hardscape construction, all piers, footings, and walls are to be surveyed, laid out, and staked in field for approval by landscape architect. Contractor shall assume responsibility for any demolition, adjustments, or reconstruction resulting from unauthorized construction activities.

3. Contractor is responsible for all final quantities per drawings and specifications. Any quantities provided by MESA Design Group are provided as a convenience only and shall not be considered absolute. Landscape architect should be notified if any discrepancies occur. CONTRACTORS ARE TO BID THEIR OWN VERIFIED QUANTITIES.

CRITICAL: MATERIALS AND WORKMANSHIP

FLAGSTONE: LEUDERS CREME & GRAY (RANDOM FIELDSTONE PATTERN)

MORTAR: Ho-ham Masonry Cement, ASTM C270, type S / part portland cement 1/2 part hydrated lime, line 4 1/2 parts sand by volume).

WORKMANSHIP: Head and bed joints must be filled solid. Grout in pilasters must surround the rebar and completely fill the pilaster. Good workmanship is important.

SOURCE: Ho-ham Inc.
1600 Dove Lane
Marathon, Texas 76065-4455
(800) 538-1821

SITE IMPROVEMENTS LEGEND

KEY	BID ITEM	SHEET	BID ITEM
3	HIKE & BIKE TRAIL	SD-1	3
101	MANHOLE	MEP-3	101
11A	LARGE PAVILION	A-1	11A
11B	SMALL PAVILION	A-2	11B
11C	RESTROOM BUILDING	A-3	11C
11D	SUNDIAL/GNOMON	LC-15	11D
11E	CONCRETE FTG. & REN.	LC-3	11E
11F	STONE VENEER	LC-3	11F
11G	STONE RADII STEPS	LC-4	11G
11H	FLAGSTONE INSTALLATION	LC-11	11H
11I	DECOMPOSED GRANITE	LC-11	11I
11K	CONCRETE PAVING	LC-11	11K

LEGEND
RE RIM ELEVATION
TH TOP OF WALL
BH BOTTOM OF WALL

SITE MAP: N.T.S

NOTE : ALL TREES IN THIS AREA TO BE PRESERVED UNLESS REMOVAL IS APPROVED BY LANDSCAPE ARCHITECT.

STONE VENEERED RETAINING WALL

STONE VENEERED RETAINING WALL

2'-0" STONE CONCENTRIC RADII STEPS

STONE VENEERED RETAINING WALL

NATURAL WOODLAND SCENIC OVERLOOK

EXISTING SPECIMEN CEDAR ELM TREE TO BE PRESERVED

NATURAL WOODLAND SCENIC OVERLOOK

STONE VENEERED RETAINING WALL

A PAVILION PLAZA LAYOUT
SCALE: 1" = 10'-0"

NORTH

MESA
DESIGN GROUP
Landscape Architecture
Urban Design
Land Planning

3100 McKinnon Street
Suite 905
Dallas, Texas 75201
(214) 871-0568 Fax: 871-1507

ARBOR HILLS
NATURE PRESERVE
CITY OF PLANO, TEXAS

Revisions
No. Date Item

Registration

FLW/MGF/CWM
Drawn
SRC
Checked
95102   4/24/97
Project No.   Date

Sheet Title

PAVILION PLAZA
LAYOUT PLAN

BID ITEMS 11A-11L

Sheet No.
LA-5

Arbor Hills

157

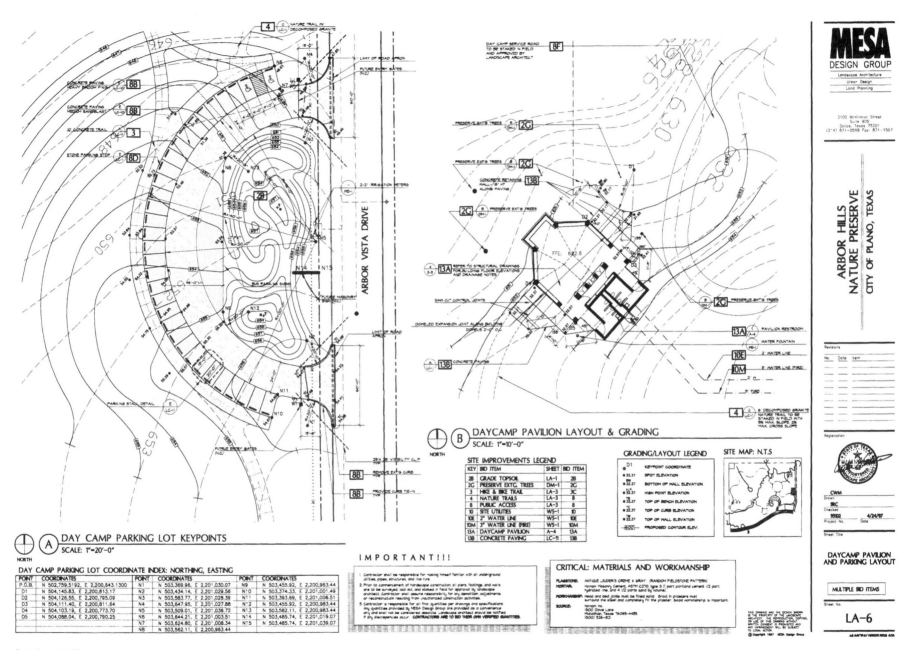

A DAY CAMP PARKING LOT KEYPOINTS
SCALE: 1"=20'-0"
NORTH

B DAYCAMP PAVILION LAYOUT & GRADING
SCALE: 1"=10'-0"
NORTH

DAY CAMP PARKING LOT COORDINATE INDEX: NORTHING, EASTING

POINT	COORDINATES	POINT	COORDINATES	POINT	COORDINATES
P.O.B.	N 502,759.5192, E 2,200,643.1300	N1	N 503,369.96, E 2,201,030.07	N9	N 503,455.92, E 2,200,963.44
D1	N 504,145.83, E 2,200,813.17	N2	N 503,434.14, E 2,201,029.56	N10	N 503,374.33, E 2,201,001.49
D2	N 504,126.55, E 2,200,795.09	N3	N 503,583.77, E 2,201,028.39	N11	N 503,393.69, E 2,201,006.51
D3	N 504,111.40, E 2,200,811.64	N4	N 503,847.95, E 2,201,027.88	N*2	N 503,455.92, E 2,200,983.44
D4	N 504,103.19, E 2,200,773.70	N5	N 503,509.01, E 2,201,036.72	N13	N 503,562.11, E 2,201,019.07
D5	N 504,088.04, E 2,200,790.25	N6	N 503,844.21, E 2,201,003.51	N14	N 503,485.74, E 2,201,019.07
		N7	N 503,624.80, E 2,201,008.34	N15	N 503,485.74, E 2,201,039.07
		N8	N 503,562.11, E 2,200,963.44		

SITE IMPROVEMENTS LEGEND

KEY	BID ITEM	SHEET	BID ITEM
2B	GRADE TOPSOIL	LA-1	2B
2G	PRESERVE EXTG. TREES	DM-1	2G
3	HIKE & BIKE TRAIL	LA-3	3C
4	NATURE TRAILS	LA-3	8
8	PUBLIC ACCESS	LA-3	8
10	SITE UTILITIES	WS-1	10
10E	2" WATER LINE	WS-1	10E
10M	3" WATER LINE (FIRE)	WS-1	10M
13A	DAYCAMP PAVILION	A-4	13A
13B	CONCRETE PAVING	LC-11	13B

GRADING/LAYOUT LEGEND

SITE MAP: N.T.S

IMPORTANT!!!

CRITICAL: MATERIALS AND WORKMANSHIP

MESA DESIGN GROUP
Landscape Architecture
Urban Design
Land Planning

3100 McKinnon Street
Suite 905
Dallas, Texas 75201
(214) 871-0568 Fax 871-1507

ARBOR HILLS
NATURE PRESERVE
CITY OF PLANO, TEXAS

Sheet Title

DAYCAMP PAVILION
AND PARKING LAYOUT

MULTIPLE BID ITEMS

Sheet No.

LA-6

▌Arbor Hills

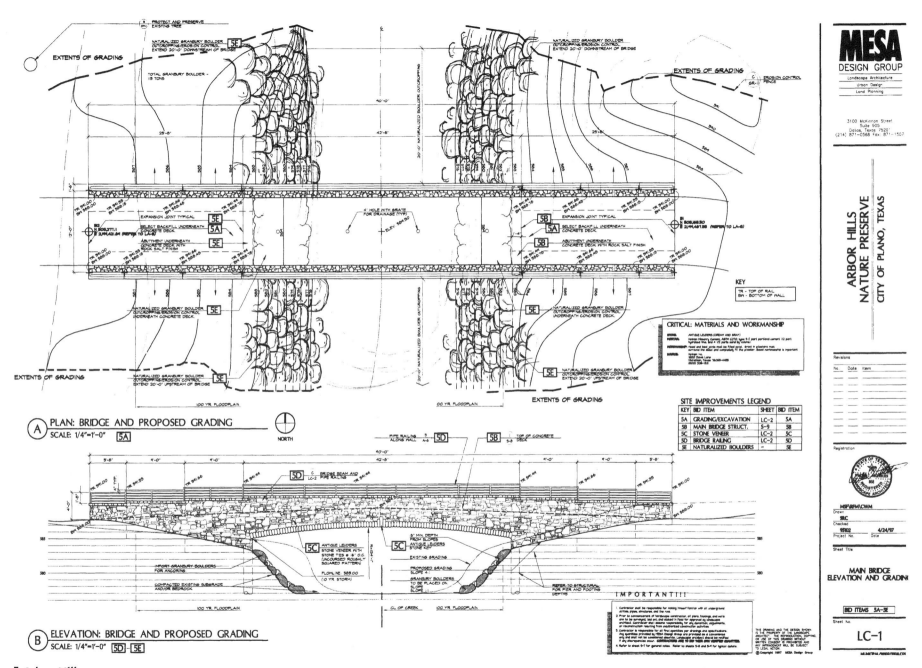

MESA
DESIGN GROUP

Landscape Architecture
Urban Design
Land Planning

3100 McKinnon Street
Suite 905
Dallas, Texas 75201
(214) 871-0568 Fax: 871-1507

ARBOR HILLS
NATURE PRESERVE
CITY OF PLANO, TEXAS

A PLAN: BRIDGE AND PROPOSED GRADING
SCALE: 1/4"=1'-0" 5A

B ELEVATION: BRIDGE AND PROPOSED GRADING
SCALE: 1/4"=1'-0" 5D 5E

NORTH

SITE IMPROVEMENTS LEGEND

KEY	BID ITEM	SHEET	BID ITEM
5A	GRADING/EXCAVATION	LC-2	5A
5B	MAIN BRIDGE STRUCT.	S-9	5B
5C	STONE VENEER	LC-2	5C
5D	BRIDGE RAILING	LC-2	5D
5E	NATURALIZED BOULDERS	–	5E

KEY
TR - TOP OF RAIL
BR - BOTTOM OF WALL

CRITICAL: MATERIALS AND WORKMANSHIP

Revisions
No. Date Item

Registration

Drawn
SRC
Checked
95102   4/24/97
Project No.   Date

Sheet Title

MAIN BRIDGE
ELEVATION AND GRADING

BID ITEMS 5A-5E

Sheet No.
LC-1

IMPORTANT!!!

Arbor Hills

159

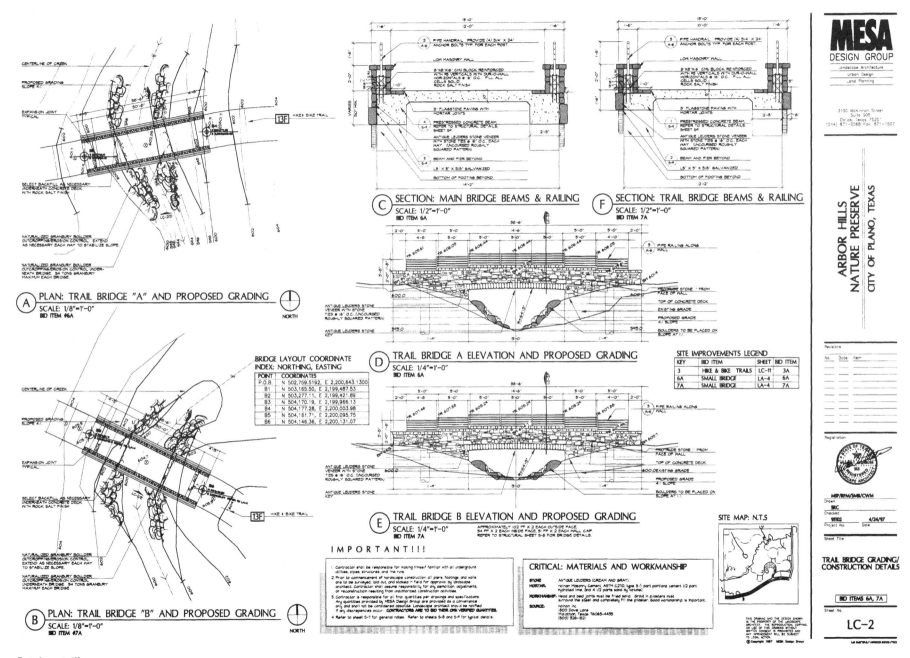

PLAN: TRAIL BRIDGE "A" AND PROPOSED GRADING
A SCALE: 1/8"=1'-0"
BID ITEM #6A

NORTH

PLAN: TRAIL BRIDGE "B" AND PROPOSED GRADING
B SCALE: 1/8"=1'-0"
BID ITEM #7A

NORTH

SECTION: MAIN BRIDGE BEAMS & RAILING
C SCALE: 1/2"=1'-0"
BID ITEM 6A

SECTION: TRAIL BRIDGE BEAMS & RAILING
F SCALE: 1/2"=1'-0"
BID ITEM 7A

TRAIL BRIDGE A ELEVATION AND PROPOSED GRADING
D SCALE: 1/4"=1'-0"
BID ITEM 6A

TRAIL BRIDGE B ELEVATION AND PROPOSED GRADING
E SCALE: 1/4"=1'-0"
BID ITEM 7A

APPROXIMATELY 102 FF X 2 EACH OUTSIDE FACE,
54 FF X 2 EACH INSIDE FACE, 51 FF X 2 EACH WALL CAP
REFER TO STRUCTURAL SHEET S-8 FOR BRIDGE DETAILS

BRIDGE LAYOUT COORDINATE INDEX: NORTHING, EASTING

POINT	COORDINATES
P.O.B.	N 502,759.5192, E 2,200,643.1300
B1	N 503,165.50, E 2,199,487.53
B2	N 503,277.11, E 2,199,421.89
B3	N 504,170.19, E 2,199,966.13
B4	N 504,177.28, E 2,200,003.98
B5	N 504,181.71, E 2,200,095.75
B6	N 504,146.36, E 2,200,131.07

SITE IMPROVEMENTS LEGEND

KEY	BID ITEM	SHEET	BID ITEM
3	HIKE & BIKE TRAILS	LC-11	3A
6A	SMALL BRIDGE	LA-4	6A
7A	SMALL BRIDGE	LA-4	7A

SITE MAP: N.T.S

IMPORTANT!!!

1. Contractor shall be responsible for making himself familiar with all underground utilities, pipes, structures, and line runs.
2. Prior to commencement of hardscape construction, all piers, footings, and walls are to be surveyed, laid out, and staked in field for approval by landscape architect. Contractor shall assume responsibility for any demolition, adjustments, or reconstruction resulting from unauthorized construction activities.
3. Contractor is responsible for all final quantities per drawings and specifications. Any quantities provided by MESA Design Group are provided as a convenience only, and shall not be considered absolute. Landscape architect should be notified if any discrepancies occur. **CONTRACTORS ARE TO BID THEIR OWN VERIFIED QUANTITIES.**
4. Refer to sheet S-1 for general notes. Refer to sheets S-8 and S-4 for typical details.

CRITICAL: MATERIALS AND WORKMANSHIP

STONE: ANTIQUE LEUDERS (CREAM AND GRAY).
MORTAR: Holnam Masonry Cement, ASTM C270, type S (1 part portland cement 1/2 part hydrated lime, and 4 1/2 parts sand by volume).
WORKMANSHIP: Head and bed joints must be filled solid. Grout in pilasters must surround the steel and completely fill the pilaster. Good workmanship is important.
SOURCE: Holnam Inc.
800 Dove Lane
Midlothian, Texas 76065-4438
(800) 926-1821

MESA DESIGN GROUP
Landscape Architecture
Urban Design
Land Planning

3100 McKinnon Street
Suite 905
Dallas, Texas 75201
(214) 871-0568 Fax. 871-1507

ARBOR HILLS
NATURE PRESERVE
CITY OF PLANO, TEXAS

Revisions
No. Date Item

Registration

MSF/RFM/SMB/CWM
Drawn
SRC
Checked
Project No. 95102 Date 4/24/97

Sheet Title

TRAIL BRIDGE GRADING/
CONSTRUCTION DETAILS

BID ITEMS 6A, 7A

Sheet No.

LC-2

Arbor Hills

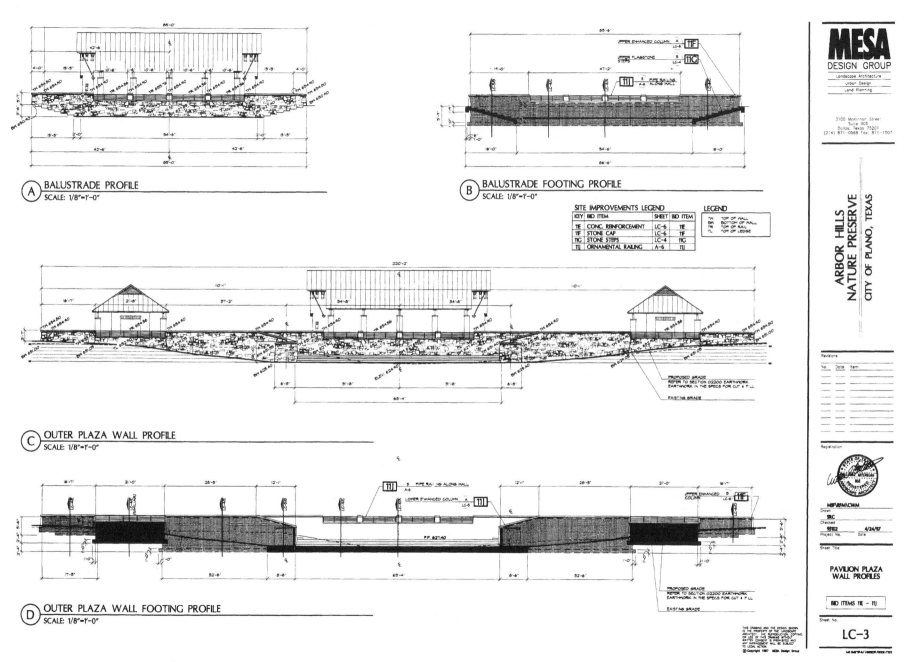

Arbor Hills

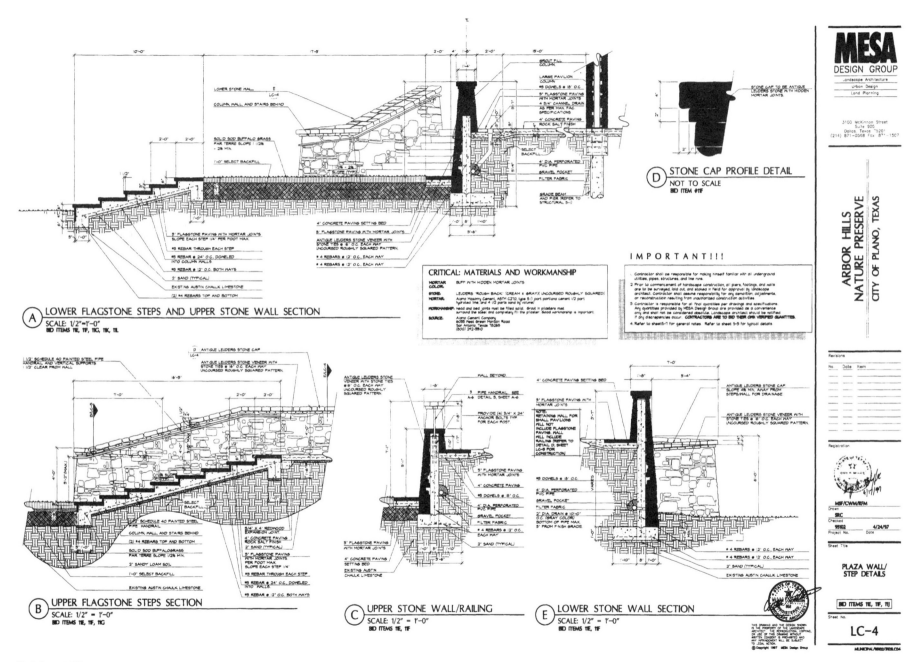

A LOWER FLAGSTONE STEPS AND UPPER STONE WALL SECTION
SCALE: 1/2"=1'-0"
BID ITEMS 11E, 11F, 11G, 11K, 11L

B UPPER FLAGSTONE STEPS SECTION
SCALE: 1/2" = 1'-0"
BID ITEMS 11E, 11F, 11G

C UPPER STONE WALL/RAILING
SCALE: 1/2" = 1'-0"
BID ITEMS 11E, 11F

E LOWER STONE WALL SECTION
SCALE: 1/2" = 1'-0"
BID ITEMS 11E, 11F

D STONE CAP PROFILE DETAIL
NOT TO SCALE
BID ITEM #11F

CRITICAL: MATERIALS AND WORKMANSHIP

IMPORTANT!!!

MESA
DESIGN GROUP
Landscape Architecture
Urban Design
Land Planning

3100 McKinnon Street
Suite 905
Dallas, Texas 75201
(214) 871-0568 Fax 871-1507

ARBOR HILLS
NATURE PRESERVE
CITY OF PLANO, TEXAS

Revisions
No. Date Item

Registration

MSF/CWM/RFM
Drawn
SRC
Checked
95102   4/24/97
Project No.   Date

Sheet Title

PLAZA WALL/
STEP DETAILS

BID ITEMS 11E, 11F, 11J

Sheet No.

LC-4

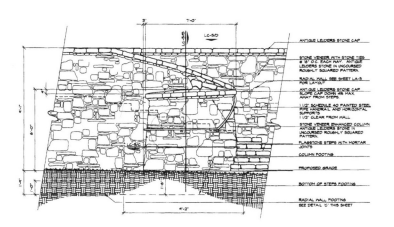

A. LOWER ENHANCED COLUMN ELEVATION
SCALE: 1/2"=1'-0"

ANTIQUE LEUDERS STONE CAP

STONE VENEER WITH STONE TIES
@ 16" O.C. EACH WAY, ANTIQUE
LEUDERS STONE IN UNCOURSED
ROUGHLY SQUARED PATTERN.

RADIAL WALL SEE SHEET LA-5
FOR LAYOUT

ANTIQUE LEUDERS STONE CAP
SLOPE CAP DOWN 4% MAX.
AWAY FROM STEPS

1 1/2" SCHEDULE 40 PAINTED STEEL
PIPE HANDRAIL AND HORIZONTAL
SUPPORTS
1 1/2" CLEAR FROM WALL

STONE VENEER ENHANCED COLUMN
ANTIQUE LEUDERS STONE IN
UNCOURSED ROUGHLY SQUARED
PATTERN.

FLAGSTONE STEPS WITH MORTAR
JOINTS

COLUMN FOOTING

PROPOSED GRADE

BOTTOM OF STEPS FOOTING

RADIAL WALL FOOTING
SEE DETAIL 'C' THIS SHEET

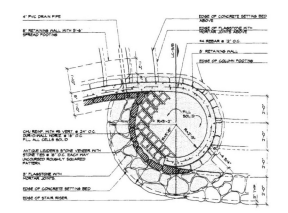

4" PVC DRAIN PIPE

8" RETAINING WALL WITH 3'-0"
SPREAD FOOTING

EDGE OF CONCRETE SETTING BED
ABOVE

EDGE OF FLAGSTONE WITH
MORTAR JOINTS ABOVE

#4 REBAR @ 12" O.C.

8" RETAINING WALL

EDGE OF COLUMN FOOTING

CMU REINF. WITH #5 VERT. @ 24" O.C.
DUR-O-WALL HORIZ. @ 16" O.C.
FILL ALL CELLS SOLID

ANTIQUE LEUDERS STONE VENEER WITH
STONE TIES @ 16" O.C. EACH WAY
UNCOURSED ROUGHLY SQUARED
PATTERN.

3" FLAGSTONE WITH
MORTAR JOINTS

EDGE OF CONCRETE SETTING BED

EDGE OF STAIR RISER

C. LOWER ENHANCED COLUMN PLAN SECTION
SCALE: 1/2"=1'-0"

CRITICAL: MATERIALS AND WORKMANSHIP

MORTAR COLOR: BUFF WITH HIDDEN MORTAR JOINTS

STONE: LEUDERS "ROUGH BACK" (CREAM & GRAY)(UNCOURSED ROUGHLY SQUARED)

MORTAR: Alamo Masonry Cement, ASTM C270 type S (1 part portland cement 1/2 part hydrated lime, and 4 1/2 parts sand by volume)

WORKMANSHIP: Head and bed joints must be filled solid. Grout in pilasters must surround the steel and completely fill the pilaster. Good workmanship is important.

SOURCE: Alamo Cement Company
6055 Aust Green Mountain Road
San Antonio, Texas 78265
(800) 292-5810

IMPORTANT!!!

1. Contractor shall be responsible for making himself familiar with all underground utilities, pipes, structures, and line runs.

2. Prior to commencement of hardscape construction, all piers, footings, and walls are to be surveyed, laid out, and staked in field for approval by landscape architect. Contractor shall assume responsibility for any demolition, adjustments, or reconstruction resulting from unauthorized construction activities.

3. Contractor is responsible for all final quantities per drawings and specifications. Any quantities provided by MESA Design Group are provided as a convenience only and shall not be considered absolute. Landscape architect should be notified if any discrepancies occur. CONTRACTORS ARE TO BID THEIR OWN VERIFIED QUANTITIES.

4. Refer to sheets 1-7 for general notes. Refer to sheet 5-8 for typical details.

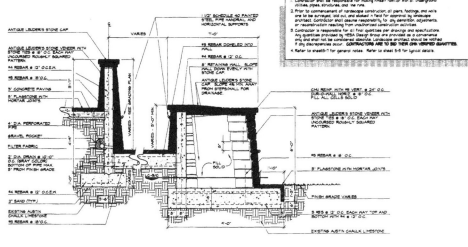

B. LOWER ENHANCED COLUMN SECTION
SCALE: 1/2"=1'-0"

ANTIQUE LEUDERS STONE CAP

ANTIQUE LEUDERS STONE VENEER WITH
STONE TIES @ 16" O.C. EACH WAY
UNCOURSED ROUGHLY SQUARED
PATTERN.

#4 REBAR @ 12" O.C.E.W.

#5 REBAR @ 18"O.C.

3" CONCRETE PAVING

3" FLAGSTONE WITH
MORTAR JOINTS

4" DIA. PERFORATED
PIPE

GRAVEL POCKET

FILTER FABRIC

3" DIA. DRAIN @ 10'-0"
O.C. (GRAY COLOR)
BOTTOM OF PIPE MAX.
3" FROM FINISH GRADE

#4 REBAR @ 12" O.C.E.W.

2" SAND (TYP.)

EXISTING AUSTIN
CHALK LIMESTONE

#5 REBAR @ 18"O.C.

1 1/2" SCHEDULE 40 PAINTED
STEEL PIPE HANDRAIL AND
HORIZONTAL SUPPORTS

#9 REBAR DOWELED INTO
WALL

#4 REBAR @ 12" O.C.

8" RETAINING WALL, SLOPE
WALL DOWN EVENLY WITH
STONE CAP.

ANTIQUE LEUDERS STONE
CAP. SLOPE 4% MIN. AWAY
FROM STEPS/WALL FOR
DRAINAGE

CMU REINF. WITH #5 VERT. @ 24" O.C.
DUR-O-WALL HORIZ. @ 16" O.C.
FILL ALL CELLS SOLID

ANTIQUE LEUDERS STONE VENEER WITH
STONE TIES @ 16" O.C. EACH WAY
UNCOURSED ROUGHLY SQUARED
PATTERN.

#5 REBAR @ 18" O.C.

3" FLAGSTONE WITH MORTAR JOINTS

FILL SOLID

FINISH GRADE VARIES

5 #5 @ 12" O.C. EACH WAY TOP AND
BOTTOM WITH #4 @ 12" O.C.

EXISTING AUSTIN CHALK LIMESTONE

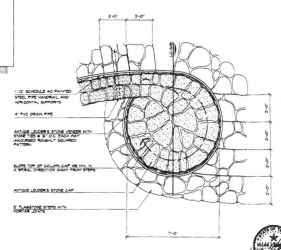

1 1/2" SCHEDULE 40 PAINTED
STEEL PIPE HANDRAIL AND
HORIZONTAL SUPPORTS

4" PVC DRAIN PIPE

ANTIQUE LEUDERS STONE VENEER WITH
STONE TIES @ 16" O.C. EACH WAY
UNCOURSED ROUGHLY SQUARED
PATTERN.

SLOPE TOP OF COLUMN CAP 4% MIN. IN
A SPIRAL DIRECTION AWAY FROM STEPS

ANTIQUE LEUDERS STONE CAP

3" FLAGSTONE STEPS WITH
MORTAR JOINTS

D. LOWER ENHANCED COLUMN PLAN
SCALE: 1/2"=1'-0"

MESA
DESIGN GROUP
Landscape Architecture
Urban Design
Land Planning

3100 McKinnon Street
Suite 905
Dallas, Texas 75201
(214) 871-0568 Fax: 871-1507

ARBOR HILLS
NATURE PRESERVE
CITY OF PLANO, TEXAS

Revisions
No.   Date   Item

Registration

MGF/RPM/CWM
Drawn
SRC
Checked
95122   4/24/97
Project No.   Date

Sheet Title

PLAZA STAIR/
COLUMN DETAILS

BID ITEMS 11E, F, G

Sheet No.

LC-5

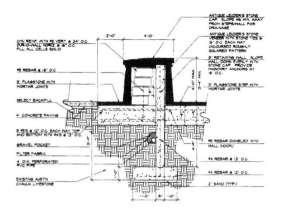

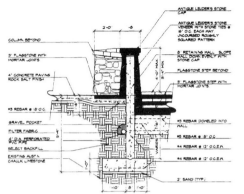

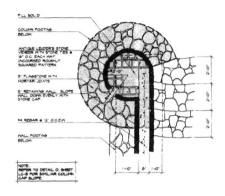

A UPPER STAIRS ENHANCED COLUMN SECTION
SCALE: 1/2"=1'-0"

C UPPER STAIRS WALL/COLUMN SECTION
SCALE: 1/2"=1'-0"

E UPPER STAIRS COLUMN PLAN SECTION
SCALE: 1/2"=1'-0"

CRITICAL: MATERIALS AND WORKMANSHIP

MORTAR
COLOR: Buff with hidden mortar joints

MATERIAL SPEC.

MORTAR: Holnam Masonry Cement, ASTM C270, type S (1 part portland cement 1/2 part hydrated lime, and 4 1/2 parts sand by volume).

WORKMANSHIP: Head and bed joints must be filled solid. Grout in pilasters must surround the steel and completely fill the pilaster. Good workmanship is important.

SOURCE: Holnam Inc.
1800 Dove Lane
Midlothian, Texas 76065-4485
(800) 926-82I

IMPORTANT!!!

1. Contractor shall be responsible for making himself familiar with all underground utilities, pipes, structures, and line runs.

2. Prior to commencement of hardscape construction, all piers, footings, and walls are to be surveyed, laid out, and staked in field for approval by landscape architect. Contractor shall assume responsibility for any demolition, adjustments, or reconstruction resulting from unauthorized construction activities.

3. Contractor is responsible for all final quantities per drawings and specifications. Any quantities provided by MESA Design Group are provided as a convenience only and shall not be considered absolute. Landscape architect should be notified if any discrepancies occur. CONTRACTORS ARE TO BID THEIR OWN VERIFIED QUANTITIES.

4. Refer to sheets 5-7 for general notes. Refer to sheet 5-5 for typical details.

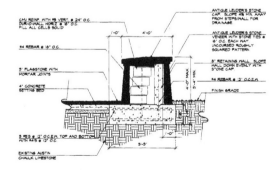

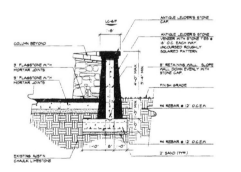

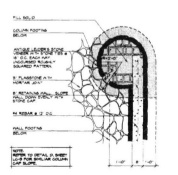

B LOWER WALL SMALL ENHANCED COLUMN SECTION
SCALE: 1/2"=1'-0"

D LOWER WALL/SMALL COLUMN SECTION
SCALE: 1/2"=1'-0"

F LOWER WALL SMALL COLUMN PLAN SECTION
SCALE: 1/2"=1'-0"

MESA
DESIGN GROUP
Landscape Architecture
Urban Design
Land Planning

3100 McKinnon Street
Suite 905
Dallas, Texas 75201
(214) 871-0568 Fax: 871-1507

ARBOR HILLS
NATURE PRESERVE
CITY OF PLANO, TEXAS

Revisions
No. Date Item

Registration

MSP/CWM
Drawn
SRC
Checked
95102   4/24/97
Project No.   Date

Sheet Title
PLAZA SMALL
COLUMN DETAILS

BID ITEMS 11E, F, G

Sheet No.
LC-6

Arbor Hills

164

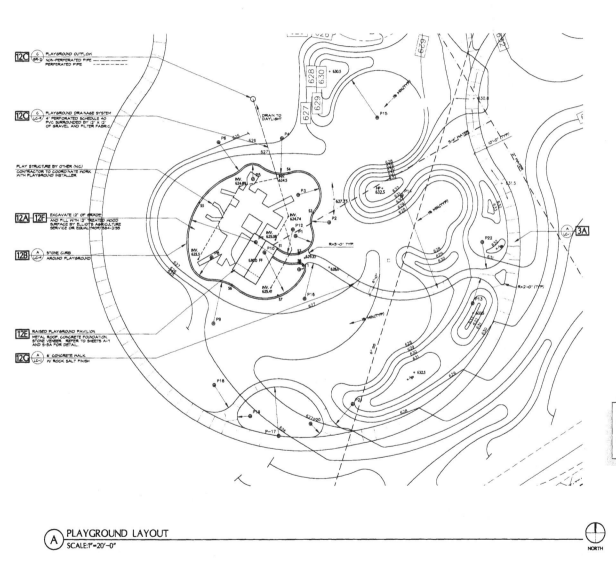

12C — (c SR-2) PLAYGROUND OUTFLOW
NON-PERFERATED PIPE
PERFERATED PIPE

12C — (c LC-9) PLAYGROUND DRAINAGE SYSTEM
4" PERFORATED SCHEDULE 40
PVC SURROUNDED BY 12" x 12"
OF GRAVEL AND FILTER FABRIC

PLAY STRUCTURE BY OTHER (NIC)
CONTRACTOR TO COORDINATE WORK
WITH PLAYGROUND INSTALLER

12A — 12F EXCAVATE 12" OF GRADE
AND FILL WITH 12" TREATED WOOD
SURFACE BY ELLIOTT AGRICULTURE
SERVICE OR EQUAL (MOR) 984-2158

12B — (A LC-9) STONE CURB
AROUND PLAYGROUND

12E RAISED PLAYGROUND PAVILION
METAL ROOF, CONCRETE FOUNDATION,
STONE VENEER. REFER TO SHEETS A-7
AND S-8A FOR DETAIL.

12C — (A LC-11) 6' CONCRETE WALK
W/ ROCK SALT FINISH

(A) PLAYGROUND LAYOUT
SCALE: 1"=20'-0"

NORTH

Arbor Hills

PLAYGROUND LAYOUT COORDINATE INDEX: NORTHING, EASTING

POINT	NORTHING	EASTING	RADIUS
P.O.B.	502,759.5192	2,200,643.1300	NA
P1	502,749.39	2,199,821.43	13.23'
P2	502,750.46	2,199,847.59	14.84'
P3	502,780.06	2,199,825.49	16.86'
P4	502,822.31	2,199,810.82	27.24'
P5	502,791.79	2,199,788.39	10.63'
P6	502,819.27	2,199,761.82	27.60'
P7	502,744.81	2,199,790.63	52.24'
P8	502,733.49	2,199,756.49	16.27'
P9	502,684.89	2,199,756.49	32.34'
P10	502,737.12	2,199,797.21	33.89'
P11	502,724.48	2,199,824.21	4.09'
P12	502,754.15	2,199,819.33	18.00'
P13	502,699.14	2,199,959.57	20.00'
P14	502,779.53	2,199,904.03	75.00'
P15	502,837.64	2,199,885.23	32.50'
P16	502,702.66	2,199,828.40	27.20'
P17	502,600.90	2,199,808.16	36.45'
P18	502,638.66	2,199,758.42	9.73'
P19	502,615.76	2,199,786.28	10.00'
P20	502,609.85	2,199,833.05	10.00'
P21	502,624.61	2,199,865.93	20.00'
P22	502,744.51	2,199,967.17	20.00'

NOTE: ALL RADIUS DIMENSIONS ARE TO THE INSIDE OF THE PLAYGROUND CURB.

PLAYGROUND SPOT ELEVATION INDEX: IN FEET

POINT	TOP OF CURB	BOTTOM OF CURB	SURFACE
S1	30.16	26.25	27.5
S2	30.16	26.25	27.5
S3	28.0	26.25	27.5
S4	28.0	26.25	27.5
S5	28.0	26.25	27.5
S6	28.0	26.25	27.5
S7	28.0	26.25	27.5
S8	30.16	26.25	27.5

SITE IMPROVEMENTS LEGEND

KEY	BID ITEM	SHEET	BID ITEM
3A	HIKE & BIKE TRAIL	LC-9	3A
12A	GRADING & EXCAVATION	LC-9	12A
12B	PLAYGROUND CURBS	LC-9	12B
12C	DRAINAGE SYSTEM	LC-9	12C
12D	6' CONCRETE WALK	LC-9	12D
12E	21'X27' PAVILION	A-7	12E
12F	WOOD SURFACE	LC-9	12F

IMPORTANT!!!

1. Contractor shall be responsible for making himself familiar with all underground utilities, pipes, structures, and lines.
2. Prior to commencement of hardscape construction, all piers, footings, and walls are to be surveyed, laid out, and staked in field for approval by landscape architect. Contractor shall assume responsibility for any demolition, adjustments, or reconstruction resulting from unauthorized construction activities.
3. Contractor is responsible for all final quantities per drawings and specifications. Any quantities provided by MESA Design Group are provided as a convenience only and shall not be considered absolute. Landscape architect should be notified if any discrepancies occur. CONTRACTORS ARE TO BID THEIR OWN VERIFIED QUANTITIES.

SITE MAP: N.T.S

MESA
DESIGN GROUP
Landscape Architecture
Urban Design
Land Planning

3100 McKinney Street
Suite 905
Dallas, Texas 75201
(214) 871-0568 Fax 871-1507

ARBOR HILLS
NATURE PRESERVE
CITY OF PLANO, TEXAS

Revisions

No.	Date	Item

Registration

ES/PC/CWM/SMB/JTR
Drawn
SRC
Checked
95102   4/24/97
Project No.   Date

Sheet Title

PLAYGROUND LAYOUT/
GRADING PLAN

BID ITEMS 12A-12F

Sheet No.

LC-8

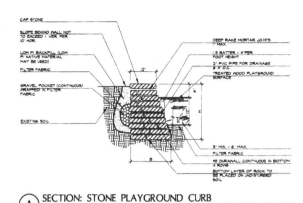

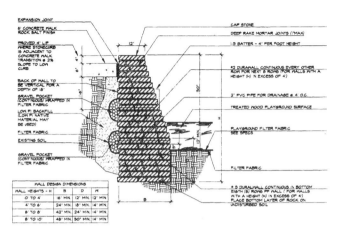

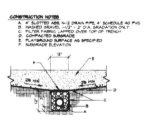

(A) SECTION: STONE PLAYGROUND CURB
N.T.S.

(B) SECTION: ENHANCED STONE PLAYGROUND CURB
N.T.S.

CONSTRUCTION NOTES
A. 4" SLOTTED ABS N-12 DRAIN PIPE, 4" SCHEDULE 40 PVC
B. WASHED GRAVEL 1-1/2" - 2" DIA. GRADATION ONLY.
C. FILTER FABRIC LAPPED OVER TOP OF TRENCH.
D. COMPACTED SUBGRADE.
E. PLAYGROUND SURFACE AS SPECIFIED.
F. SUBGRADE ELEVATION.

(C) SECTION: SUBSURFACE DRAIN LINE
N.T.S.

MESA
DESIGN GROUP
Landscape Architecture
Urban Design
Land Planning

3100 McKinnon Street
Suite 905
Dallas, Texas 75201
(214) 871-0568 Fax 871-1507

ARBOR HILLS
NATURE PRESERVE
CITY OF PLANO, TEXAS

Revisions
No. Date Item

Registration

ES/JTR/CWM
Drawn
SRC
Checked
95102   4/24/97
Project No.   Date

Sheet Title

PLAYGROUND
DETAILS

BID ITEMS 12

Sheet No.

LC-9

▌Arbor Hills

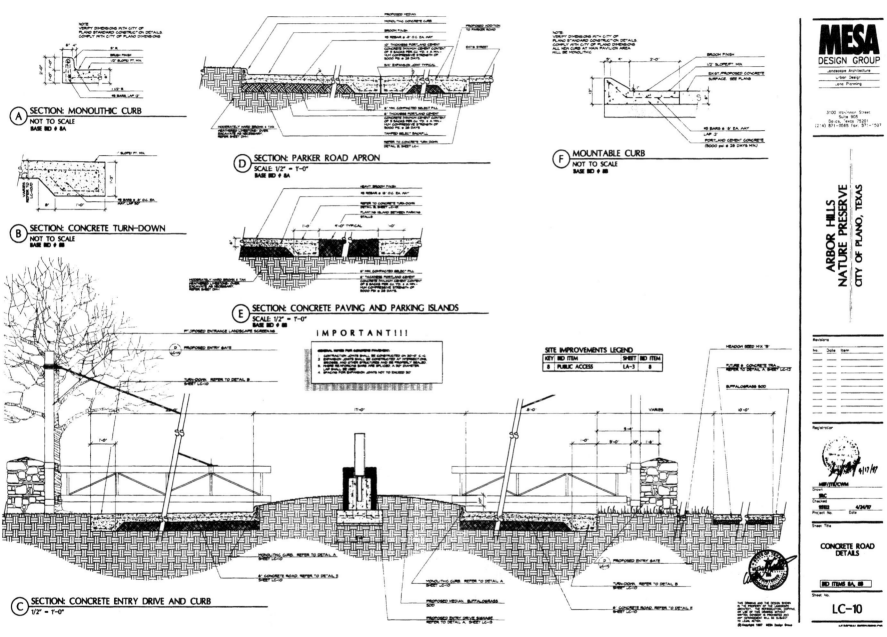

A SECTION: MONOLITHIC CURB
NOT TO SCALE
BASE BID # 8A

B SECTION: CONCRETE TURN-DOWN
NOT TO SCALE
BASE BID # 8B

D SECTION: PARKER ROAD APRON
SCALE: 1/2" = 1'-0"
BASE BID # 8A

E SECTION: CONCRETE PAVING AND PARKING ISLANDS
SCALE: 1/2" = 1'-0"
BASE BID # 8B

F MOUNTABLE CURB
NOT TO SCALE
BASE BID # 8B

C SECTION: CONCRETE ENTRY DRIVE AND CURB
1/2" = 1'-0"

IMPORTANT!!!

SITE IMPROVEMENTS LEGEND

KEY	BID ITEM	SHEET	BID ITEM
8	PUBLIC ACCESS	LA-3	8

MESA
DESIGN GROUP

Landscape Architecture
Urban Design
Land Planning

3100 McKinnon Street
Suite 905
Dallas, Texas 75201
(214) 871-0568 Fax: 871-1507

ARBOR HILLS
NATURE PRESERVE
CITY OF PLANO, TEXAS

Revisions
No. Date Item

Registration

Drawn
Checked
Project No.   Date

Sheet Title

CONCRETE ROAD
DETAILS

BID ITEMS 8A, 8B

Sheet No.

LC-10

Arbor Hills

167

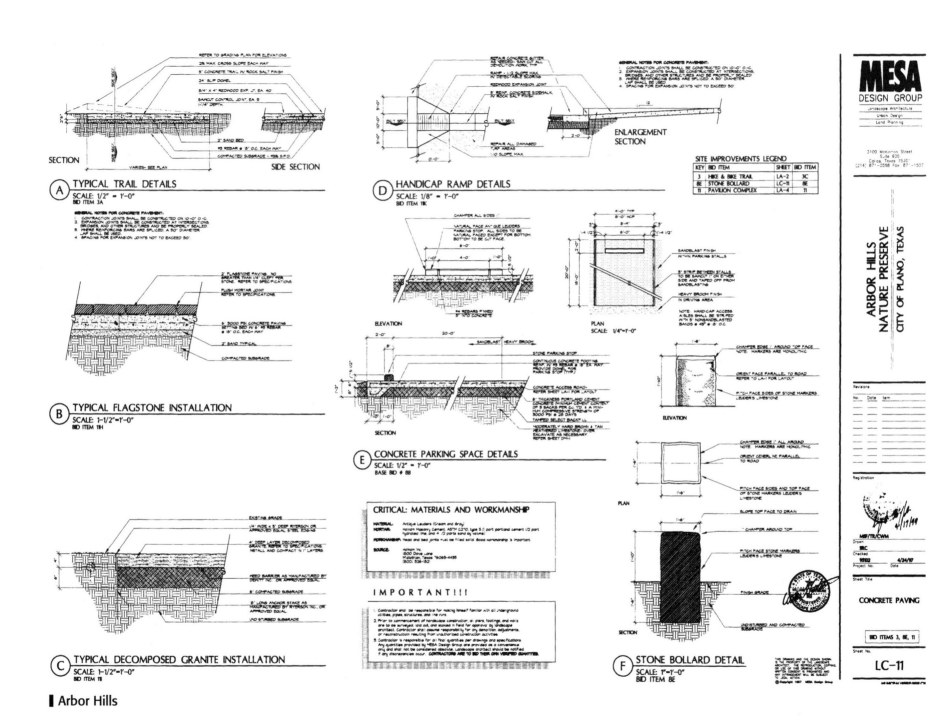

Arbor Hills

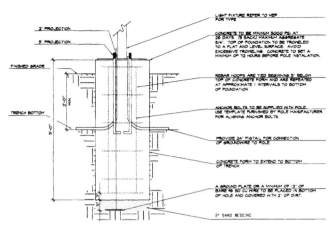

LIGHT FIXTURE REFER TO MEP FOR TYPE

CONCRETE TO BE MINIMUM 3000 PSI AT 28 DAYS (5 SACK) MAXIMUM AGGREGATE 3/4". TOP OF FOUNDATION TO BE TROWELED TO A FLAT AND LEVEL SURFACE. AVOID EXCESSIVE TROWELING. CONCRETE TO SET A MINIMUM OF 12 HOURS BEFORE POLE INSTALATION.

REBAR HOOPS ARE TIED BEGINNING 3" BELOW TOP OF CONCRETE FORM AND ARE REPEATED AT APPROXIMATE 1' INTERVALS TO BOTTOM OF FOUNDATION.

ANCHOR BOLTS TO BE SUPPLIED WITH POLE. USE TEMPLATE FURNISHED BY POLE MANUFACTURER FOR ALIGNING ANCHOR BOLTS.

PROVIDE 24" PIGTAIL FOR CONNECTION OF GROUNDWIRE TO POLE.

CONCRETE FORM TO EXTEND TO BOTTOM OF TRENCH.

A GROUND PLATE OR A MINIMUM OF 12' OF BARE #6 SO CU WIRE TO BE PLACED IN BOTTOM OF HOLE AND COVERED WITH 2" OF DIRT.

2" SAND BEDDING

2' PROJECTION
5" PROJECTION
FINISHED GRADE
TRENCH BOTTOM

(A) SECTION: LIGHT POLE & SOLAR PHONE FOOTING
SCALE: 1"=1'-0"
BID ITEMS 8C

IMPORTANT!
DURING EXCAVATION FOR POLE FOOTINGS, ROCK MAY BE FOUND.

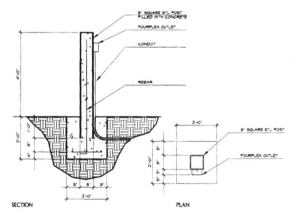

8" SQUARE ST. POST FILLED WITH CONCRETE
FOURPLEX OUTLET
CONDUIT
REBAR

8" SQUARE ST. POST
FOURPLEX OUTLET

SECTION   PLAN

(B) CONCRETE POST DETAILS
SCALE: 3/4"=1'-0"
BID ITEMS

FURNITURE SCHEDULE	BASE BID QUANTITY	BASE BID ITEM
STONE SLAB BENCHES BY CONTRACTED MASON	3	15A
PICNIC TABLES MODEL 508-08820 JOHN TAFT (817) 461-1889	4	15B
GRILLS MODEL BC-28 B2 THE PLAYWELL GROUP 800 726-1816	4	15C
DRINKING FOUNTAINS HAWS 3300FR THE THOMPSON CO. (214) 351-5911	2	15D
SOLAR PHONES	2	10L

SITE IMPROVEMENTS LEGEND

KEY	BID ITEM	SHEET	BID ITEM
8C	LIGHTING	MEP-3	8C
10L	SOLAR PHONE	MEP-2	10L
15A	STONE BENCH	N/A	15A
15B	PICNIC TABLE	N/A	15B
15C	GRILLS	N/A	15C
15D	DRINKING FOUNTAIN	LA-5,6	15C

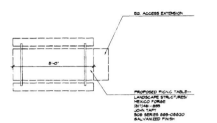

8'-0"

EQ. ACCESS EXTENSION

PROPOSED PICNIC TABLE-- LANDSCAPE STRUCTURES/ MEXICO FORGE (817)461-1889 JOHN TAFT 508 SERIES 508-08820 GALVANIZED FINISH

(C) PLAN: PICNIC TABLE LAYOUT
SCALE: 3/8"=1'-0"
BID ITEMS 15B

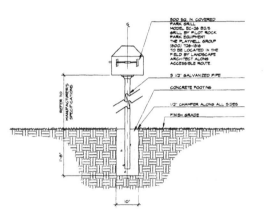

900 SQ. IN. COVERED PARK GRILL MODEL BC-28 B2/5 GRILL BY PILOT ROCK PARK EQUIPMENT THE PLAYWELL GROUP (800) 726-1816 TO BE LOCATED IN THE FIELD BY LANDSCAPE ARCHITECT ALONG ACCESSIBLE ROUTE

3 1/2" GALVANIZED PIPE
CONCRETE FOOTING
1/2" CHAMFER ALONG ALL SIDES
FINISH GRADE

REFER TO MANUFACTURER'S SPECIFICATIONS

(D) GRILL PAD DETAIL
SCALE: 1"=1'-0"
BID ITEMS 15C

IMPORTANT!!!

1. Contractor shall be responsible for making himself familiar with all underground utilities, pipes, structures, and line runs.

2. Prior to commencement of hardscape construction, all piers, footings, and walls are to be surveyed, laid out, and staked in field for approval by Landscape architect. Contractor shall assume responsibility for any demolition, adjustments, or reconstruction resulting from unauthorized construction activities.

3. Contractor is responsible for all final quantities per drawings and specifications. Any quantities provided by MESA Design Group are provided as a convenience only and shall not be considered absolute. Landscape architect should be notified if any discrepancies occur. CONTRACTORS ARE TO BID THEIR OWN VERIFIED QUANTITIES.

IMPORTANT!!!

1. Written dimensions prevail over scaled dimensions.

THIS DRAWING AND THE DESIGN SHOWN IS THE PROPERTY OF THE LANDSCAPE ARCHITECT. THE REPRODUCTION, COPYING, OR USE OF THIS DRAWING WITHOUT WRITTEN CONSENT IS PROHIBITED AND ANY INFRINGEMENT WILL BE SUBJECT TO LEGAL ACTION.
© Copyright 1997 MESA Design Group

MESA
DESIGN GROUP
Landscape Architecture
Urban Design
Land Planning

3100 McKinnon Street
Suite 905
Dallas, Texas 75201
(214) 871-0568 Fax: 871-1507

ARBOR HILLS
NATURE PRESERVE
CITY OF PLANO, TEXAS

Revisions
No. Date Item

Registration

FLW/CWM/RFM
Drawn
SRC
Checked
95102   4/24/97
Project No.   Date

Sheet Title

SITE FURNITURE
CONSTRUCTION DETAILS

BID ITEMS 8C, 16A-16D

Sheet No.

LC-12

MUNICIPAL\95REVFURB.CTL.DWG

Arbor Hills

169

IMPORTANT!!!

1. Contractor shall be responsible for making himself familiar with all underground utilities, pipes, structures, and line runs.
2. Prior to commencement of hardscape construction, all piers, footings, and walls are to be surveyed, laid out, and staked in field for approval by landscape architect. Contractor shall assume responsibility for any demolition, adjustments, or reconstruction resulting from unauthorized construction activities.
3. Contractor is responsible for all final quantities per drawings and specifications. Any quantities provided by MESA Design Group are provided as a convenience only and shall not be considered absolute. Landscape architect should be notified if any discrepancies occur. **CONTRACTORS ARE TO BID THEIR OWN VERIFIED QUANTITIES.**

CRITICAL: MATERIALS AND WORKMANSHIP

MATERIAL   SPEC.
MORTAR: Holnam Masonry Cement, ASTM C270, type N (1 part portland cement 1/2 part hydrated lime, and 4 1/2 parts sand by volume). Mortar color Buff w/ hidden joints.

WORKMANSHIP: Head and bed joints must be filled solid. Grout in pilasters must surround the steel and completely fill the pilaster. Good workmanship is important.

SOURCE: Holnam Inc.
              1600 Dove Lane
              Midlothian, Texas 76065-4455
              (800) 526-1821

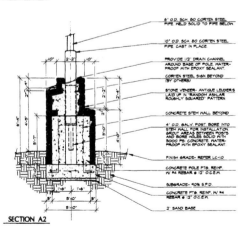

SECTION A1

SECTION A2

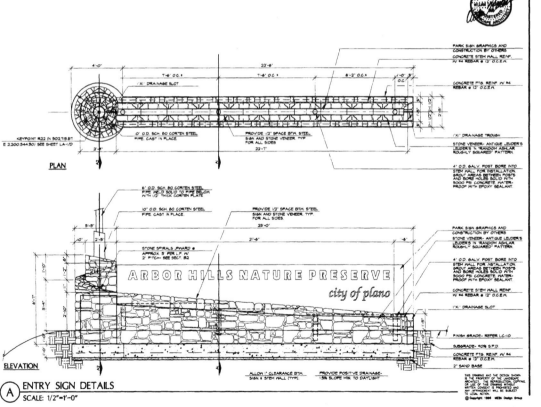

PLAN

ELEVATION

ARBOR HILLS NATURE PRESERVE
city of plano

(A) ENTRY SIGN DETAILS
SCALE: 1/2"=1'-0"

MESA
DESIGN GROUP
Landscape Architecture
Urban Design
Land Planning

3100 McKinnon Street
Suite 905
Dallas, Texas 75201
(214) 871-0568 Fax: 871-1507

ARBOR HILLS
NATURE PRESERVE
CITY OF PLANO, TEXAS

Revisions

No.	Date	Item

Registration

Drawn   PLW/CWM/JTR
Checked SRC
Project No. 95102   Date 4/24/97

Sheet Title

MASONRY/SIGNAGE
DETAILS

BID ITEM #16 & 17

Sheet No.

LC-13

| Arbor Hills

170

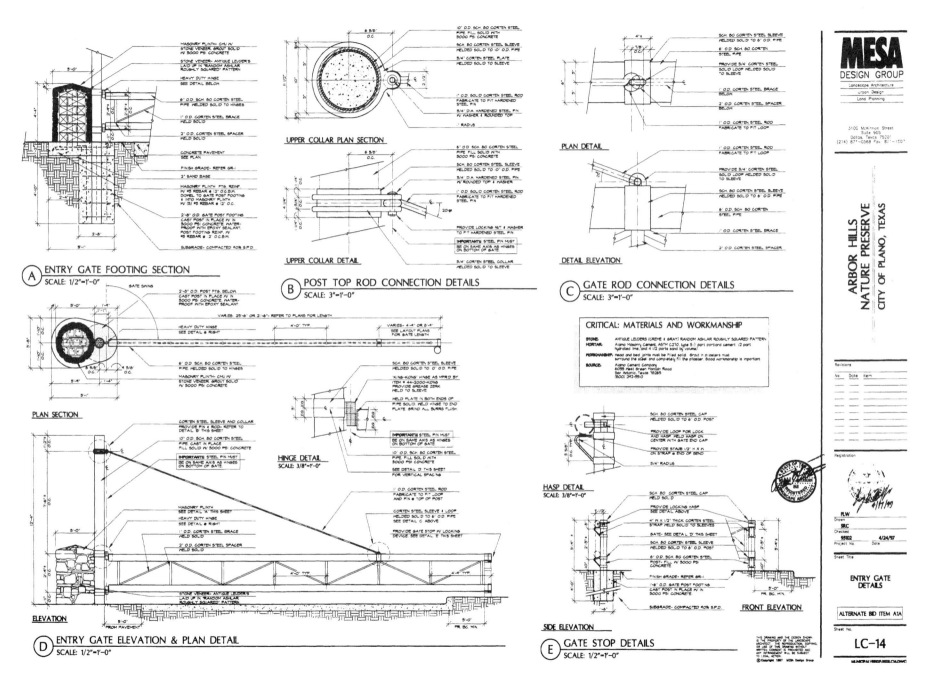

A ENTRY GATE FOOTING SECTION
SCALE: 1/2"=1'-0"

UPPER COLLAR PLAN SECTION

UPPER COLLAR DETAIL

B POST TOP ROD CONNECTION DETAILS
SCALE: 3"=1'-0"

PLAN DETAIL

DETAIL ELEVATION

C GATE ROD CONNECTION DETAILS
SCALE: 3"=1'-0"

PLAN SECTION

HINGE DETAIL
SCALE: 3/8"=1'-0"

ELEVATION

D ENTRY GATE ELEVATION & PLAN DETAIL
SCALE: 1/2"=1'-0"

CRITICAL: MATERIALS AND WORKMANSHIP

HASP DETAIL
SCALE: 3/8"=1'-0"

SIDE ELEVATION

FRONT ELEVATION

E GATE STOP DETAILS
SCALE: 1/2"=1'-0"

MESA DESIGN GROUP
Landscape Architecture
Urban Design
Land Planning

3100 McKinnon Street
Suite 905
Dallas, Texas 75201
(214) 871-0568 Fax 871-1507

ARBOR HILLS
NATURE PRESERVE
CITY OF PLANO, TEXAS

ENTRY GATE
DETAILS

ALTERNATE BID ITEM A1A

Sheet No.
LC-14

Arbor Hills

171

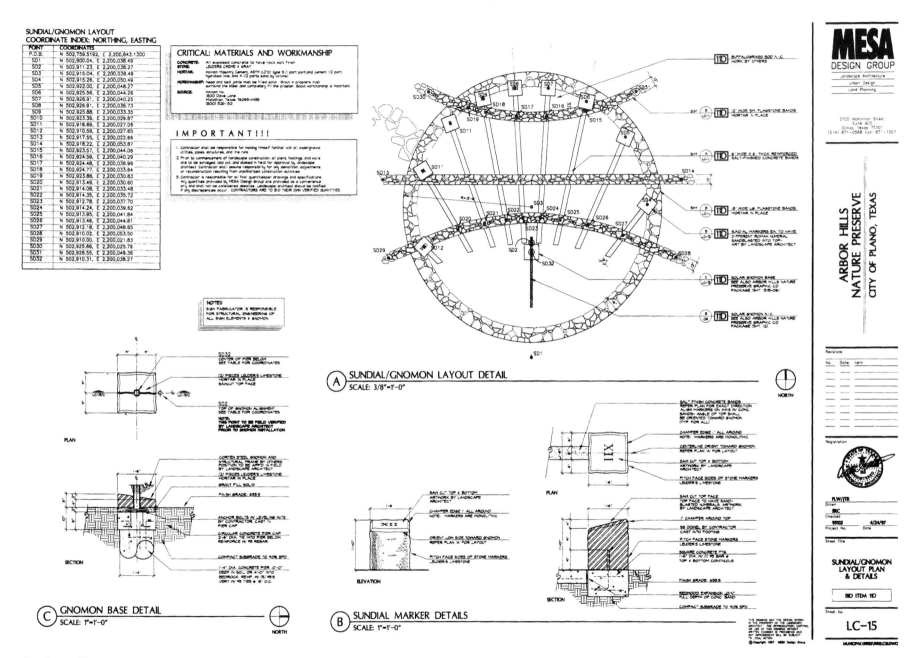

SUNDIAL/GNOMON LAYOUT
COORDINATE INDEX: NORTHING, EASTING

POINT	COORDINATES
P.O.B.	N 502,759.5192, E 2,200,643.1300
SD1	N 502,900.04, E 2,200,038.49
SD2	N 502,911.23, E 2,200,038.27
SD3	N 502,915.04, E 2,200,038.27
SD4	N 502,915.26, E 2,200,050.49
SD5	N 502,922.00, E 2,200,048.27
SD6	N 502,925.56, E 2,200,044.26
SD7	N 502,926.91, E 2,200,040.25
SD8	N 502,926.91, E 2,200,036.73
SD9	N 502,925.88, E 2,200,033.35
SD10	N 502,923.39, E 2,200,030.49
SD11	N 502,918.69, E 2,200,027.06
SD12	N 502,910.59, E 2,200,027.65
SD13	N 502,917.55, E 2,200,022.66
SD14	N 502,918.22, E 2,200,053.87
SD15	N 502,923.57, E 2,200,044.06
SD16	N 502,924.59, E 2,200,040.29
SD17	N 502,924.48, E 2,200,036.99
SD18	N 502,923.88, E 2,200,030.83
SD19	N 502,921.49, E 2,200,030.60
SD20	N 502,914.08, E 2,200,033.48
SD21	N 502,914.35, E 2,200,036.72
SD22	N 502,912.78, E 2,200,037.70
SD23	N 502,914.24, E 2,200,039.62
SD24	N 502,913.95, E 2,200,041.84
SD25	N 502,913.46, E 2,200,044.81
SD26	N 502,912.18, E 2,200,048.65
SD27	N 502,910.02, E 2,200,053.50
SD28	N 502,910.00, E 2,200,021.83
SD29	N 502,910.16, E 2,200,025.79
SD30	N 502,925.66, E 2,200,049.36
SD31	N 502,925.55, E 2,200,049.36
SD32	N 502,910.31, E 2,200,038.27

CRITICAL: MATERIALS AND WORKMANSHIP

CONCRETE: All exposed concrete to have rock salt finish
STONE: LEUDERS CREME & GRAY
MORTAR: Honron Masonry Cement, ASTM C270 type S (1 part portland cement 1/2 part hydrated lime, and 4 1/2 parts sand by volume)
WORKMANSHIP: Head and bed joints must be filled solid. Grout in pilasters must surround the steel and completely fill the pilaster. Good workmanship is important.
SOURCE: Hanson Inc.
1800 Dove Lane
Midlothian, Texas 76065-4435
(800) 526-621

IMPORTANT!!!

1. Contractor shall be responsible for making himself familiar with all underground utilities, pipes, structures, and line runs.
2. Prior to commencement of hardscape construction, all piers, footings, and walls are to be surveyed, laid out, and staked in field for approval by landscape architect. Contractor shall assume responsibility for any demolition, adjustments, or reconstruction resulting from unauthorized construction activities.
3. Contractor is responsible for all final quantities per drawings and specifications. Any quantities provided by MESA Design Group are provided as a convenience only and shall not be considered absolute. Landscape architect should be notified if any discrepancies occur. CONTRACTORS ARE TO BID THEIR OWN VERIFIED QUANTITIES.

NOTE!!
SIGN FABRICATOR IS RESPONSIBLE FOR STRUCTURAL ENGINEERING OF ALL SIGN ELEMENTS & GNOMON

BUFFALOGRASS SOD N.G.
WORK BY OTHERS

12" WIDE SM. FLAGSTONE BANDS
MORTAR IN PLACE

6" WIDE X 6" THICK REINFORCED
SALT-FINISHED CONCRETE BANDS

18" WIDE LG. FLAGSTONE BANDS
MORTAR IN PLACE

SUNDIAL MARKERS EA. TO HAVE
DIFFERENT ROMAN NUMERAL
SANDBLASTED INTO TOP.
ART BY LANDSCAPE ARCHITECT

SOLAR GNOMON BASE
SEE ALSO ARBOR HILLS NATURE
PRESERVE GRAPHIC CD
PACKAGE (SHT. 13/S-06)

SOLAR GNOMON N.I.C.
SEE ALSO ARBOR HILLS NATURE
PRESERVE GRAPHIC CD
PACKAGE (SHT. 12)

(A) SUNDIAL/GNOMON LAYOUT DETAIL
SCALE: 3/8"=1'-0"

NORTH

SD32
CENTER OF PIER BELOW
SEE TABLE FOR COORDINATES

(2) PIECES LEUDERS LIMESTONE
MORTAR IN PLACE
SAWCUT TOP FACE

SD2
TOP OF GNOMON ALIGNMENT
SEE TABLE FOR COORDINATES

NOTE:
THIS POINT TO BE FIELD VERIFIED
BY LANDSCAPE ARCHITECT
PRIOR TO GNOMON INSTALLATION

PLAN

CORTEN STEEL GNOMON AND
STRUCTURAL FRAME BY OTHERS
POSITION TO BE APP'D IN FIELD
BY LANDSCAPE ARCHITECT

(2) PIECES LEUDERS LIMESTONE
MORTAR IN PLACE

GROUT FILL SOLID

FINISH GRADE: 659.5

ANCHOR BOLTS W/ LEVELING NUTS
BY CONTRACTOR CAST IN
PIER CAP

CIRCULAR CONCRETE PIER CAP
2'-6" DIA. TIE INTO PIER BELOW
REINFORCE W/ #5 REBAR

COMPACT SUBGRADE TO 90% SPD

1'-4" DIA. CONCRETE PIER 10'-0"
DEEP IN SOIL, OR 4'-0" INTO
BEDROCK REINF. W/ (5) #5
VERT W/ #3 TIES @ 18" O.C.

SECTION

(C) GNOMON BASE DETAIL
SCALE: 1"=1'-0"

NORTH

SAW CUT TOP & BOTTOM
ARTWORK BY LANDSCAPE
ARCHITECT

CHAMFER EDGE 1" ALL AROUND
NOTE: MARKERS ARE MONOLITHIC

ORIENT LOW SIDE TOWARD GNOMON
REFER PLAN 'A' FOR LAYOUT

PITCH FACE SIDES OF STONE MARKERS
LEUDERS LIMESTONE

ELEVATION

(B) SUNDIAL MARKER DETAILS
SCALE: 1"=1'-0"

SALT FINISH CONCRETE BANDS
REFER PLAN FOR EXACT DIRECTION
ALIGN MARKERS ON AXIS W/ CONC.
BANDS- ANGLE OF TOP SHALL
BE ORIENTED TOWARD GNOMON
(TYP FOR ALL)

CHAMFER EDGE 1" ALL AROUND
NOTE: MARKERS ARE MONOLITHIC

CENTERLINE ORIENT TOWARD GNOMON.
REFER PLAN 'A' FOR LAYOUT

SAW CUT TOP & BOTTOM
ARTWORK BY LANDSCAPE
ARCHITECT

PITCH FACE SIDES OF STONE MARKERS
LEUDERS LIMESTONE

PLAN

SAW CUT TOP FACE
TOP FACE TO HAVE SAND-
BLASTED NUMERALS. ARTWORK
BY LANDSCAPE ARCHITECT

1" CHAMFER AROUND TOP

SS DONE BY CONTRACTOR
CAST INTO FOOTING

PITCH FACE STONE MARKERS
LEUDERS LIMESTONE

SQUARE CONCRETE FTG.
1'-6" DIA. W/ (4) #5 BAR @
TOP & BOTTOM CONTINUOUS

FINISH GRADE: 659.5

REDWOOD EXPANSION JOINT
FULL DEPTH OF CONC. BAND

COMPACT SUBGRADE TO 90% SPD

SECTION

MESA
DESIGN GROUP
Landscape Architecture
Urban Design
Land Planning

3100 McKinnon Street;
Suite 905
Dallas, Texas 75201
(214) 871-0568 Fax: 871-1507

ARBOR HILLS
NATURE PRESERVE
CITY OF PLANO, TEXAS

Revisions
No. Date Item

Registration

PLW/ITR
Drawn
SRC
Checked
95102   4/24/97
Project No.   Date

Sheet Title

SUNDIAL/GNOMON
LAYOUT PLAN
& DETAILS

BID ITEM 11D

Sheet No.
LC-15

❚ Arbor Hills

172

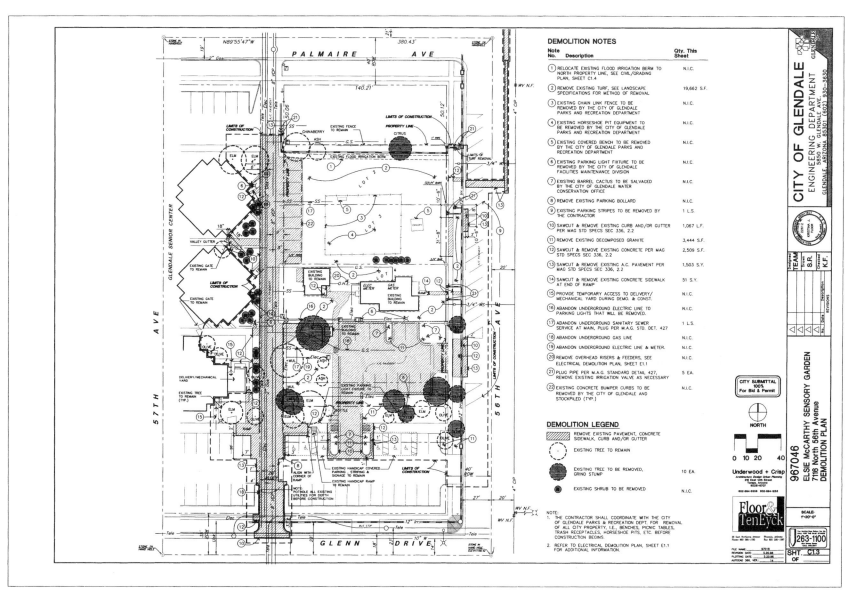

Elsie McCarthy Sensory Garden. Note that the conceptual design drawings are illustrated on page 124.

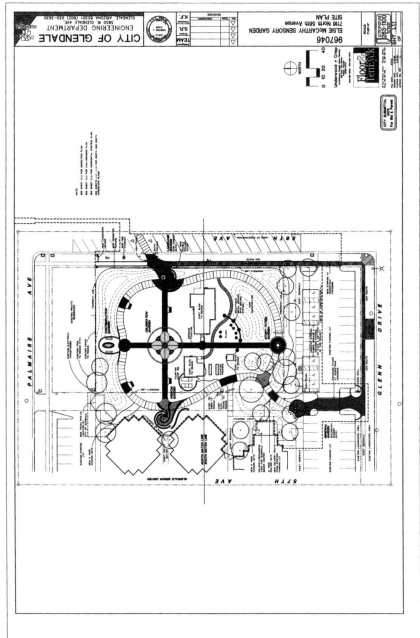

Elsie McCarthy

174

Elsie McCarthy

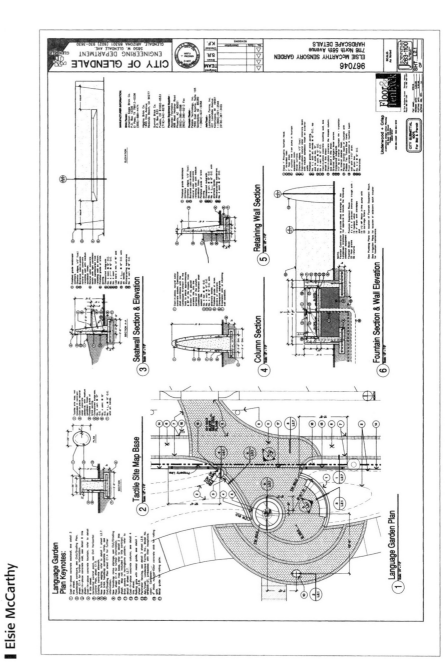

Elsie McCarthy

Elsie McCarthy

175

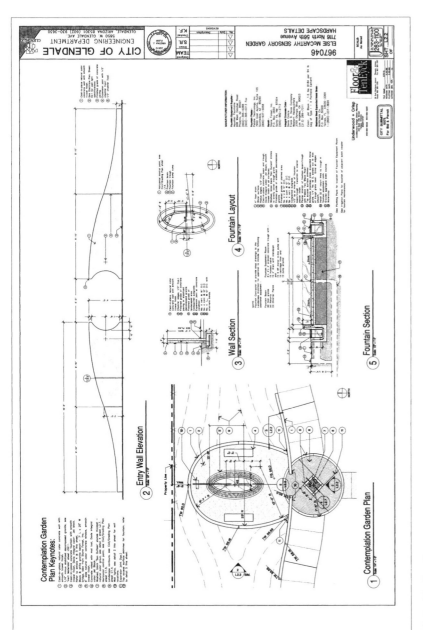

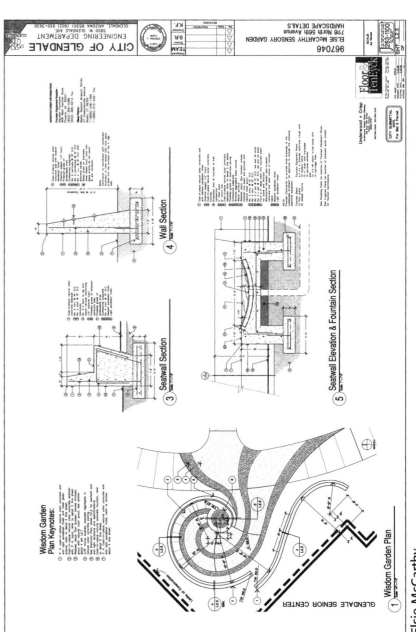

Elsie McCarthy

Elsie McCarthy

176

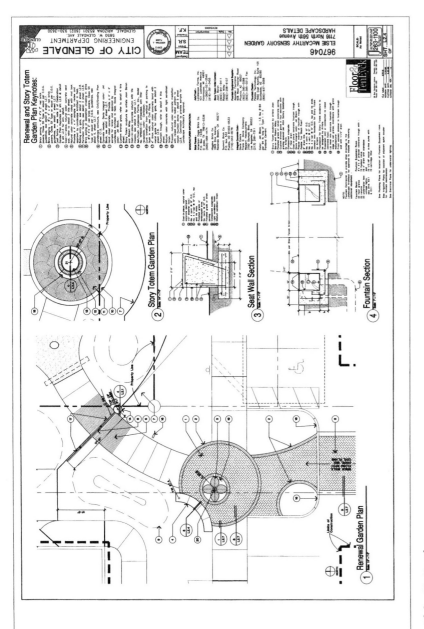

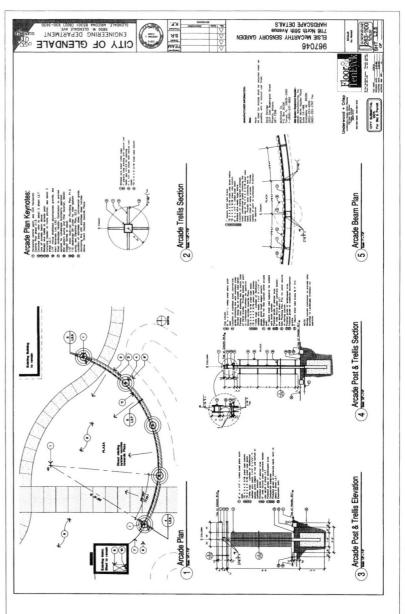

Elsie McCarthy

Elsie McCarthy

177

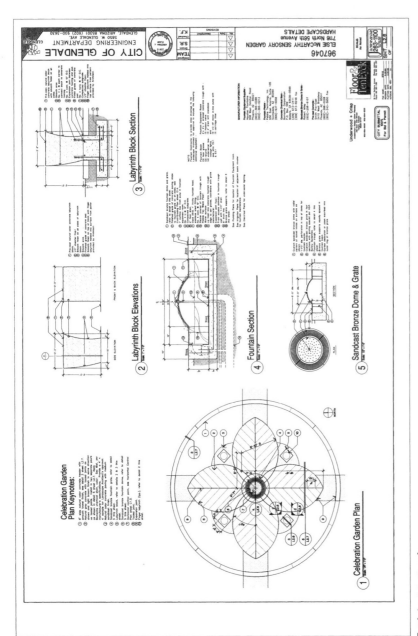

Elsie McCarthy

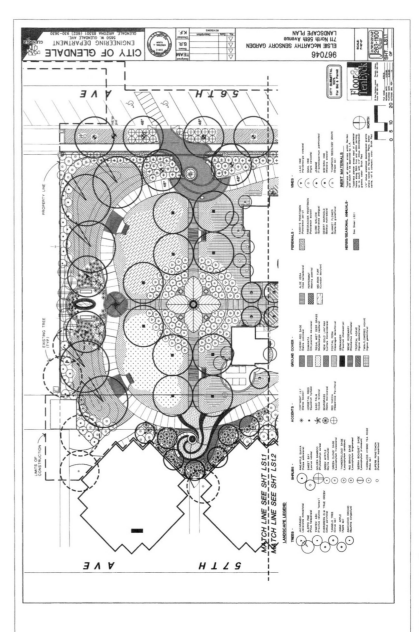

Elsie McCarthy

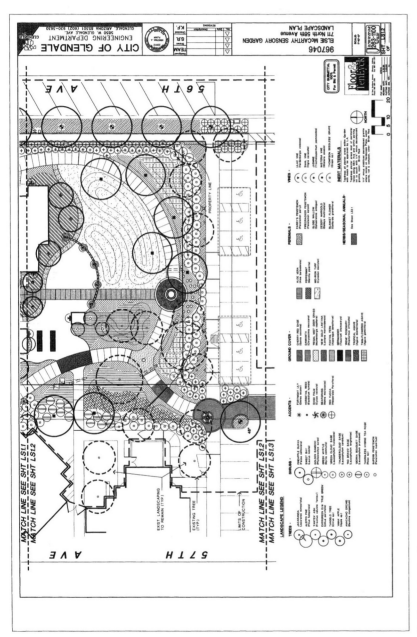

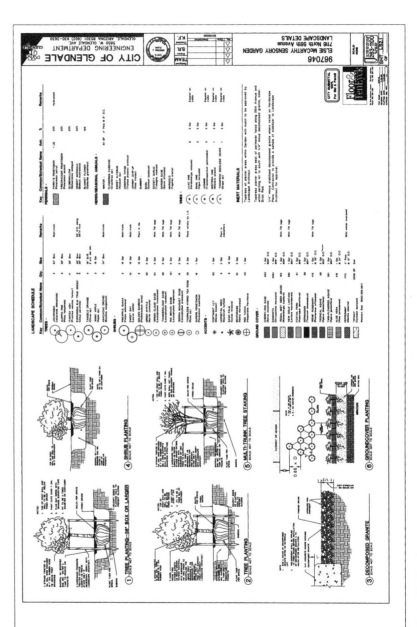

Elsie McCarthy

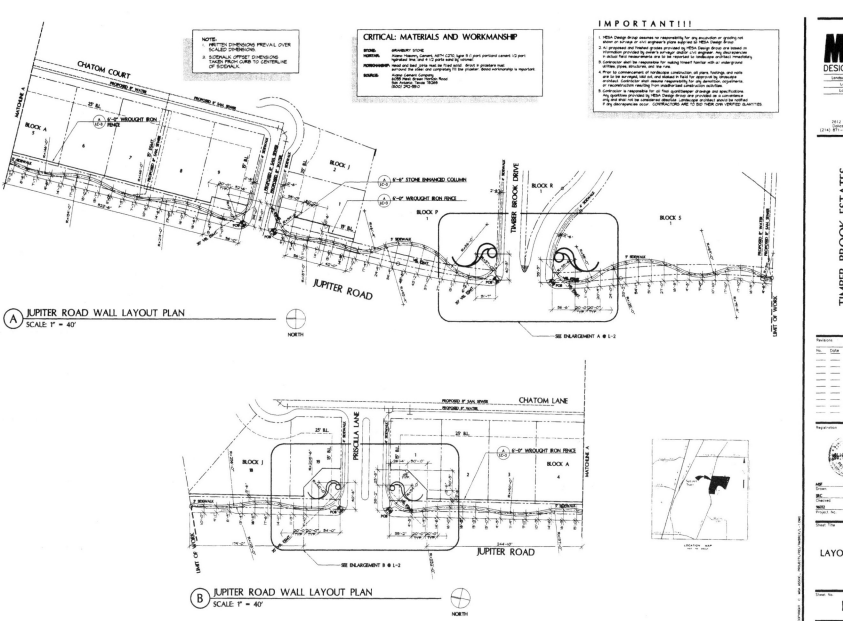

Timber Brook Estates

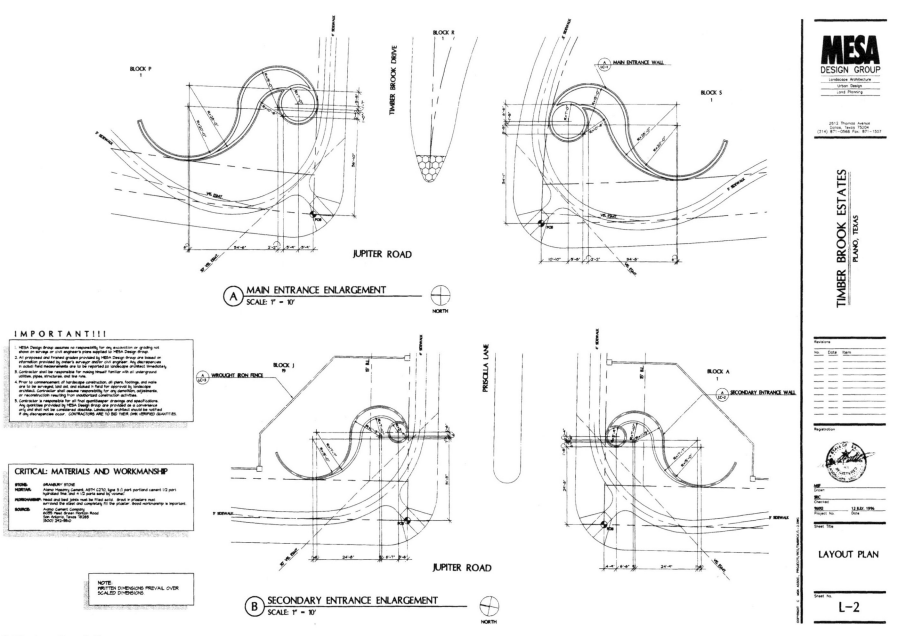

Timber Brook Estates

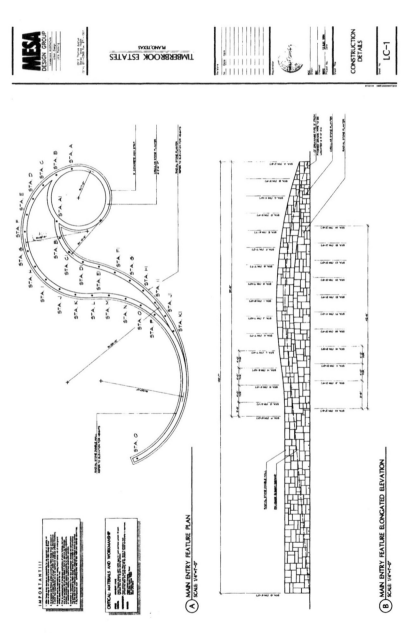

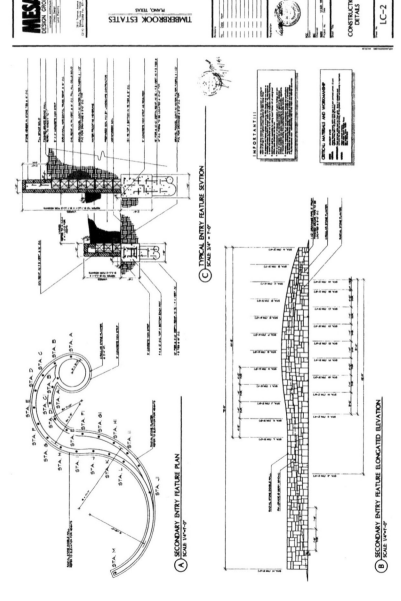

Timber Brook Estates

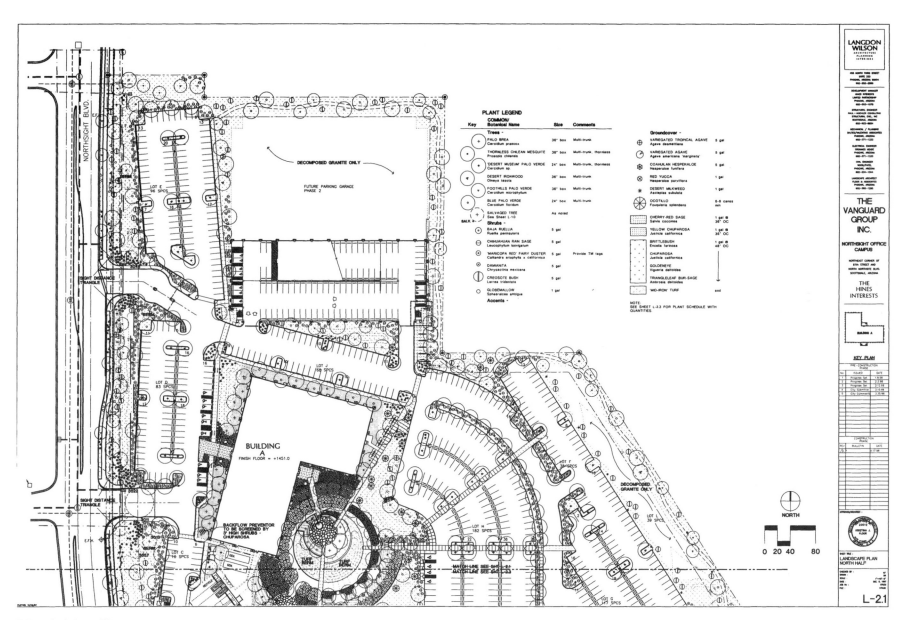

Northsight Office Campus

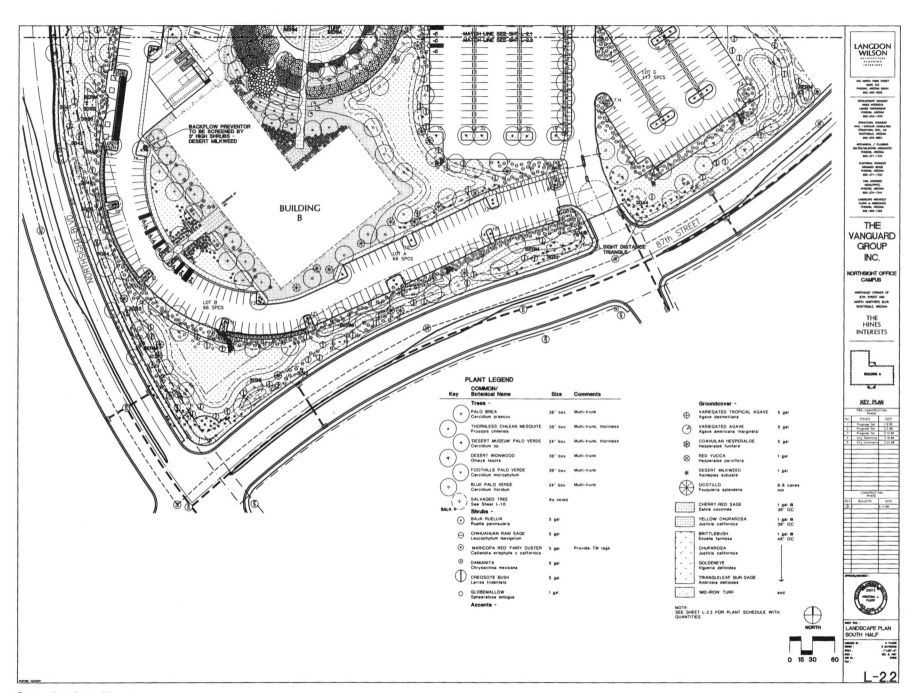

Northsight Office Campus

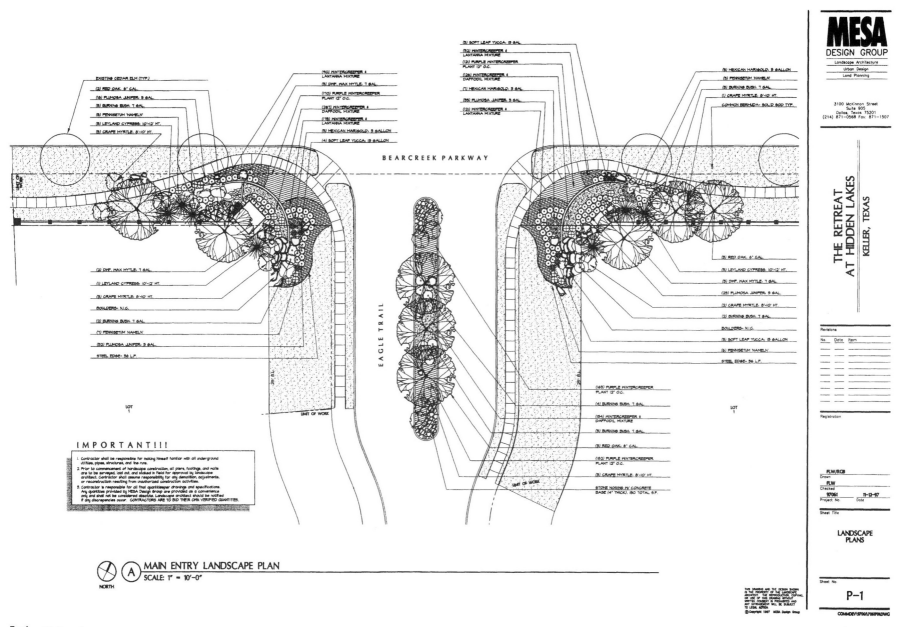

BEARCREEK PARKWAY

EAGLE TRAIL

MESA
DESIGN GROUP

Landscape Architecture
Urban Design
Land Planning

3100 McKinnon Street
Suite 905
Dallas, Texas 75201
(214) 871-0568 Fax: 871-1507

THE RETREAT
AT HIDDEN LAKES — KELLER, TEXAS

Revisions

No.   Date   Item

Registration

FLW/RGB
Drawn
FLW
Checked
97061   11-12-97
Project No.   Date

Sheet Title

LANDSCAPE
PLANS

Sheet No.

P-1

I M P O R T A N T ! ! !

A   MAIN ENTRY LANDSCAPE PLAN
SCALE: 1" = 10'-0"
NORTH

■ The Retreat

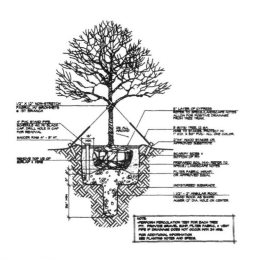

A CANOPY TREE PLANTING DETAIL
NOT TO SCALE

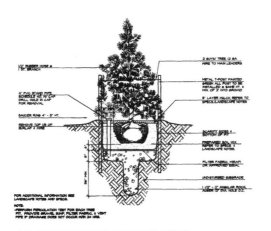

B EVERGREEN TREE PLANTING DETAIL
NOT TO SCALE

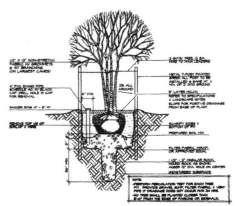

C ORNAMENTAL TREE PLANTING DETAIL
NOT TO SCALE

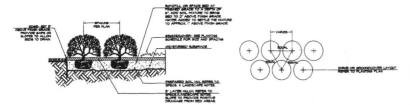

D SHRUBS & GROUNDCOVERS PLANTING DETAIL
NOT TO SCALE

LANDSCAPE NOTES

PLANT LIST

PLANT	PLANT QUANTITY	COMMON NAME / BOTANICAL NAME	SIZE	HEIGHT	SPREAD	COMMENTS
		LARGE TREES- INSTALL PER DETAIL P-3/A				
N/A	12	SHUMARD RED OAK / QUERCUS SHUMARDII	6" CAL.	14'-16'	10'-12'	NURSERY GROWN, MATCHED FULL BROAD HEADS. CONTAINER OR B & B, STRAIGHT & SYMMETRICAL TRUNKS.
		ORNAMENTAL TREES- INSTALL PER INDICATED ON NOTES				
	22	CRAPEMYRTLE / LAGARSTROEMIA INDICA		8'-10'	6'-8'	NURSERY GROWN, MATCHED FULL BROAD HEADS. CONTAINER OR B & B, 5 LEADERS MIN. P-3/C
	18	LEYLAND CYPRESS / CUPRESSOCYPARIS LEYLANDII		10'-12'	6'-8'	NURSERY GROWN, MATCHED FULL BROAD HEADS. STRAIGHT LEADER, SYMMETRICAL. P-3/B
		SHRUBS- INSTALL PER P-3/D				
	81	BURNING BUSH / EUONYMUS ALATUS	7 GAL.	24"-30"	18"-34"	NURSERY GROWN, MATCHED. FULL BROAD HEADS. MATURE ROOT SYSTEM, NON-ROTBOUND.
	9	DWARF WAX MYRTLE / MYRICA PUSILLA	7 GAL.	24"-30"	18"-34"	NURSERY GROWN, MATCHED. FULL BROAD HEADS. MATURE ROOT SYSTEM, NON-ROTBOUND.
	228	PLUMOSA JUNIPER / JUNIPEROUS HORIZONTALIS	5 GAL.	18"	18"-34"	NURSERY GROWN, MATCHED. FULL BROAD HEADS. MATURE ROOT SYSTEM, NON-ROTBOUND.
	54	SOFT LEAF YUCCA / YUCCA RECURVIFOLIA	15 GAL.	30"-36"	36"-44"	NURSERY GROWN, MATCHED FULL BROAD HEADS. MATURE ROOT SYSTEM, NON-ROTBOUND.
		PERENNIALS & ORNAMENTAL GRASSES- INSTALL PER				
	542	DAFFODIL / NARCISSUS SPP.	GAL.	10"-12"	10"-12"	YELLOW & WHITE MIX BLEND 50-50 WITH PURPLE WINTERCREEPER IN AREAS INDICATED.
	481	TEXAS LANTANA / LANTANA SPP.	1 GAL.	10"	12"	NURSERY GROWN. HARDY PERENNIAL VARIETY. MIX 50-50 WITH WINTERCREEPER WHERE INDICATED.
	17	MEXICAN MINT MARIGOLD / TAGETES LUCIDA	1 GAL.	18"-34"	18"-34"	NURSERY GROWN, MATCHED FULL BROAD HEADS. CONTAINER MATURE ROOT SYSTEM.
	58	HAMELN FOUNTAIN GRASS / PENNISETUM ALOPECUROIDES 'HAMELN'	5 GAL.	18"-34"	18"-34"	CONTAINER GROWN, MATURE ROOT SYSTEM. FULL AND ROUND.
	1,448	PURPLE WINTERCREEPER / EUONYMUS COLORATUS	1 GAL.	8"-10"	12"	GOOD ROOT DEVELOPMENT, NON-ROOTBOUND. FIVE LEADERS MIN. MIX 50-50 W/ OTHERS AS SHOWN.
	15,455	COMMON BERMUDA / CYNODON DACTYLOIDES	SOLID SOD			OVERSEED W/ PERENNIAL RYE. APPLY PER MFR'S SPEC. ROLL TWICE OR UNTIL SMOOTH.
	144 LF	STEEL EDGE / RYERSON OR BETTER				PAINTED GREEN.
		SHREDDED CYPRESS MULCH				APPLY TO 3" THICKNESS AFTER WATERING IN.

MESA
DESIGN GROUP
Landscape Architecture
Urban Design
Land Planning

3100 McKinnon Street
Suite 905
Dallas, Texas 75201
(214) 871-0568 Fax: 871-1507

THE RETREAT
OF HIDDEN LAKES
KELLER, TEXAS

Revisions
No. Date Item

Registration

RLW
Drawn
RLW
Checked
97061   11-12-97
Project No.   Date

Sheet Title

LANDSCAPE
DETAILS

Sheet No.

P-3

The Retreat

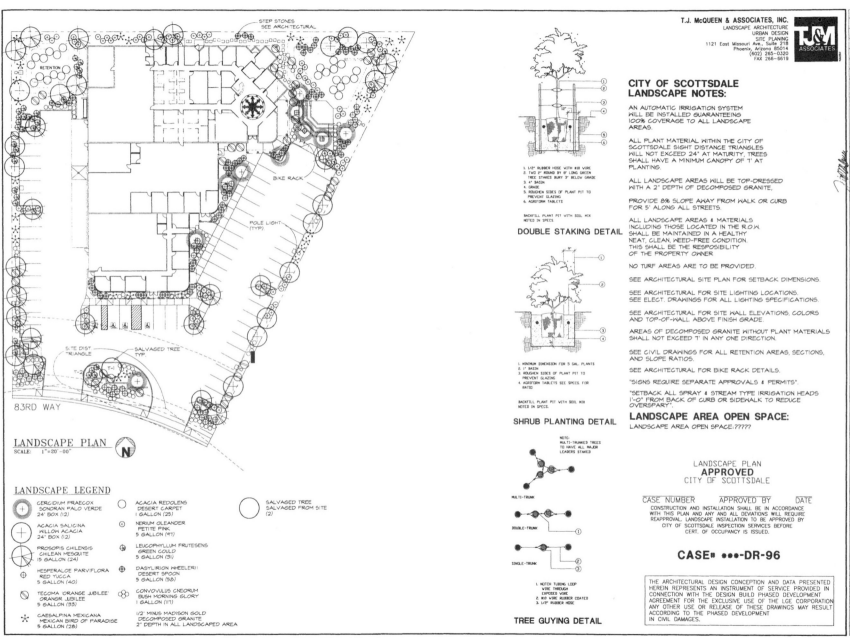

LANDSCAPE PLAN
SCALE: 1"=20'-00"

LANDSCAPE LEGEND

CERCIDIUM PRAECOX SONORAN PALO VERDE 24" BOX (12)		ACACIA REDOLENS DESERT CARPET 1 GALLON (25)		SALVAGED TREE SALVAGED FROM SITE (2)
ACACIA SALICINA WILLOW ACACIA 24" BOX (12)		NERIUM OLEANDER PETITE PINK 5 GALLON (97)		
PROSOPIS CHILENSIS CHILEAN MESQUITE 15 GALLON (24)		LEUCOPHYLLUM FRUTESENS GREEN GOULD 5 GALLON (31)		
HESPERALOE PARVIFLORA RED YUCCA 5 GALLON (40)		DASYLIRION WHEELERII DESERT SPOON 5 GALLON (53)		
TECOMA 'ORANGE JUBILEE' ORANGE JUBILEE 5 GALLON (33)		CONVOVULUS CNEORUM BUSH MORNING GLORY 1 GALLON (117)		
CAESALPINA MEXICANA MEXICAN BIRD OF PARADISE 5 GALLON (28)		1/2" MINUS MADISON GOLD DECOMPOSED GRANITE 2" DEPTH IN ALL LANDSCAPED AREA		

DOUBLE STAKING DETAIL

1. 1/2" RUBBER HOSE WITH #10 WIRE
2. TWO 2" ROUND BY 8' LONG GREEN TREE STAKES BURY 3' BELOW GRADE
3. 4" BASIN
4. GRADE
5. ROUGHEN SIDES OF PLANT PIT TO PREVENT GLAZING
6. AGRIFORM TABLETS

BACKFILL PLANT PIT WITH SOIL MIX NOTED IN SPECS.

SHRUB PLANTING DETAIL

1. MINIMUM DIMENSION FOR 5 GAL. PLANTS
2. 1" BASIN
3. ROUGHEN SIDES OF PLANT PIT TO PREVENT GLAZING
4. AGRIFORM TABLETS SEE SPECS. FOR RATIO

BACKFILL PLANT PIT WITH SOIL MIX NOTED IN SPECS.

TREE GUYING DETAIL

NOTE:
MULTI-TRUNKED TREES TO HAVE ALL MAJOR LEADERS STAKED

MULTI-TRUNK

DOUBLE-TRUNK

SINGLE-TRUNK

1. NOTCH TUBING LOOP WIRE THROUGH
2. #10 WIRE RUBBER COATED
3. 1/2" RUBBER HOSE

T.J. McQUEEN & ASSOCIATES, INC.
LANDSCAPE ARCHITECTURE
URBAN DESIGN
SITE PLANING
1121 East Missouri Ave., Suite 218
Phoenix, Arizona 85014
(602) 265-0320
FAX 266-6619

CITY OF SCOTTSDALE LANDSCAPE NOTES:

AN AUTOMATIC IRRIGATION SYSTEM WILL BE INSTALLED GUARANTEEING 100% COVERAGE TO ALL LANDSCAPE AREAS.

ALL PLANT MATERIAL WITHIN THE CITY OF SCOTTSDALE SIGHT DISTANCE TRIANGLES WILL NOT EXCEED 24" AT MATURITY, TREES SHALL HAVE A MINIMUM CANOPY OF 7' AT PLANTING.

ALL LANDSCAPE AREAS WILL BE TOP-DRESSED WITH A 2" DEPTH OF DECOMPOSED GRANITE,

PROVIDE 8% SLOPE AWAY FROM WALK OR CURB FOR 5' ALONG ALL STREETS.

ALL LANDSCAPE AREAS & MATERIALS INCLUDING THOSE LOCATED IN THE R.O.W. SHALL BE MAINTAINED IN A HEALTHY NEAT, CLEAN, WEED-FREE CONDITION. THIS SHALL BE THE RESPOSIBILITY OF THE PROPERTY OWNER

NO TURF AREAS ARE TO BE PROVIDED.

SEE ARCHITECTURAL SITE PLAN FOR SETBACK DIMENSIONS.

SEE ARCHITECTURAL FOR SITE LIGHTING LOCATIONS. SEE ELECT. DRAWINGS FOR ALL LIGHTING SPECIFICATIONS.

SEE ARCHITECTURAL FOR SITE WALL ELEVATIONS, COLORS AND TOP-OF-WALL ABOVE FINISH GRADE.

AREAS OF DECOMPOSED GRANITE WITHOUT PLANT MATERIALS SHALL NOT EXCEED 7' IN ANY ONE DIRECTION.

SEE CIVIL DRAWINGS FOR ALL RETENTION AREAS, SECTIONS, AND SLOPE RATIOS.

SEE ARCHITECTURAL FOR BIKE RACK DETAILS.

"SIGNS REQUIRE SEPARATE APPROVALS & PERMITS".

"SETBACK ALL SPRAY & STREAM TYPE IRRIGATION HEADS 1'-0" FROM BACK OF CURB OR SIDEWALK TO REDUCE OVERSPARY".

LANDSCAPE AREA OPEN SPACE:

LANDSCAPE AREA OPEN SPACE:?????

LANDSCAPE PLAN
APPROVED
CITY OF SCOTTSDALE

CASE NUMBER   APPROVED BY   DATE
CONSTRUCTION AND INSTALLATION SHALL BE IN ACCORDANCE WITH THIS PLAN AND ANY AND ALL DEVIATIONS WILL REQUIRE REAPPROVAL. LANDSCAPE INSTALLATION TO BE APPROVED BY CITY OF SCOTTSDALE INSPECTION SERVICES BEFORE CERT. OF OCCUPANCY IS ISSUED.

CASE# *-DR-96**

REVISIONS

A NEW FACILITY FOR
MIDNIGHT HOLDINGS
15650 83RD WAY, SCOTTSDALE, ARIZONA 85244

Date 2-17-96
Scale AS NOTED
Drawn T.D.B.
Job 9602

L-1

■ Midnight Holdings

Crib wall section. Hand-drawn sitework detail with graphite on mylar.

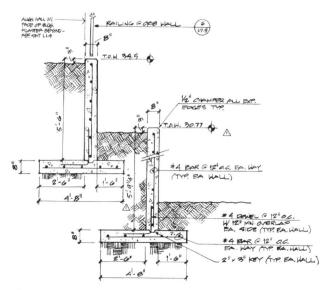

ALIGN WALL W/ FACE OF BLDG. PILASTER BEYOND - REF SHT. L1.4
RAILING @ CRIB WALL
8"
T.O.W. 34.5
1/2" CHAMFER ALL EXP. EDGES TYP.
8"
T.O.W. 30.77
#4 BAR @ 12" O.C. EA. WAY (TYP. EA. WALL)
2'-6"
1'-6"
4'-8"
#4 DOWEL @ 12" O.C. W/ 12" MIN OVERLAP EA. SIDE (TYP. EA. WALL)
#4 BAR @ 12" O.C. EA. WAY (TYP. EA. WALL)
2" X 3" KEY (TYP. EA. WALL)
8"
2'-0"
1'-6"
4'-8"

11 Crib Wall Section
SCALE: 1/2" = 1'-0"

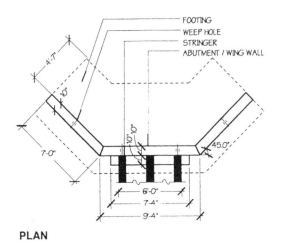

FOOTING
WEEP HOLE
STRINGER
ABUTMENT / WING WALL
4'-7"
10"
7'-0"
10" 10"
45.0°
6'-0"
7'-4"
9'-4"

PLAN

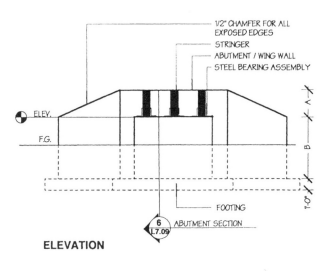

1/2" CHAMFER FOR ALL EXPOSED EDGES
STRINGER
ABUTMENT / WING WALL
STEEL BEARING ASSEMBLY
ELEV.
F.G.
A
B
1'-0"
FOOTING
6 ABUTMENT SECTION
L7.09

ELEVATION

4 Trail Bridge Abutment
1/4" = 1' - 0"

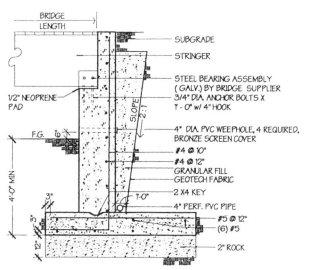

BRIDGE LENGTH
SUBGRADE
STRINGER
STEEL BEARING ASSEMBLY (GALV.) BY BRIDGE SUPPLIER
3/4" DIA. ANCHOR BOLTS X 1'- 0" w/ 4" HOOK
4" DIA. PVC WEEPHOLE, 4 REQUIRED, BRONZE SCREEN COVER
#4 @ 10"
#4 @ 12"
GRANULAR FILL
GEOTECH FABRIC
2 X 4 KEY
4" PERF. PVC PIPE
#5 @ 12"
(6) #5
2" ROCK
1/2" NEOPRENE PAD
F.G.
SLOPE 2:1
4'-0" MIN
3"
3"
12"
1'-0"

6 Trail Bridge Abutment - Section
1/2" = 1' - 0"

Bridge detail. Sitework details generated in AutoCADD.

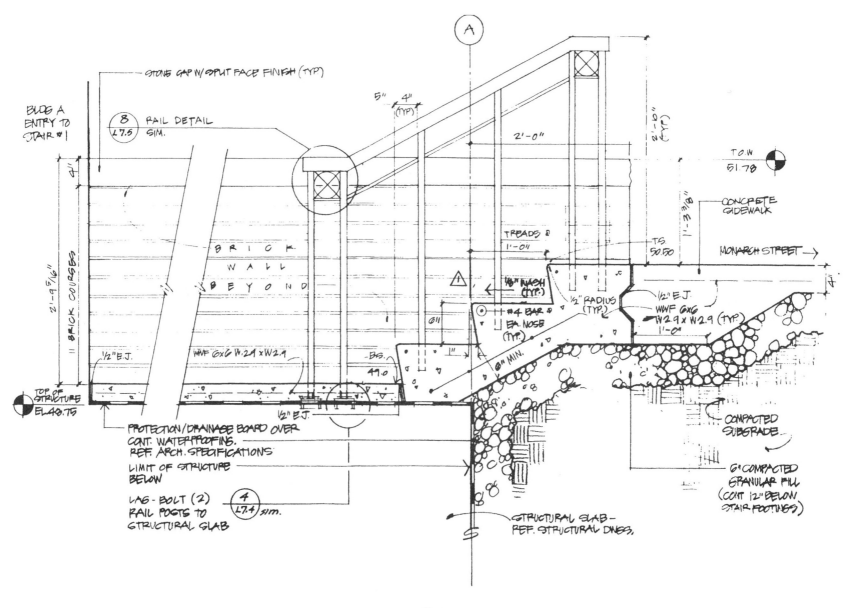

STONE CAP W/ SPLIT FACE FINISH (TYP.)

BLDG A ENTRY TO STAIR #1

8 / L7.5 — RAIL DETAIL SIM.

A

5" 4" (TYP.)

2'-0"

2'-0" (TYP.)

T.O.W. 51.78

2'-9 5/16" = BRICK COURSES

4"

CONCRETE SIDEWALK

B R I C K W A L L B E Y O N D

TREADS @ 1'-0"

T.S. 50.50

MONARCH STREET →

1

1/8" WASH (TYP.)

1/2" RADIUS (TYP.)

#4 BAR EA. NOSE (TYP.)

1/2" E.J. (TYP.)

WWF 6x6 W2.9 x W2.9 (TYP.) 1'-0"

1/2" E.J.

WWF 6x6 W2.9 x W2.9

B.S.

49.0

6" MIN.

1"

TOP OF STRUCTURE EL 48.75

1/2" E.J.

PROTECTION/DRAINAGE BOARD OVER CONT. WATERPROOFING. REF. ARCH. SPECIFICATIONS.

LIMIT OF STRUCTURE BELOW

LAG - BOLT (2) RAIL POSTS TO STRUCTURAL SLAB

4 / L7.4 sim.

STRUCTURAL SLAB - REF. STRUCTURAL DWGS.

COMPACTED SUBGRADE

6" COMPACTED GRANULAR FILL (CONT. 12" BELOW STAIR FOOTINGS)

8 Stair Detail at Bldg. Stair #1

SCALE: 1" = 1'-0"

Stair detail. Hand-drawn sitework detail with graphite on mylar.

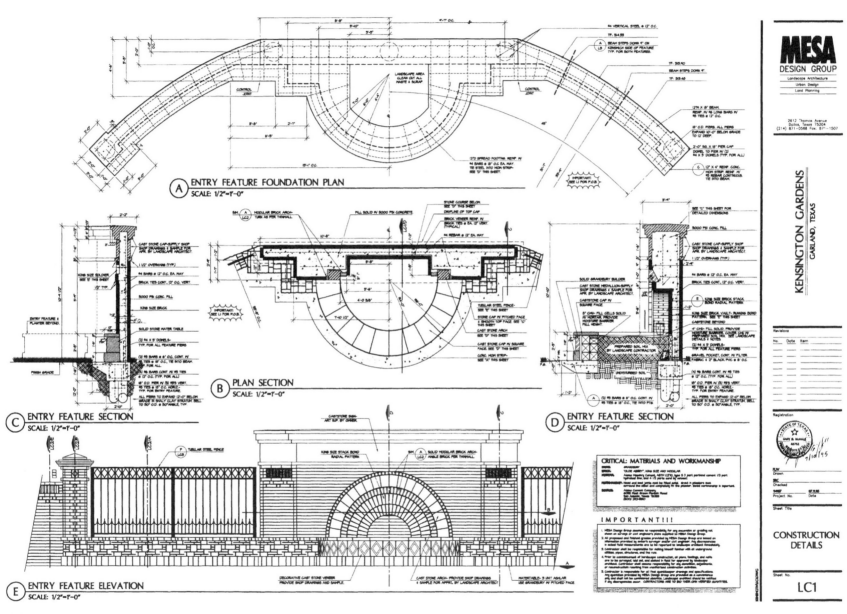

ENTRY FEATURE FOUNDATION PLAN
SCALE: 1/2"=1'-0"

ENTRY FEATURE SECTION
SCALE: 1/2"=1'-0"

PLAN SECTION
SCALE: 1/2"=1'-0"

ENTRY FEATURE SECTION
SCALE: 1/2"=1'-0"

ENTRY FEATURE ELEVATION
SCALE: 1/2"=1'-0"

CRITICAL: MATERIALS AND WORKMANSHIP

IMPORTANT!!!

MESA
DESIGN GROUP
Landscape Architecture
Urban Design
Land Planning

KENSINGTON GARDENS
GARLAND, TEXAS

CONSTRUCTION
DETAILS

Sheet No.

LC1

Kensington Gardens

190

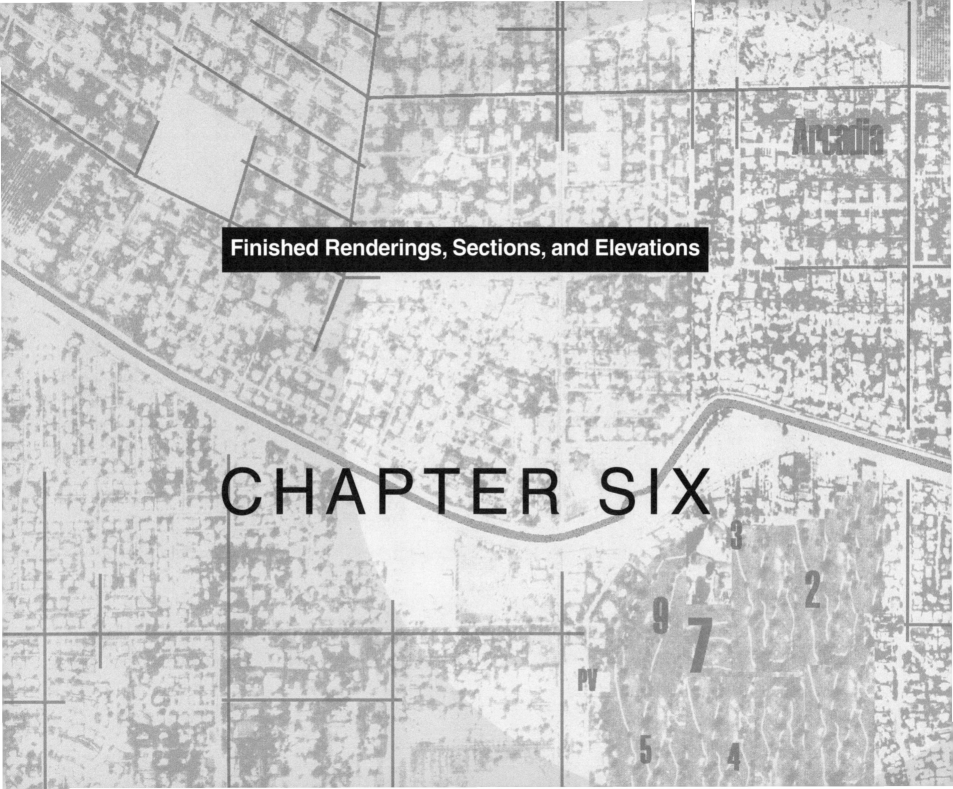

Finished Renderings, Sections, and Elevations

CHAPTER SIX

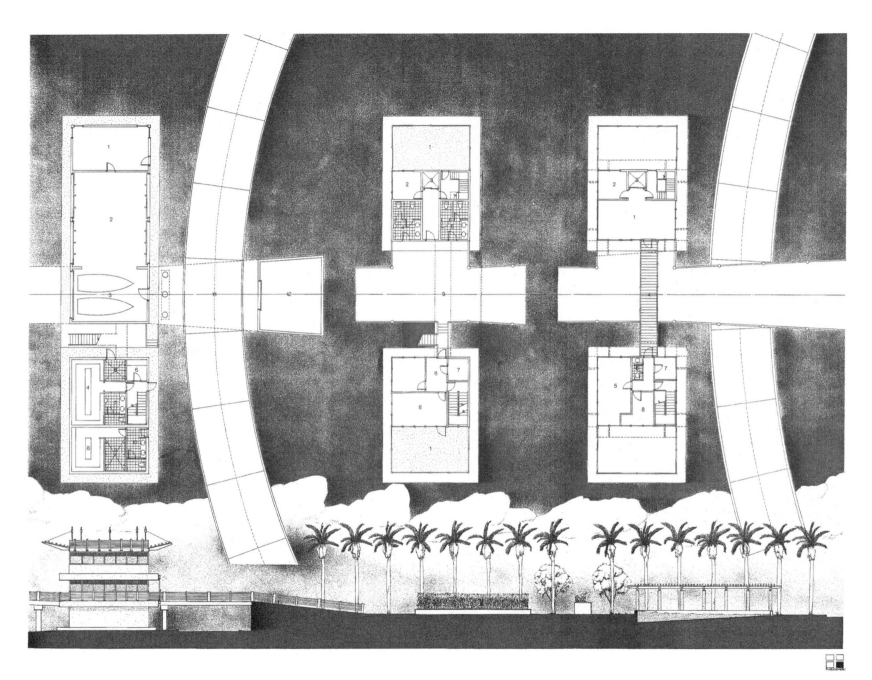

Hermosa Beach Pier. The following four images were created
for a design competition. Ink and airbrushed ink on mylar.

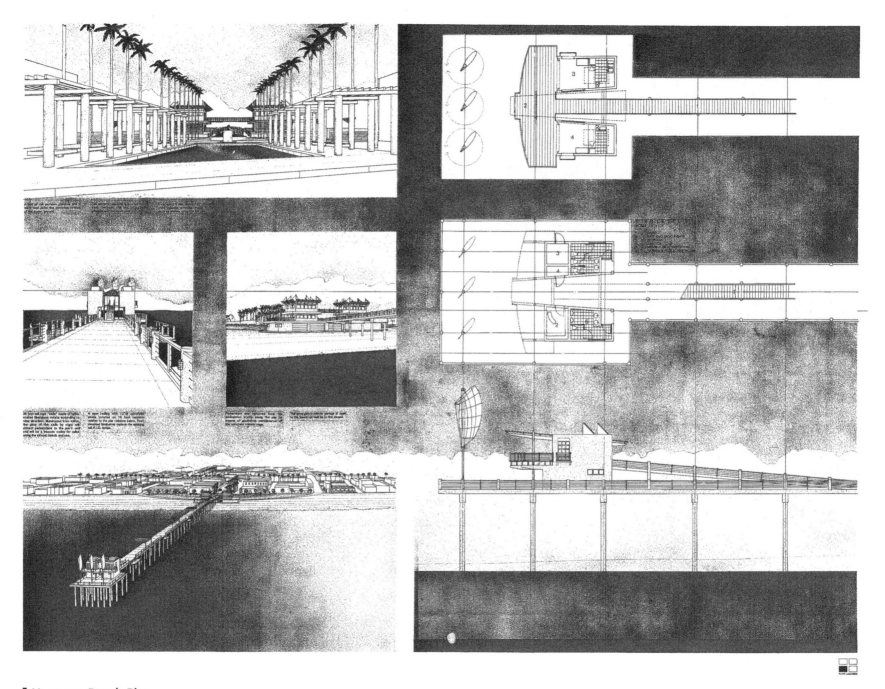

▌ Hermosa Beach Pier

Hermosa Beach and its neighboring oceanfront communities make up a narrow sliver of restfulness at the edge of a dry, tense, seemingly endless metropolis. A breeze and an uninterrupted view of the horizon are all that are necessary to draw large numbers of visitors from inland. We hope however to create an experience which is more than just an escape.

Our scheme invites residents and visitors alike to celebrate the meeting of continent and ocean. Within a proposed new plaza located between the pier and Pier Avenue, both realms coexist. The perpetual motion of the ocean waves is echoed in a bed of tall pampas grasses swaying with the breezes and again in a pool in which horizontal waves are created. The city likewise reaches out to the Ocean with defined lines of regularly spaced palm trees. To suggest the continuity of the city avenue, we have allowed the pier to bisect

the lifeguard building and the structure at the pier's end. Along this axis, a succession of forced perspectives directs one's sight and thoughts to the open Pacific, where there is no visible end. A circular promenade overlooking the ocean surrounds two amphitheaters. As if affected by the same gravitational pulls which rule the tides, the circular forms break away from their concentric order. This shift results in an expansion of the promenade's north side where volleyball spectators are likely to congregate. Low beach grasses are introduced along the sloping planes to the west of the promenade. In contrast with the the two formal amphitheaters within the plaza, the grassy slopes provide for a more relaxed area for sitting and viewing the beach. The faster moving circulation along the strand has been redirected towards the life guard buildings allowing for slower pedestrian and retail activities to take near the plaza.

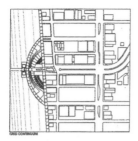

GRID CONTINUUM

AMPHITHEATER RACE LOCATIONS

PLAZA AND STRAND RACE LOCATIONS

FORCED PERSPECTIVE DATUM

PLATE NUMBER

❚ Hermosa Beach Pier

194

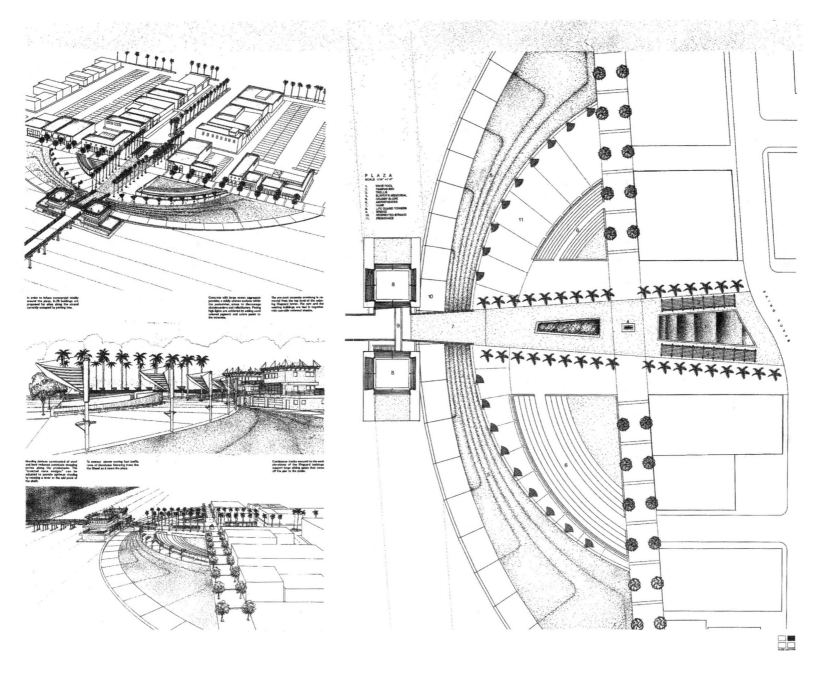

PLAZA
SCALE 1/16" = 1'-0"

1. WAVE POOL
2. RAMPING BED
3. TRELLIS
4. BUYER'S MEMORIAL
5. GRASSY SLOPE
6. AMPHITHEATER
7. RAMP
8. LIFE GUARD TOWERS
9. BRIDGE
10. RESPECTED STRAND
11. PROMENADE

▌Hermosa Beach Pier

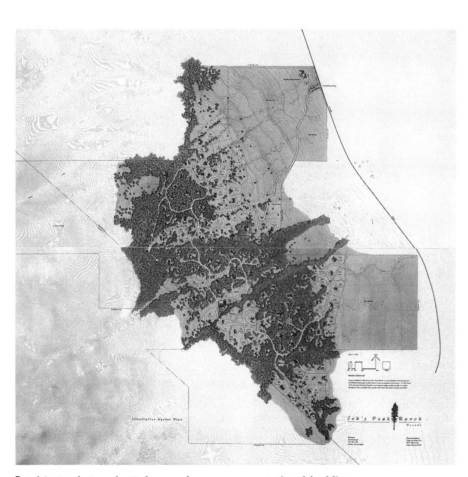

Job's Peak Ranch. Color marker on presentation blackline.

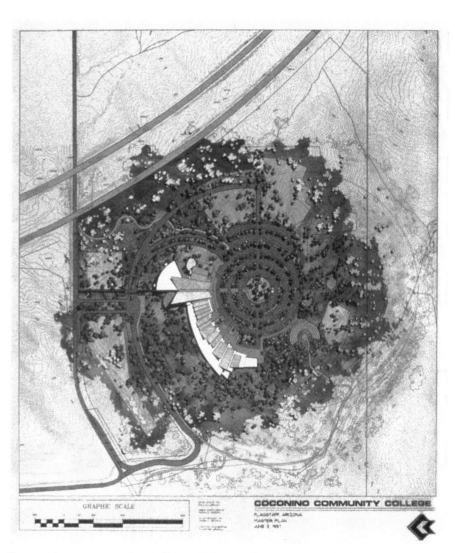

Coconino Community College. Color marker on presentation blackline over AutoCADD base drawing.

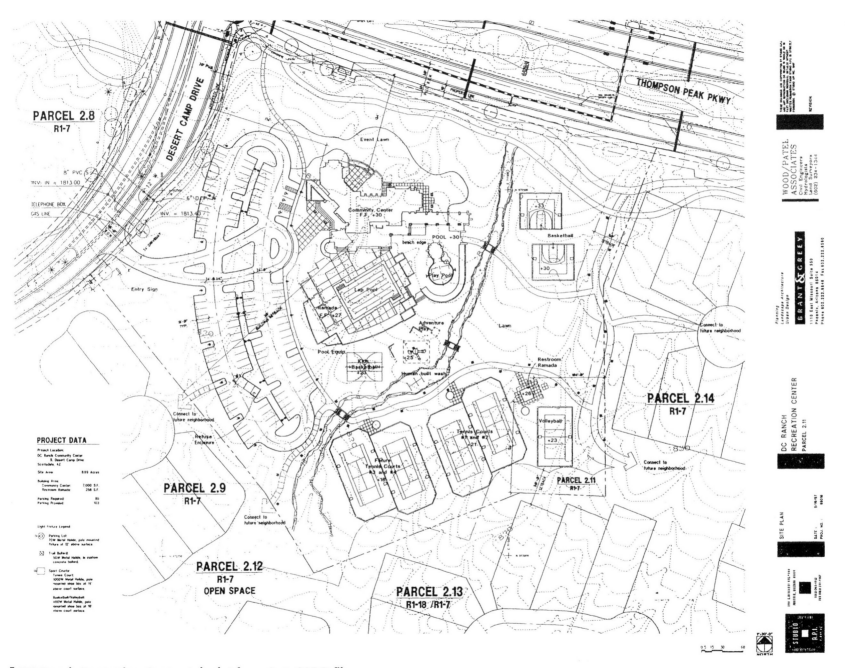

▌DC Ranch Recreation Center. Ink plot from AutoCADD file.

MASTER PLAN

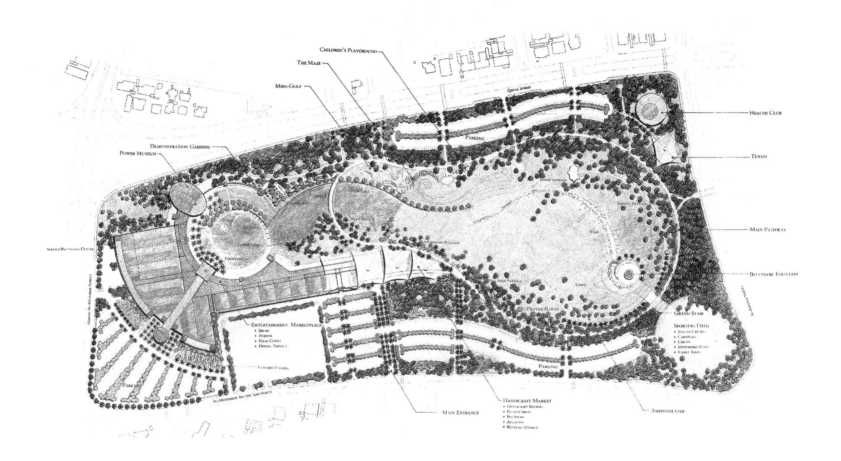

Entertainment and Gardens

Kuwait City, Kuwait

Kuwait Finance House
PACE • EDAW
January 1998

Salmiya Park. Color pencil on bond base. The master plan is hand drawn over a screened CADD base on vellum. The final line drawing is an OCE photocopy to bond.

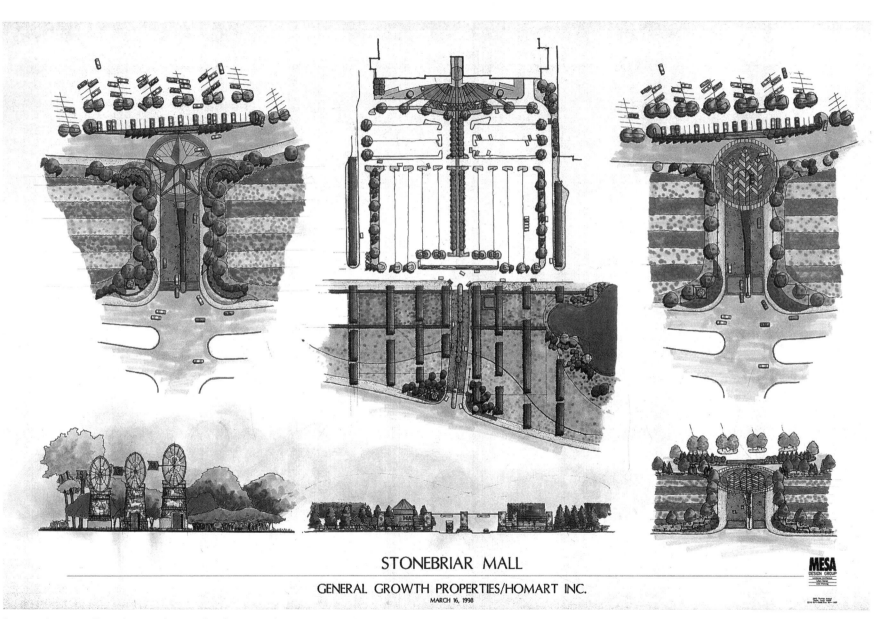

STONEBRIAR MALL

GENERAL GROWTH PROPERTIES/HOMART INC.

MARCH 16, 1998

Stonebriar Mall. Color marker and color pencil on presentation
blackline over hand-drawn base drawing.

Las Casitas. Color marker on presentation blackline over Auto-CADD base drawing.

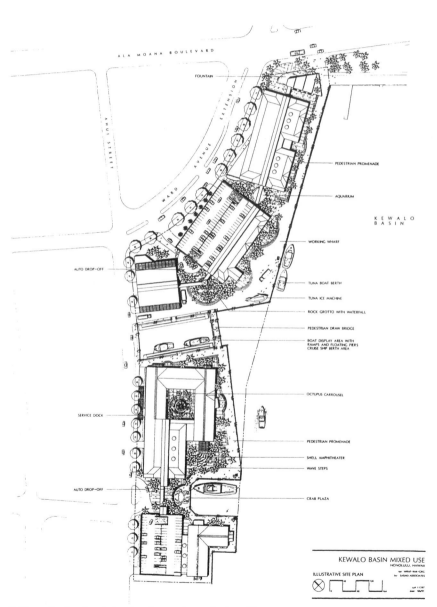

Kewalo Basin. Ink plot from AutoCADD file.

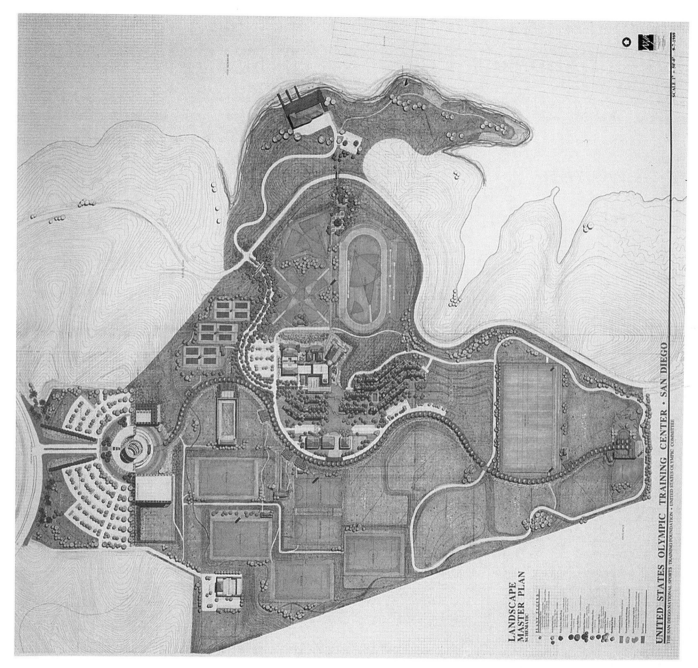

San Diego Olympic Training Center. Color pencil on bond over
AutoCADD base drawing.

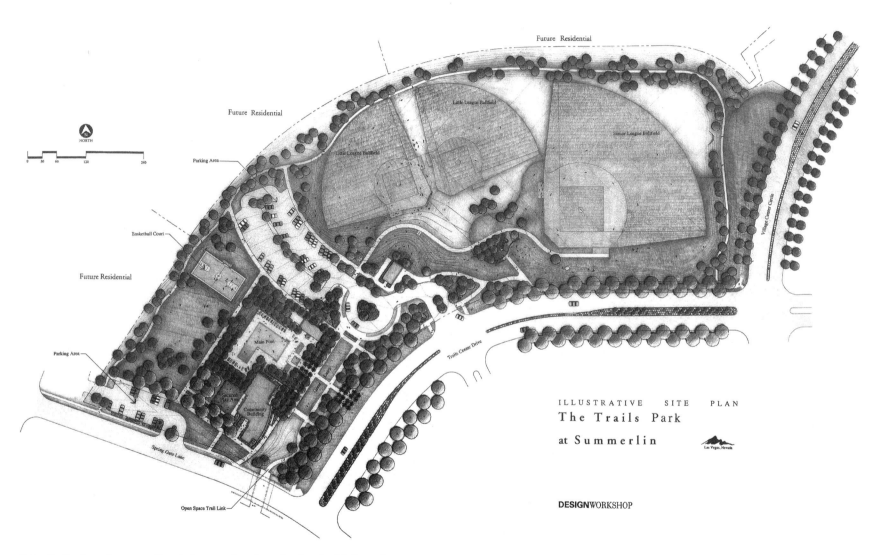

Trails Park at Summerlin. Color marker (on the back side) and color pencil on mylar. The base plot, from an AutoCADD file, is printed on single-side frosted mylar. Ink baselines and color marker are applied to the back, nonfrosted side.

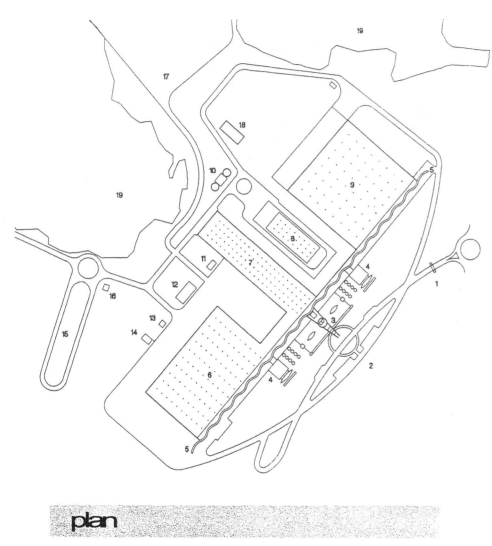

1   main entrance / check point
2   arrival arc
3   administration
4   cafeteria
5   masonry wall
6   final assembly
7   paint
8   energy plant
9   body
10   water reservoir
11   chemical storage
12   fluids station
13   maintenance station
14   fire station
15   truck parking
16   trucker's lodging
17   parking for 3000 cars
18   fuel station
19   existing trees
20   axial entry point at narrow end
     of the wedge
21   rotunda courtyard
22   conference room
23   reception
24   workroom
25   restrooms
26   undulating masonry wall
27   conveyor system in 'Spine' of
     building
28   paint structure

plan

▌ Renault in Brazil. Ink plot from AutoCADD file.

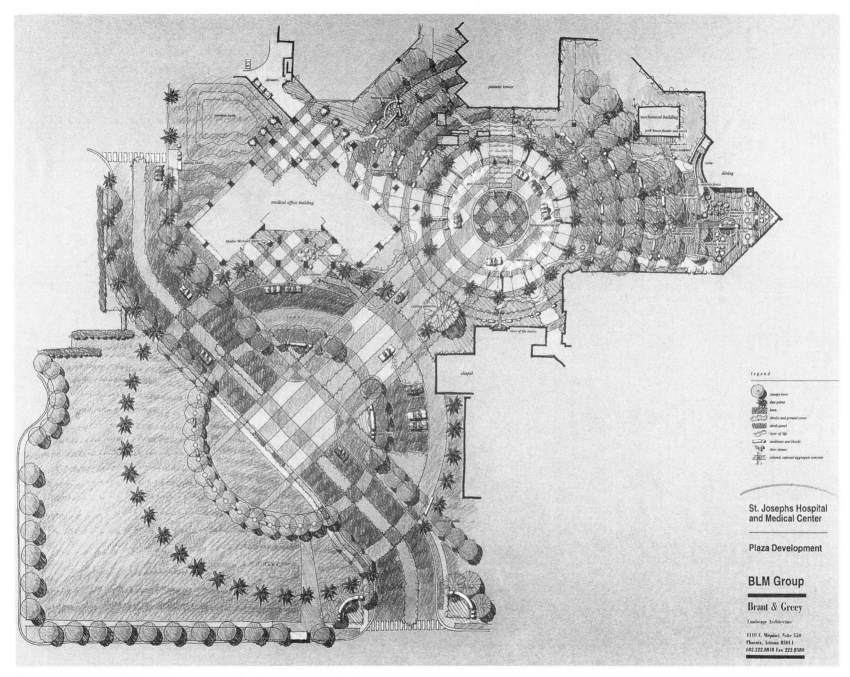

St. Joseph's Hospital. Color pencil on kraft paper over freehand
base drawing.

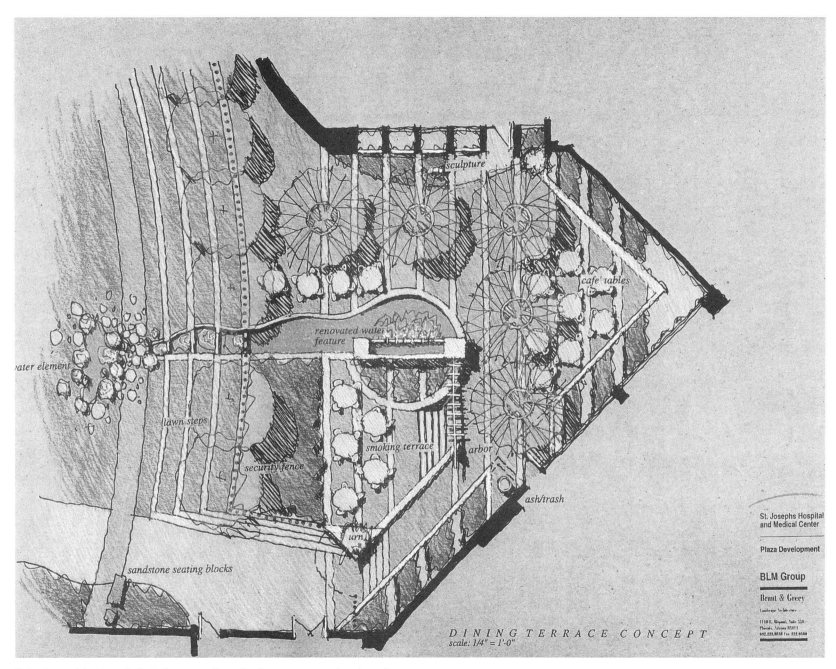

sculpture

cafe tables

renovated water feature

water element

lawn steps

security fence

smoking terrace

arbor

ash/trash

urn

sandstone seating blocks

DINING TERRACE CONCEPT
scale: 1/4" = 1'-0"

St. Josephs Hospital
and Medical Center

Plaza Development

BLM Group

Brant & Greey
Landscape Architecture
1110 E. Missouri, Suite 550
Phoenix, Arizona 85014
602.222.8818 Fax 222.8586

St. Joseph's Hospital. Color pencil on kraft paper over freehand
base drawing.

Wyndham Rose Hall. Color marker on presentation blackline over AutoCADD base drawing.

WATER TAXI

PEDESTRIAN CROSSING

THEME LIGHTHOUSE

TO AIRPORT

LANDSCAPED BOULEVARD/PROJECT ENTRY

TO MARIGOT & PHILIPSBURG

ARRIVAL COURT

TURNING LANE

SIDEWALK

LANDSCAPED MEDIAN

SERVICE ACCESS

SERVICE BUILDING

EMPLOYEE PARKING

CABANAS

CASCADES

WATERSPORTS

CAFE/BAR

PEDESTRIAN PROMENADE

WATER TAXI

CABANAS

GATE HOUSE

RESORT RESIDENCES

BEACH SHOPS/CAFE/BAR

EXPANDED BEACH AND BEACH PLANTINGS

MARIGOT

SIMSON BAY

KEY MAP

TO PELICAN RESORT

NORTH

0M   10M   50M
SCALE 1:300
4/89

BEACH CLUB

Beach Club. Color marker and color pencil on presentation
blackline. The base drawing is hand drawn on mylar with
computer-generated text added manually.

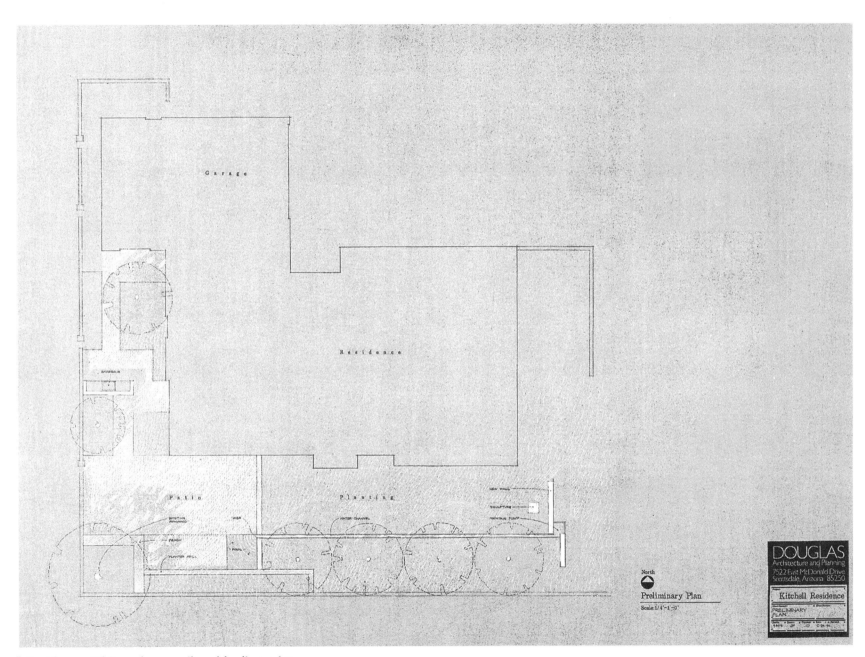

Residence. White color pencil on blueline print.

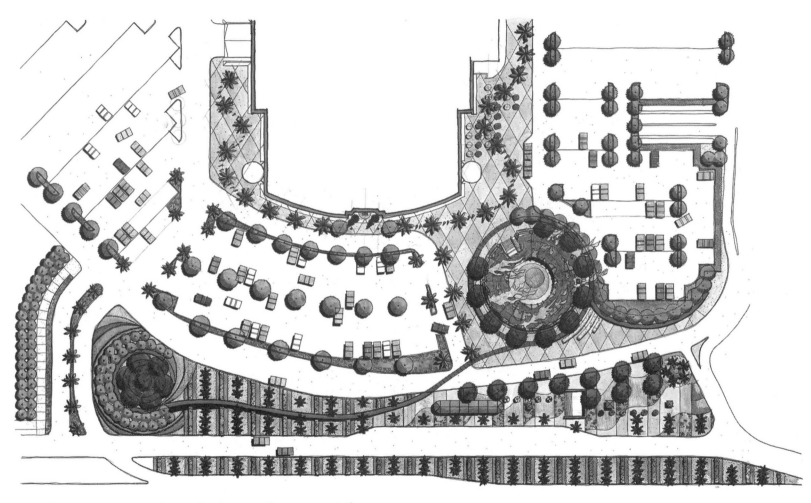

Retail center. Color marker and color pencil on presentation
blackline over hand-drawn base drawing.

Early Winters Resort. Color marker on presentation blackline.

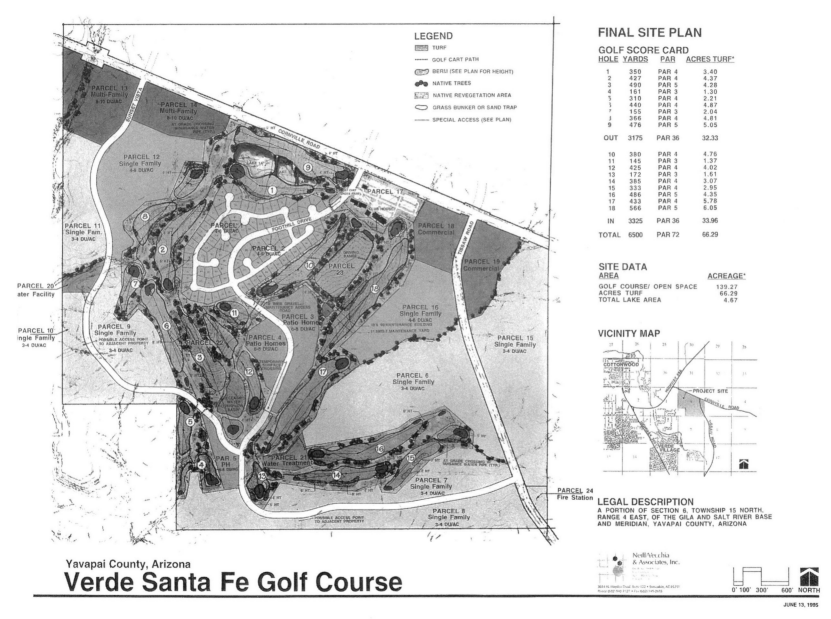

LEGEND

- ▨ TURF
- ⋯ GOLF CART PATH
- ⬭ BERM (SEE PLAN FOR HEIGHT)
- ● NATIVE TREES
- ▨ NATIVE REVEGETATION AREA
- ⬭ GRASS BUNKER OR SAND TRAP
- ⋯ SPECIAL ACCESS (SEE PLAN)

PARCEL 13
Multi-Family
8-10 DU/AC

PARCEL 14
Multi-Family
8-10 DU/AC

AT GRADE CROSSING
NUISANCE WATER
PIPE (TYP.)

CORNVILLE ROAD

PARCEL 12
Single Family
4-8 DU/AC

LAKE 1A

LAKE 1B

PARCEL 17

PARCEL 11
Single Fam.
3-4 DU/AC

CLUB HOUSE

FOOTHILL DRIVE

PARCEL
6 DU/AC

PARCEL
4-6 DU/AC

PARCEL 18
Commercial

PARCEL 20
ater Facility

DRIVING
RANGE

PARCEL
23

PARCEL 19
Commercial

WIDE GRAVEL
MAINTENANCE ACCESS
ROAD

PARCEL 16
Single Family
4-6 DU/AC

PARCEL 10
ingle Family
3-4 DU/AC

PARCEL 9
Single Family

PARCEL 3
Patio Homes
6-8 DU/AC

48' X 90' MAINTENANCE BUILDING
11,880 S.F. MAINTENANCE YARD

PARCEL 15
Single Family
3-4 DU/AC

POSSIBLE ACCESS POINT
TO ADJACENT PROPERTY
3-4 DU/AC

PARCEL 22

PARCEL 4
Patio Homes
6-8 DU/AC

TEMPORARY
SURFACE
CROSSING

PARCEL 6
Single Family
3-4 DU/AC

DECLINING
WATER
DISPERSAL
BASIN

PAR 5
PH
6-8 DU/AC

PARCEL 21
Water Treatment

AT GRADE CROSSING
NUISANCE WATER PIPE (TYP.)

PARCEL 7
Single Family
3-4 DU/AC

PARCEL 24
Fire Station

POSSIBLE ACCESS POINT
TO ADJACENT PROPERTY

PARCEL 8
Single Family
3-4 DU/AC

FINAL SITE PLAN

GOLF SCORE CARD

HOLE	YARDS	PAR	ACRES TURF*
1	350	PAR 4	3.40
2	427	PAR 4	4.37
3	490	PAR 5	4.28
4	161	PAR 3	1.30
5	310	PAR 4	2.21
6	440	PAR 4	4.87
7	155	PAR 3	2.04
8	366	PAR 4	4.81
9	476	PAR 5	5.05
OUT	3175	PAR 36	32.33
10	380	PAR 4	4.76
11	145	PAR 3	1.37
12	425	PAR 4	4.02
13	172	PAR 3	1.61
14	385	PAR 4	3.07
15	333	PAR 4	2.95
16	486	PAR 5	4.35
17	433	PAR 4	5.78
18	566	PAR 5	6.05
IN	3325	PAR 36	33.96
TOTAL	6500	PAR 72	66.29

SITE DATA

AREA	ACREAGE*
GOLF COURSE/ OPEN SPACE	139.27
ACRES TURF	66.29
TOTAL LAKE AREA	4.67

VICINITY MAP

COTTONWOOD

PROJECT SITE

CORNVILLE ROAD

VERDE
VILLAGE

LEGAL DESCRIPTION

A PORTION OF SECTION 6, TOWNSHIP 15 NORTH,
RANGE 4 EAST, OF THE GILA AND SALT RIVER BASE
AND MERIDIAN, YAVAPAI COUNTY, ARIZONA

Neill/Vecchia
& Associates, Inc.

0' 100' 300' 600' NORTH

JUNE 13, 1995

Yavapai County, Arizona
Verde Santa Fe Golf Course

Verde Santa Fe. Color marker on presentation blackline over
AutoCADD base drawing.

211

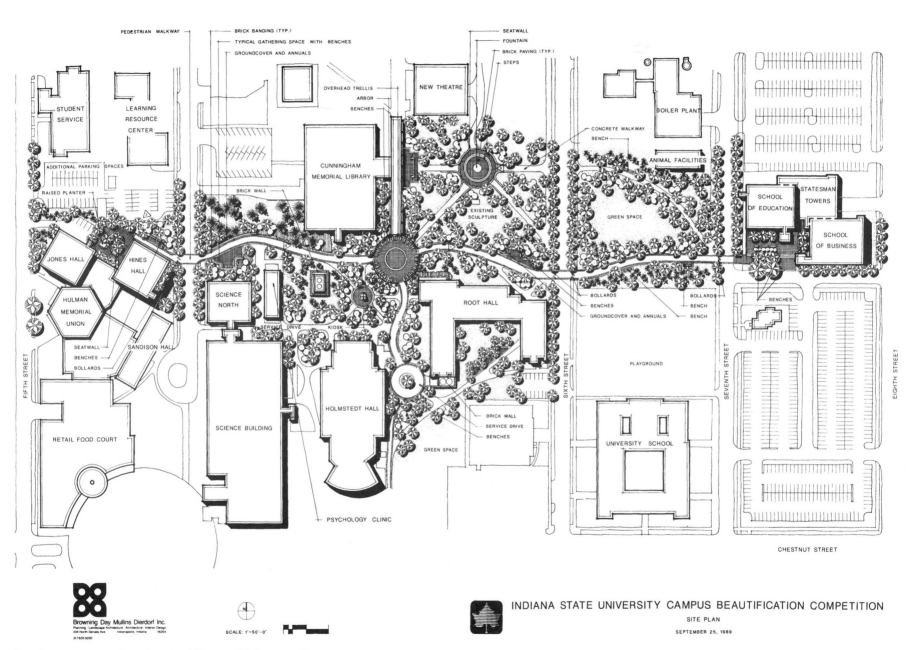

PEDESTRIAN WALKWAY
BRICK BANDING (TYP.)
TYPICAL GATHERING SPACE WITH BENCHES
GROUNDCOVER AND ANNUALS
SEATWALL
FOUNTAIN
BRICK PAVING (TYP.)
STEPS

STUDENT SERVICE
LEARNING RESOURCE CENTER
NEW THEATRE
BOILER PLANT

OVERHEAD TRELLIS
ARBOR
BENCHES

CONCRETE WALKWAY
BENCH

ANIMAL FACILITIES

ADDITIONAL PARKING SPACES
CUNNINGHAM MEMORIAL LIBRARY

RAISED PLANTER
BRICK WALL

EXISTING SCULPTURE

GREEN SPACE

SCHOOL OF EDUCATION
STATESMAN TOWERS

JONES HALL
HINES HALL

SCHOOL OF BUSINESS

HULMAN MEMORIAL UNION
SCIENCE NORTH

ROOT HALL

SEATWALL
BENCHES
BOLLARDS
SANDISON HALL

SERVICE DRIVE
KIOSK

BOLLARDS
BENCHES
GROUNDCOVER AND ANNUALS

BOLLARDS
BENCH
BENCH

BENCHES

FIFTH STREET

SIXTH STREET

SEVENTH STREET

EIGHTH STREET

PLAYGROUND

SCIENCE BUILDING
HOLMSTEDT HALL

BRICK WALL
SERVICE DRIVE
BENCHES

GREEN SPACE

UNIVERSITY SCHOOL

RETAIL FOOD COURT

PSYCHOLOGY CLINIC

CHESTNUT STREET

Browning Day Mullins Dierdorf Inc.
Planning · Landscape Architecture · Architecture · Interior Design
334 North Senate Ave   Indianapolis Indiana   46204
317-635-5030

N

SCALE: 1"=50'-0"

INDIANA STATE UNIVERSITY CAMPUS BEAUTIFICATION COMPETITION
SITE PLAN
SEPTEMBER 25, 1989

▌Indiana State University. Hard-line and ink on mylar.

212

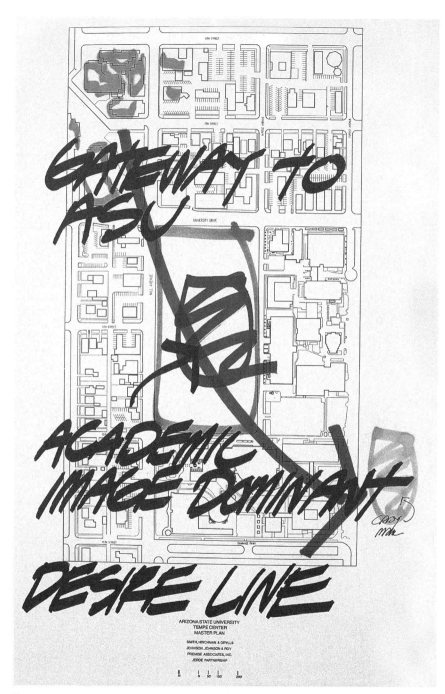

ASU Tempe Center. Color marker and ink on 11″ × 17″ bristol board.

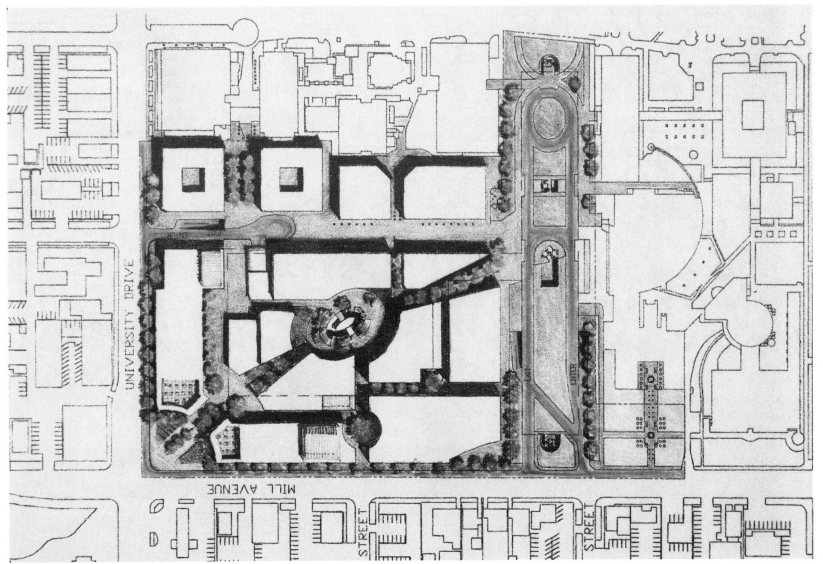

ASU Tempe Center. Color pencil on bond over AutoCADD base drawing.

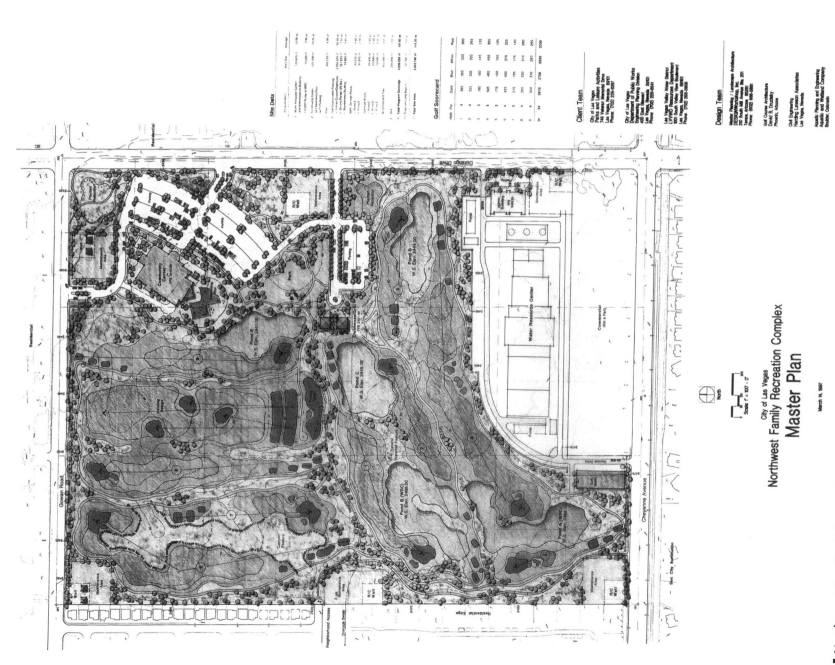

City of Las Vegas
Northwest Family Recreation Complex
Master Plan

March 14, 1997

Northwest Family. Color marker (on the back side) and color pencil on mylar. The Auto-CADD base is plotted on single-side frosted mylar.

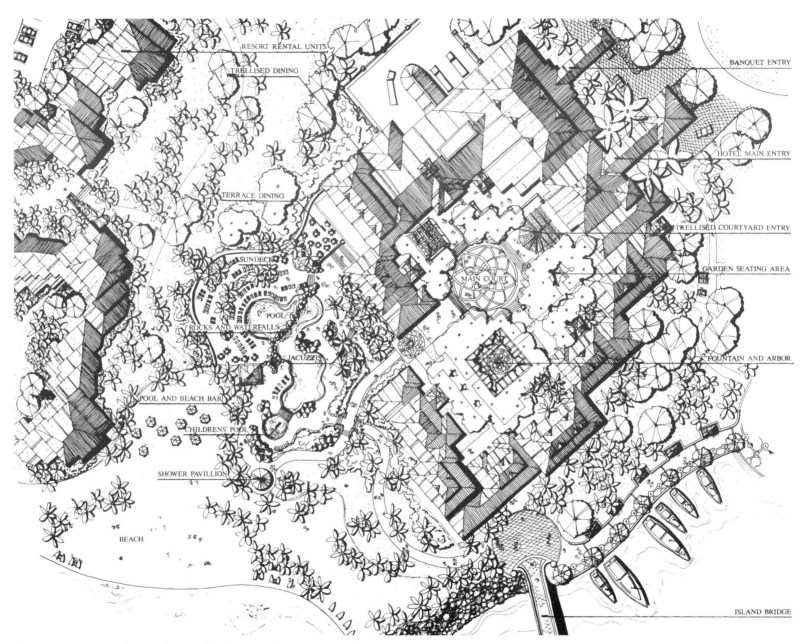

RESORT RENTAL UNITS

TRELLISED DINING

BANQUET ENTRY

HOTEL MAIN ENTRY

TERRACE DINING

TRELLISED COURTYARD ENTRY

SUNDECK

MAIN COURT

GARDEN SEATING AREA

POOL

ROCKS AND WATERFALLS

JACUZZIS

FOUNTAIN AND ARBOR

POOL AND BEACH BAR

CHILDRENS' POOL

SHOWER PAVILLION

BEACH

ISLAND BRIDGE

Coastal resort. Color marker and color pencil on presentation
blackline. The base drawing is hand drawn on mylar with
computer-generated text added manually.

216

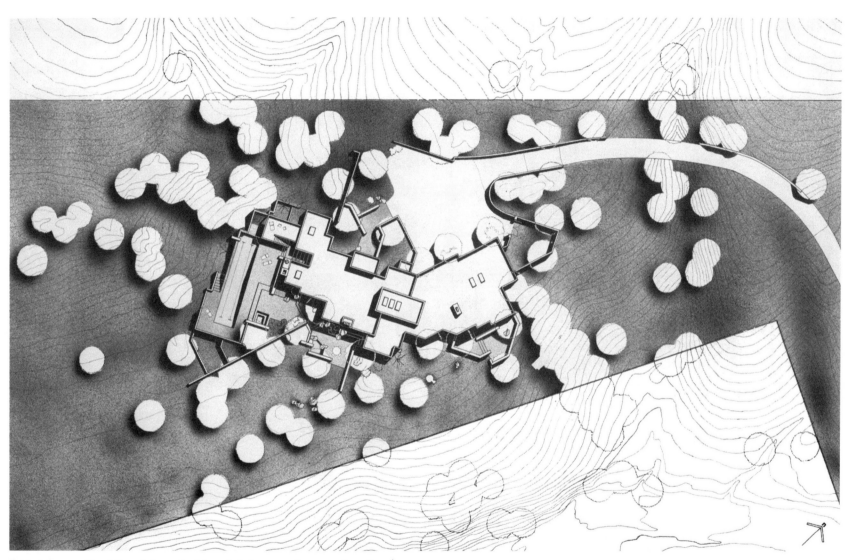

Residence. Hard-line ink and airbrush ink on mylar over hand-drawn base.

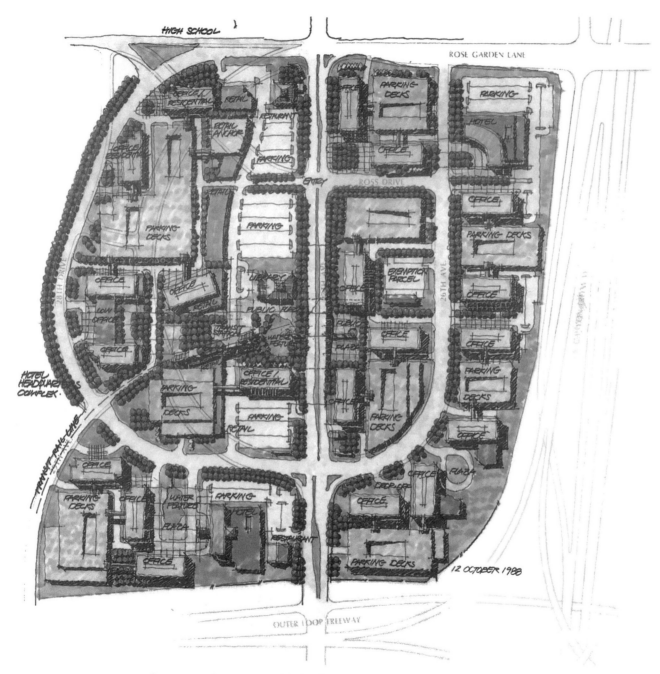

Northridge. Color marker on tracing paper with freehand base drawing.

Coastal Resort Pool. Color marker on presentation blackline
over AutoCADD perspective.

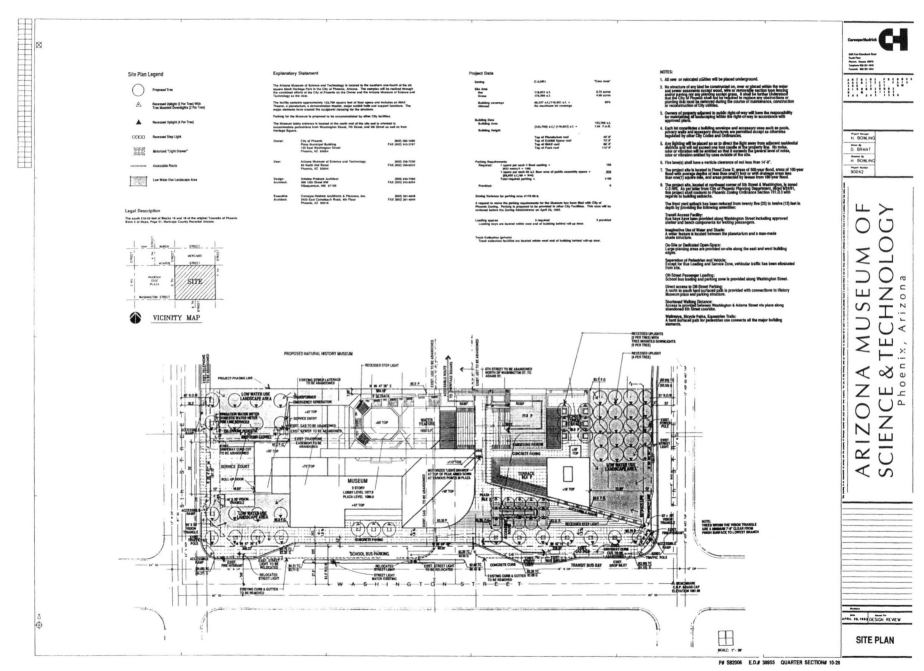

Arizona Museum. Computer-generated conceptual site plan.

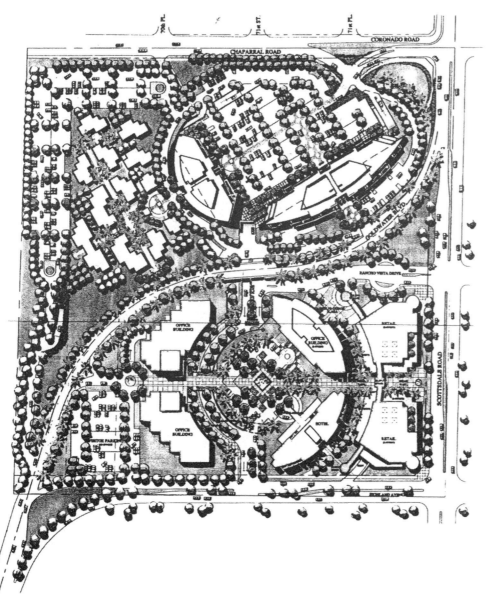

▌Scottsdale Office Park. Color marker on presentation blackline.

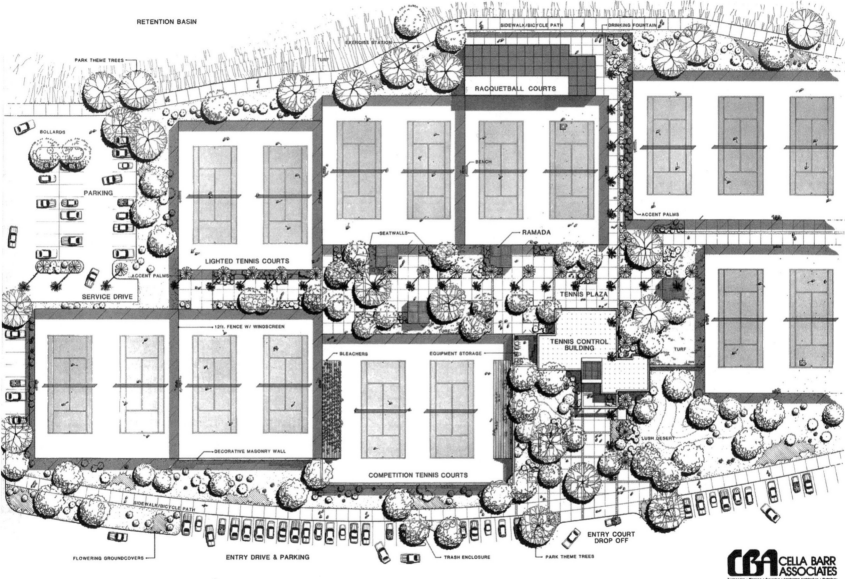

RETENTION BASIN

PARK THEME TREES

TURF

SIDEWALK/BICYCLE PATH

DRINKING FOUNTAIN

EXERCISE STATION

RACQUETBALL COURTS

BOLLARDS

BENCH

PARKING

ACCENT PALMS

LIGHTED TENNIS COURTS

ACCENT PALMS

SEATWALLS

RAMADA

SERVICE DRIVE

TENNIS PLAZA

12 ft. FENCE W/ WINDSCREEN

TURF

TENNIS CONTROL BUILDING

TURF

BLEACHERS

EQUIPMENT STORAGE

DECORATIVE MASONRY WALL

LUSH DESERT

COMPETITION TENNIS COURTS

SIDEWALK/BICYCLE PATH

ENTRY COURT DROP OFF

FLOWERING GROUNDCOVERS

ENTRY DRIVE & PARKING

TRASH ENCLOSURE

PARK THEME TREES

SCOTTSDALE RANCH PARK

TENNIS CONTROL BUILDING & PLAZA AREA

❚ Scottsdale Ranch Park. Freehand in ink on mylar.

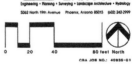

CBA CELLA BARR ASSOCIATES

Engineering • Planning • Surveying • Landscape Architecture • Hydrology

5262 North 19th Avenue   Phoenix, Arizona 85015   (602) 242-2999

0   20   40   80 feet North

CBA JOB NO.: 40936-01

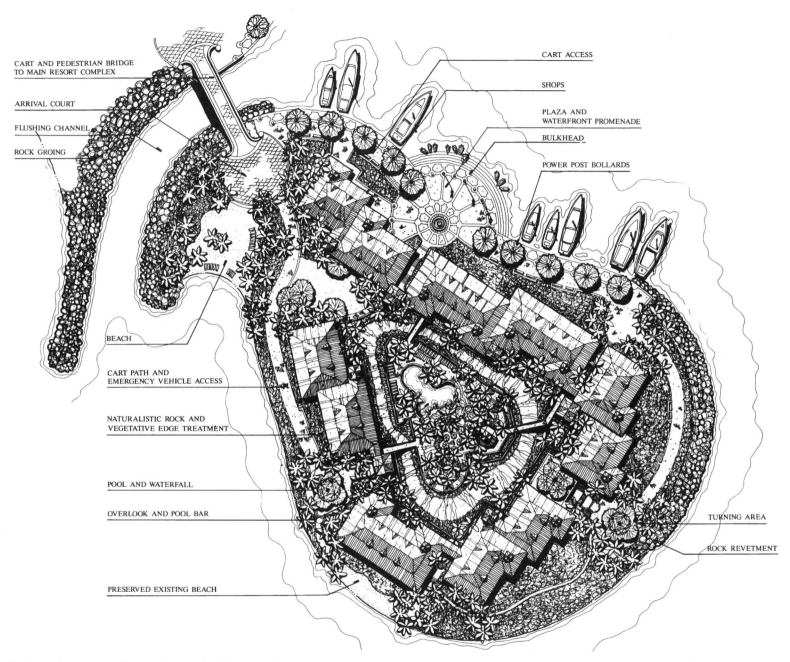

CART AND PEDESTRIAN BRIDGE
TO MAIN RESORT COMPLEX

ARRIVAL COURT

FLUSHING CHANNEL

ROCK GROING

BEACH

CART PATH AND
EMERGENCY VEHICLE ACCESS

NATURALISTIC ROCK AND
VEGETATIVE EDGE TREATMENT

POOL AND WATERFALL

OVERLOOK AND POOL BAR

PRESERVED EXISTING BEACH

CART ACCESS

SHOPS

PLAZA AND
WATERFRONT PROMENADE

BULKHEAD

POWER POST BOLLARDS

TURNING AREA

ROCK REVETMENT

Coastal resort. Color marker and color pencil on presentation
blackline. The base drawing is hand drawn on mylar with
computer-generated text added manually.

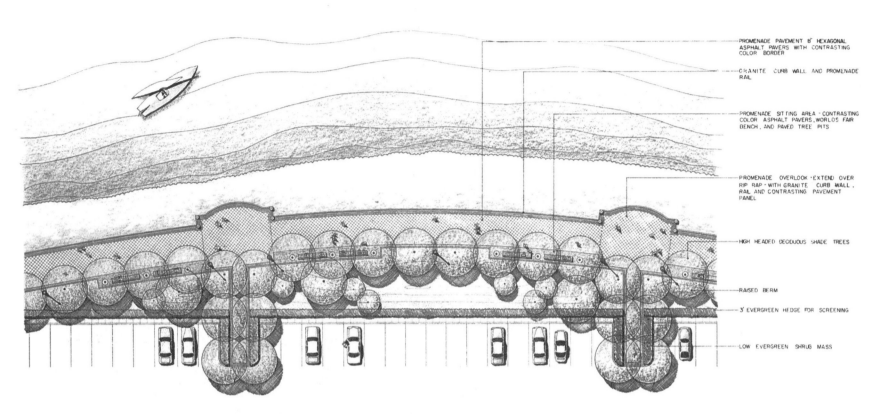

PROMENADE PAVEMENT 8" HEXAGONAL ASPHALT PAVERS WITH CONTRASTING COLOR BORDER

GRANITE CURB WALL AND PROMENADE RAIL

PROMENADE SITTING AREA - CONTRASTING COLOR ASPHALT PAVERS, WORLDS FAIR BENCH, AND PAVED TREE PITS

PROMENADE OVERLOOK - EXTEND OVER RIP RAP - WITH GRANITE CURB WALL, RAIL AND CONTRASTING PAVEMENT PANEL

HIGH HEADED DECIDUOUS SHADE TREES

RAISED BERM

3' EVERGREEN HEDGE FOR SCREENING

LOW EVERGREEN SHRUB MASS

F L U S H I N G   B A Y   P R O M E N A D E

FLUSHING MEADOWS–CORONA PARK, BOROUGH OF QUEENS
CITY OF NEW YORK PARKS & RECREATION   MICELI KULIK & ASSOCIATES, INC.

TYPICAL PROMENADE TREATMENT

Flushing Bay Promenade. Color pencil on opaque textured sketching paper. Color photographs are spray mounted onto original rendering.

FLUSHING BAY PROMENADE

FLUSHING MEADOWS–CORONA PARK, BOROUGH OF QUEENS

CITY OF NEW YORK PARKS & RECREATION ✿ MICELI KULIK & ASSOCIATES, INC.

TYPICAL PROMENADE ELEVATION

Flushing Bay Promenade. Color pencil on opaque textured
sketching paper.

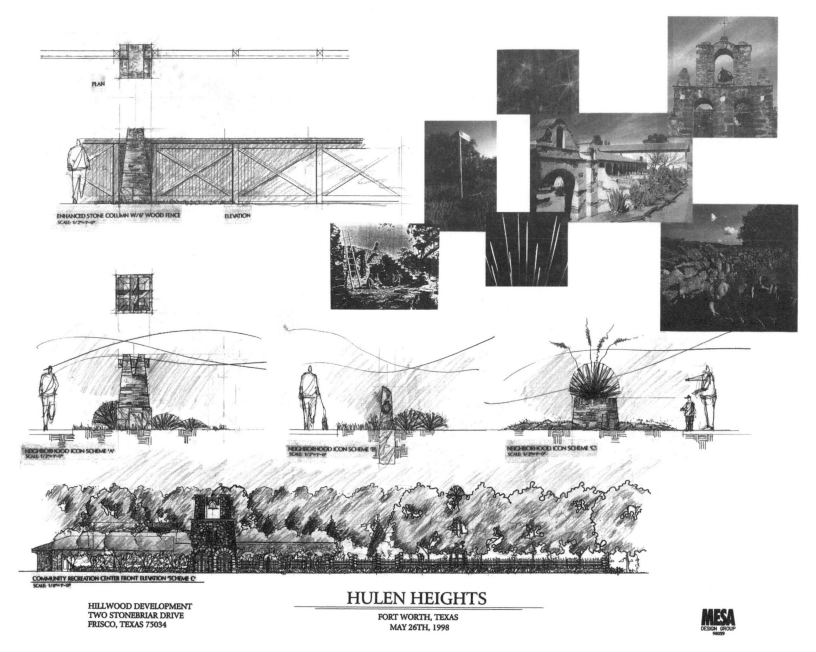

PLAN

ENHANCED STONE COLUMN W/6' WOOD FENCE
SCALE: 1/2"=1'-0"

ELEVATION

NEIGHBORHOOD ICON SCHEME 'A'
SCALE: 1/2"=1'-0"

NEIGHBORHOOD ICON SCHEME 'B'
SCALE: 1/2"=1'-0"

NEIGHBORHOOD ICON SCHEME 'C'
SCALE: 1/2"=1'-0"

COMMUNITY RECREATION CENTER FRONT ELEVATION 'SCHEME C'
SCALE: 1/8"=1'-0"

HULEN HEIGHTS

HILLWOOD DEVELOPMENT
TWO STONEBRIAR DRIVE
FRISCO, TEXAS 75034

FORT WORTH, TEXAS
MAY 26TH, 1998

MESA
DESIGN GROUP
98039

Hulen Heights. Color marker and color pencil on presentation blackline over hand-drawn
base drawing. Color photographs are spray mounted onto original rendering.

TIMESHARE CASITAS AND COURTYARD

PRESERVED EXISTING NATIVE
DESERT LANDSCAPE

PRESERVED EXISTING NATIVE
DESERT LANDSCAPE

2660
2655
2650
2645
2640
2635
2630
2625

TIMESHARE CASITA
ELEVATION 2642

PATHWAY

ARRIVAL COURT WITH
SHADE TREES

TERRACED PARKING SHADED
WITH TRELLIS AND TREES

NATIVE DESERT LANDSCAPE
SCREENS PARKING

F. TIMESHARE CASITA COURTYARD
SCALE: 1/8" = 1'-0"

FOUR SEASONS RESORT
AT TROON NORTH
EDAW

Four Seasons at Troon North. Color pencil on kraft paper. The base drawing was created in AutoCADD to accurately show topographic and engineering aspects. The proposed design is freehand with black ink. Text is created in AutoCADD; the leaders are added in freehand on the rendering.

Keynotes: Design and Construction Systems

1. Breakaway zone for future building construction
2. Subgrade utility zone
3. Future building development per Commons Urban Design Standards and Guidelines
4. Future private development area, elevated above street grade
5. Tree trench - structural soil mix with pore space and aeration sheets for improved root growth; also includes waterholding agent and nutrients
6. Improved planting medium, with topsoil, peat, woodchips, scoria and subdrainage
7. Tree lawn with full-width, continuous tree pits, irrigated sod, and subdrainage
8. Deciduous street tree, species and spacing as determined with City Forester
9. Cast-in-place concrete pavement, unreinforced, potential special aggregate or sand mix for color
10. Concrete unit pavers on sand setting bed
11. Stone or precast pavers on sand setting bed, with concrete sub-slab, weeped where shown
12. Standard cast-in-place concrete curb and gutter
13. Custom cast-in-place concrete curb and gutter
14. Light rail envelope (future construction)
15. Stone, precast or metal grate at tree
16. Precast curb at raised planter, with low iron guard
17. Planted median, with subdrainage
18. Pedestrian light, with banner where shown
19. Vehicular light
20. Street furnishings, varies per street
21. Parking meter and regulatory signage
22. Vehicular street, dimensions as determined with City Transportation planners

Little Raven Street

Section Study

Scale : 3/4" = 1' - 0"

THE COMMONS

DENVER, COLORADO

TRILLIUM CORPORATION
DESIGNWORKSHOP
MK CENTENNIAL

February 1998

The Commons. Black ink and graphite on vellum with photo-copied images of people, cars, and streetlights applied by sticky back. A bond print is rendered with color pencils.

PLANT BERM with LUSH TROPICAL PLANTINGS.

"MONSTER" FICUS, HUNDREDS OF YEARS OLD, ROOTS COVER ROCK and GROW TOWARDS WATER.

ROPE-SWINGS FROM "MONSTER" FICUS.

TO BEACH

SIGNAL FIRE POINT at top of berm.

PLANT SLOPE with PALMS and flowering shrubs.

LOUNGING TERRACES step up slope.

ZERO-ENTRY to POOL and SWIMMING AREAS.

FICUS ROOTS BETWEEN GIANT BOULDERS and ROCKS.

STAIRS from POOL to UPPER LOUNGE AREAS.

ROCK GROTTO FORMED BY WIND and EROSION.

VIEW THRU THEMATIC JUNGLE AREA
LOOKING EAST. SCALE: 1" = 5'0"

LOUNGING AREAS and TROPICAL, LUSH, FLOWERING PLANTINGS EVERYWHERE.

NEW SEAGRAPE TERRACE and TRELLIS.

GIANT ROCK FORMATION and WATERFALL BRINGS JUNGLE INTO THE RESTAURANT.

UPPER LOUNGING TERRACES.

EXISTING SEAGRAPE RESTAURANT.

"MISS BECKY'S SLIDE FOR LIFE" SNAKES THRU JUNGLE.

"SKULL DIGGERS CAVERN" with PICTOGRAPH REMNANTS OF ANCIENT INHABITANTS.

VIEW THRU THEMATIC JUNGLE AREA
LOOKING NORTH. SCALE: 1" = 5'0"

PARADISE ISLAND HOTEL AND CASINO NASSAU, BAHAMAS **E D S A**

Paradise Island Hotel and Casino. Color marker and color pencil on presentation blackline over freehand base drawing.

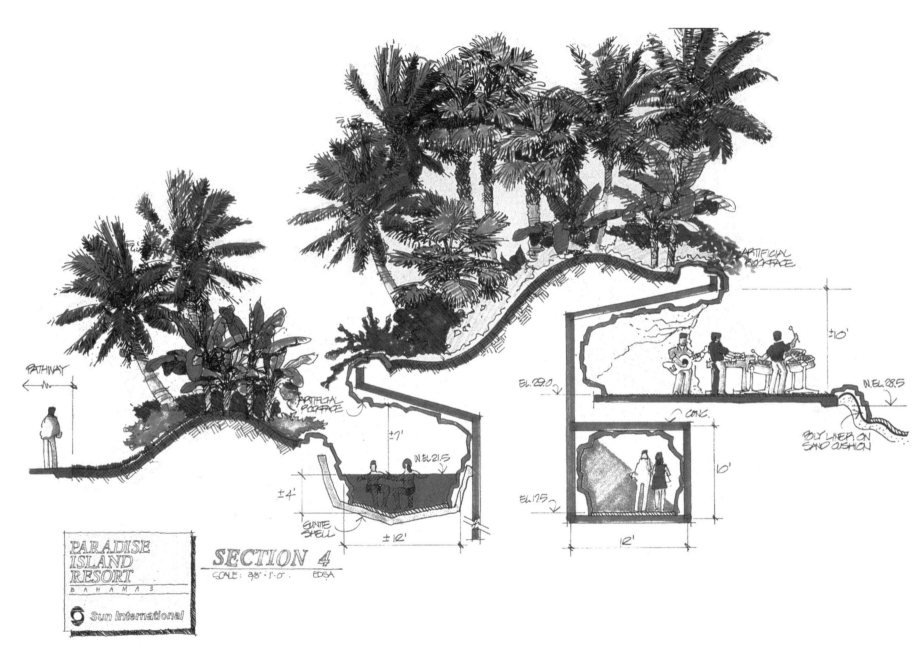

PARADISE
ISLAND
RESORT
B A H A M A S

🌀 Sun International

SECTION 4
SCALE: 3/8" · 1'-0" .   EDSA

PATHWAY

ARTIFICIAL ROCKFACE

±7'
W. EL. 21.5

±4'

±12'

GUNITE SHELL

ARTIFICIAL ROCKFACE

EL. 29.0

CONC.

EL. 17.5

12'

10'

±10'

W. EL. 28.5

POLY LINER ON SAND CUSHION

Paradise Island Hotel and Casino. Color marker and color pencil on presentation blackline over freehand base drawing.

PLANT BERM WITH LUSH TROPICAL PLANTINGS.

RO
"M

TO BEACH

SIGNAL FIRE POINT
at top of berm

PLANT SLOPE with PALMS
and flowering shrubs.

LOUNGING TERRACES
step up slope.

ZERO
POOL
AREA

Paradise Island Hotel and Casino. Color marker and color pencil on presentation blackline over freehand base drawing.

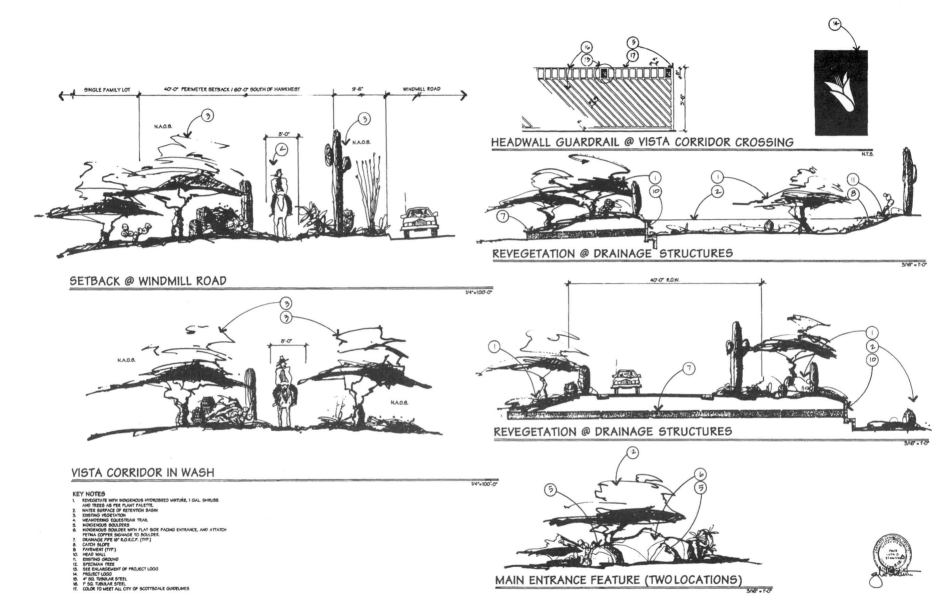

HEADWALL GUARDRAIL @ VISTA CORRIDOR CROSSING

N.T.S.

SETBACK @ WINDMILL ROAD

SINGLE FAMILY LOT | 40'-0" PERIMETER SETBACK / 60'-0" SOUTH OF HAWKNEST | 9'-6" | WINDMILL ROAD

1/4"=100'-0"

REVEGETATION @ DRAINAGE STRUCTURES

3/16" = 1'-0"

VISTA CORRIDOR IN WASH

1/4"=100'-0"

40'-0" R.O.W.

REVEGETATION @ DRAINAGE STRUCTURES

3/16" = 1'-0"

KEY NOTES
1. REVEGETATE WITH INDIGENOUS HYDROSEED MIXTURE, 1 GAL. SHRUBS AND TREES AS PER PLANT PALETTE.
2. WATER SURFACE OF RETENTION BASIN
3. EXISTING VEGETATION
4. MEANDERING EQUESTRIAN TRAIL
5. INDIGENOUS BOULDERS
6. INDIGENOUS BOULDER WITH FLAT SIDE FACING ENTRANCE, AND ATTATCH PETINA COPPER SIGNAGE TO BOULDER.
7. DRAINAGE PIPE 18" R.G.R.C.P. (TYP.)
8. CATCH SLOPE
9. PAVEMENT (TYP.)
10. HEAD WALL
11. EXISTING GROUND
12. SPECIMEN TREE
13. SEE ENLARGEMENT OF PROJECT LOGO
14. PROJECT LOGO
15. 4" SQ. TUBULAR STEEL
16. 1" SQ. TUBULAR STEEL
17. COLOR TO MEET ALL CITY OF SCOTTSDALE GUIDELINES

MAIN ENTRANCE FEATURE (TWO LOCATIONS)

3/16" = 1'-0"

CONCEPTUAL NATIVE PLANT SURVEY/RELOCATION PLAN SECTIONS

SAND FLOWER

PREPARED FOR: STARDUST DEVELOPMENT

nva nell+vecchia+associates
urban+landscape+irrigation+design

393 PA 93   6/9/94

Sand Flower. Combination freehand design sections, with
AutoCADD titles and text in detail-style format.

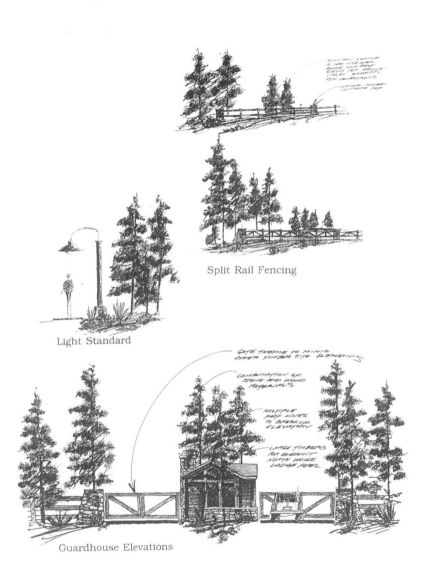

Split Rail Fencing

Light Standard

Guardhouse Elevations

T H E S U M M I T
Show Low, Arizona

vollmer & associates

The Summit. Color pencil on brownline over hand-drawn base with computer-generated titles.

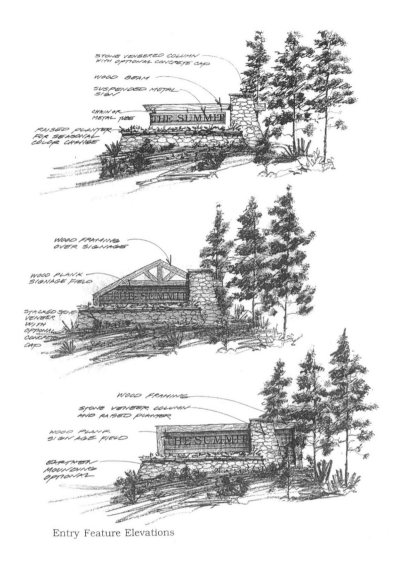

Entry Feature Elevations

T H E S U M M I T
Show Low, Arizona

vollmer & associates

The Summit. Color pencil on brownline over hand-drawn base with computer-generated titles.

€ SECTION THROUGH SPA TREATMENT CENTER
EDSA   22 JANUARY 1998   SCALE: ⅛"=1'-0"

Treatment center. Color marker and color pencil on presentation blackline.

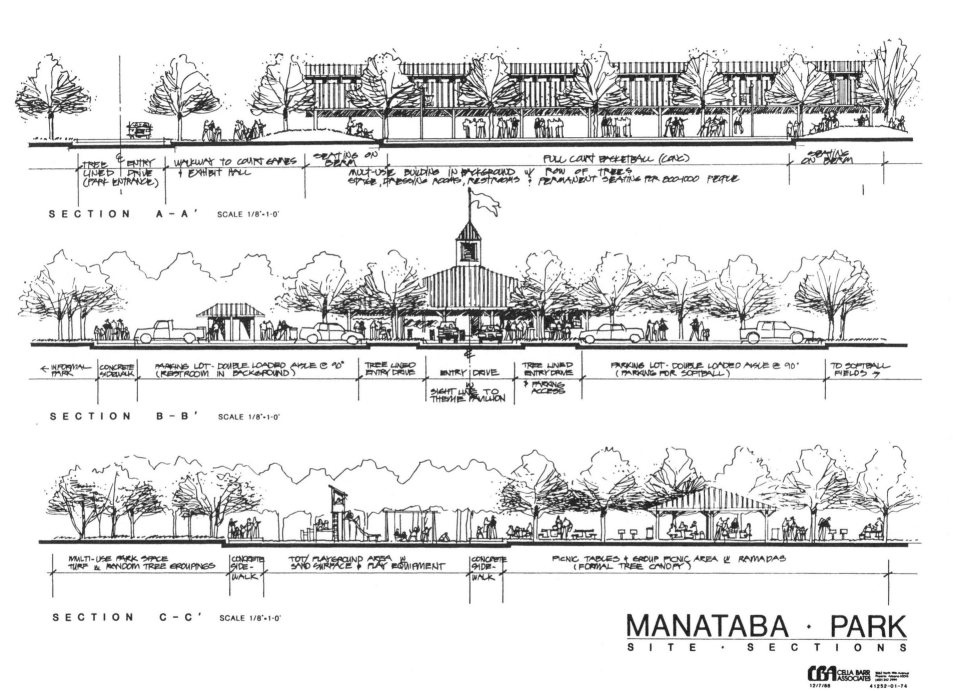

SECTION A-A' SCALE 1/8"-1-0'

TREE @ ENTRY LINED DRIVE (PARK ENTRANCE)

WALKWAY TO COURT GAMES + EXHIBIT HALL

SEATING ON BERM

FULL COURT BASKETBALL (CONC)

MULTI-USE BUILDING IN BACKGROUND W/ ROW OF TREES STAGE, DRESSING ROOMS, RESTROOMS + PERMANENT SEATING FOR 800-1000 PEOPLE

SEATING ON BERM

SECTION B-B' SCALE 1/8"-1-0'

← INFORMAL PARK

CONCRETE SIDEWALK

PARKING LOT - DOUBLE LOADED AISLE @ 90° (RESTROOM IN BACKGROUND)

TREE LINED ENTRY DRIVE

ENTRY DRIVE

SIGHT LINE TO THEME PAVILLION

TREE LINED ENTRY DRIVE + PARKING ACCESS

PARKING LOT - DOUBLE LOADED AISLE @ 90° (PARKING FOR SOFTBALL)

TO SOFTBALL FIELDS →

SECTION C-C' SCALE 1/8"-1-0'

MULTI-USE PARK SPACE TURF W/ RANDOM TREE GROUPINGS

CONCRETE SIDE-WALK

TOT/ PLAYGROUND AREA W/ SAND SURFACE + PLAY EQUIPMENT

CONCRETE SIDE-WALK

PICNIC TABLES + GROUP PICNIC AREA W/ RAMADAS (FORMAL TREE CANOPY)

MANATABA · PARK
S I T E · S E C T I O N S

CBA CELIA BARR ASSOCIATES
12/7/88   41252-01-74

Manataba Park. Combination freehand design section with
hard-line building forms on mylar.

235

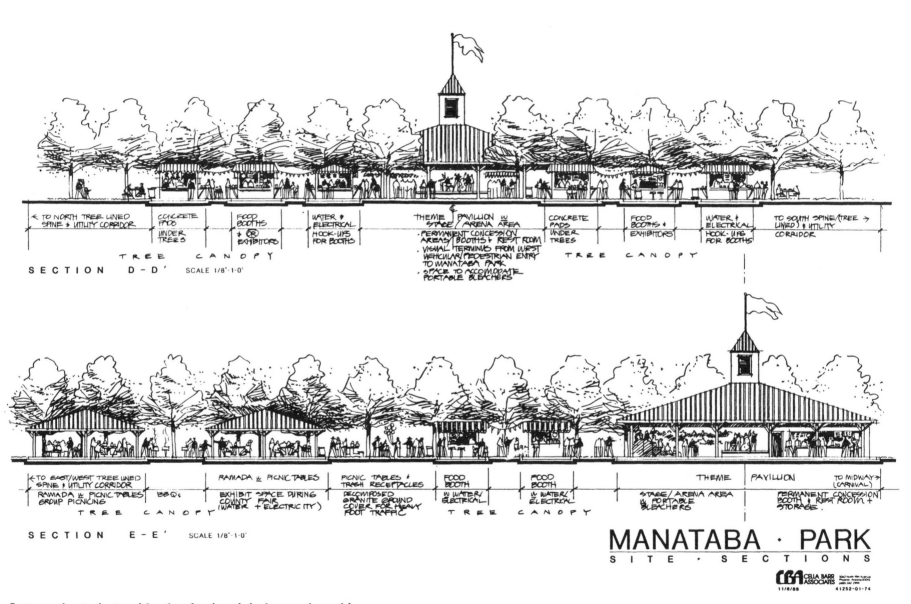

SECTION D-D' SCALE 1/8"·1-0'

← TO NORTH TREE LINED SPINE & UTILITY CORRIDOR

CONCRETE FOOD UNDER TREES

FOOD BOOTHS & ® EXHIBITORS

WATER & ELECTRICAL HOOK-UPS FOR BOOTHS

THEME PAVILLION w STAGE / ARENA AREA
· PERMANENT CONCESSION AREAS / BOOTHS & REST ROOM
· VISUAL TERMINUS FROM WEST VEHICULAR / PEDESTRIAN ENTRY TO MANATABA PARK
· SPACE TO ACCOMODATE PORTABLE BLEACHERS

CONCRETE PADS UNDER TREES

FOOD BOOTHS & EXHIBITORS

WATER & ELECTRICAL HOOK-UPS FOR BOOTHS

TO SOUTH SPINE/TREE → LINED & UTILITY CORRIDOR

TREE CANOPY   TREE CANOPY

SECTION E-E' SCALE 1/8"·1-0'

← TO EAST/WEST TREE LINED SPINE & UTILITY CORRIDOR
RAMADA w PICNIC TABLES GROUP PICNICING

BBQs

RAMADA w PICNIC TABLES
EXHIBIT SPACE DURING COUNTY FAIR (WATER + ELECTRICITY)

PICNIC TABLES & TRASH RECEPTACLES
DECOMPOSED GRANITE GROUND COVER FOR HEAVY FOOT TRAFFIC

FOOD BOOTH w WATER/ ELECTRICAL

FOOD BOOTH w WATER/ ELECTRICAL

THEME
STAGE / ARENA AREA w PORTABLE BLEACHERS

PAVILLION
PERMANENT CONCESSION BOOTH & REST ROOM + STORAGE.

TO MIDWAY → (CARNIVAL)

TREE CANOPY   TREE CANOPY

MANATABA · PARK
S I T E · S E C T I O N S

CBA CELLA BARR ASSOCIATES
11/8/88   41252-01-74

Manataba Park. Combination freehand design section with
hard-line building forms on mylar.

236

sum'mĕr·y, *a*. of, like, or characteristic of summer; summerlike.

sum'ming up, a concise summation; as, the state's attorney began his *summing up*.

sum'mist, *n*. one who makes an abridgment. [Rare.]

sum'mit, *n*. [Fr. *sommet*, dim. of OFr. *som*, a summit, from L. *summum*, the highest part.]
    1. the top or apex; the highest point, part, or elevation; as, the *summit* of a mountain.
    2. the highest state or degree; the acme; as, the general arrived at the *summit* of fame.
    3. (a) the highest level of officialdom; specifically, in connection with diplomatic negotiations, the level restricted to heads of government; as, a meeting at the *summit*; (b) a conference at the summit.
    4. in mathematics, the point at which three or more surfaces of a polyhedron meet.
    Syn.—apex, peak, top, pinnacle, crown.

sum'mit, *a*. of the heads of government; as, a *summit* parley.

sum'mit·less, *a*. having no summit.

graphic

copper cap
rose tan stucco
sommet marker

THE
SOMMET

Native vegetation-specimen cactus always with mesquite or palo verde shrubbery in natural massing groups of 10-30 plants with sympathetic combinations.

flowering native grandcovers

THE SOMMET GRAPHIC

The Sommet. Freehand in ink on vellum with freehand base drawing.

237

Parcel Entry

6'-0" HEIGHT SPLIT FACE WALL AND CAP

LARGE SPECIMEN TREE AS A FILL BACKDROP AND FRAME.

MEDIUM HEIGHT SHRUBS AND DESERT ACCENTS TO HIGHLIGHT SIGNAGE.

CAST IN PLACE INTEGRAL COLORED PARCEL SIGNWALL WITH INSET LETTERING AND LONG CONTINUOUS BEND TOWARD STREET.

TALAVERDE

Community Facility Signwalls

BUILD INTENSITY OF LANDSCAPE WITH SPECIMEN TREES, DESERT ACCENTS SUCH AS SAGUARO, BARRELS, CHOLLA AND AGAVE.

LARGE SURFACE SELECT GRANITE BOULDERS EMBANKMENT TO TERMINATE SIGNWALL

CAST IN PLACE CONCRETE SIGNWALL WITH INTEGRAL COLOR AND INSET LETTERING/ LOGO.

LOW DESERT GROUNDCOVERS SUCH AS BURSAGE, BUCKWHEAT.

SIGNWALL TO ACCOMMODATE GRADE CHANGE.

TENNIS COMPLEX

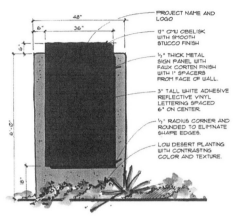

Builder Directional Signage

PROJECT NAME AND LOGO

12" CMU OBELISK WITH SMOOTH STUCCO FINISH

1/2" THICK METAL SIGN PANEL WITH FAUX CORTEN FINISH WITH 1" SPACERS FROM FACE OF WALL.

3" TALL WHITE ADHESIVE REFLECTIVE VINYL LETTERING SPACED 6" ON CENTER.

1/2" RADIUS CORNER AND ROUNDED TO ELIMINATE SHARP EDGES.

LOW DESERT PLANTING WITH CONTRASTING COLOR AND TEXTURE.

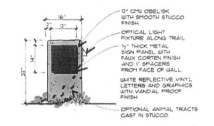

Pedestrian Trail Signage

12" CMU OBELISK WITH SMOOTH STUCCO FINISH.

OPTICAL LIGHT FIXTURE ALONG TRAIL

1/2" THICK METAL SIGN PANEL WITH FAUX CORTEN FINISH AND 1" SPACERS FROM FACE OF WALL.

WHITE REFLECTIVE VINYL LETTERS AND GRAPHICS WITH VANDAL PROOF FINISH

OPTIONAL ANIMAL TRACTS CAST IN STUCCO.

Parcel Entry and Wall Elements

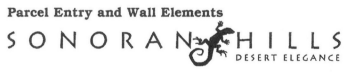

SONORAN HILLS
DESERT ELEGANCE

vollmer & associates
landscape architecture · site planning · installation mgmt.

Sonoran Hills. Color marker on presentation blackline. The base drawing is a combination of freehand site sections with computer-generated text and title blocks.

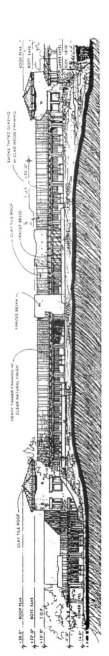

FUNCTION BUILDING
NORTH ELEVATION

FUNCTION BUILDING
WEST ELEVATION

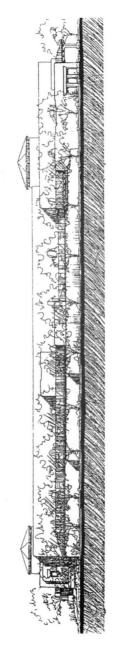

FUNCTION BUILDING
SOUTH ELEVATION

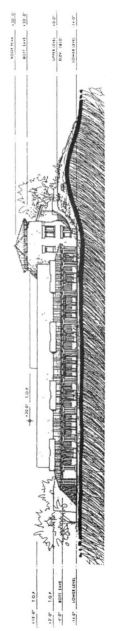

FUNCTION BUILDING
EAST ELEVATION

THE RESORT AT GRAYHAWK

EXTERIOR ELEVATIONS

DEVELOPMENT REVIEW BOARD SUBMITTAL 4.7.97

ARCHITECTURE   ADP FLUOR DANIEL
CIVIL ENGINEERING   GILBERTSON ASSOCIATES, INC
LANDSCAPE ARCHITECTURE   NEILL/VECCHIA & ASSOCIATES, INC

■ Grayhawk. Ink on vellum.

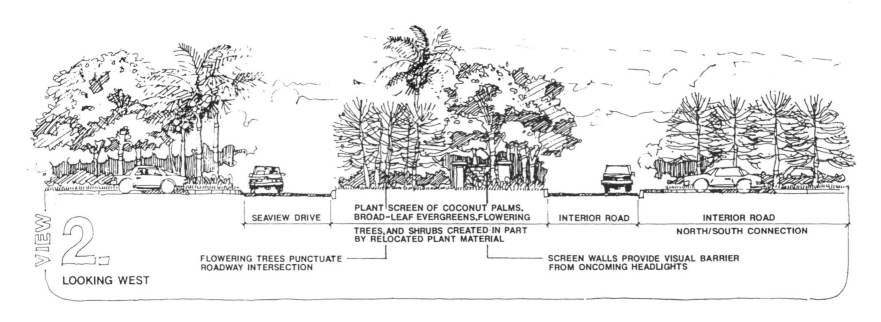

VIEW 2.
LOOKING WEST

SEAVIEW DRIVE

PLANT SCREEN OF COCONUT PALMS,
BROAD-LEAF EVERGREENS, FLOWERING
TREES, AND SHRUBS CREATED IN PART
BY RELOCATED PLANT MATERIAL

INTERIOR ROAD

INTERIOR ROAD
NORTH/SOUTH CONNECTION

FLOWERING TREES PUNCTUATE
ROADWAY INTERSECTION

SCREEN WALLS PROVIDE VISUAL BARRIER
FROM ONCOMING HEADLIGHTS

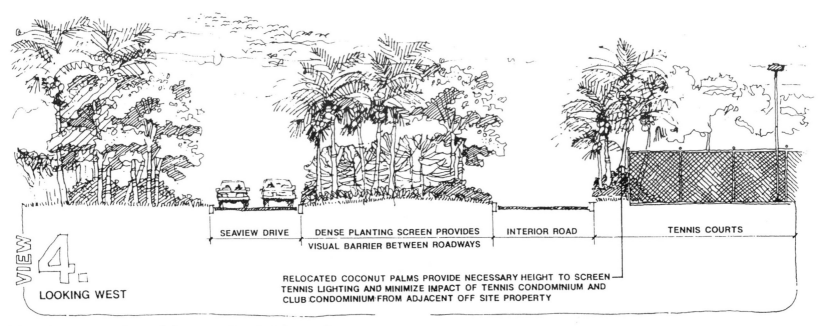

VIEW 4.
LOOKING WEST

SEAVIEW DRIVE

DENSE PLANTING SCREEN PROVIDES
VISUAL BARRIER BETWEEN ROADWAYS

INTERIOR ROAD

TENNIS COURTS

RELOCATED COCONUT PALMS PROVIDE NECESSARY HEIGHT TO SCREEN
TENNIS LIGHTING AND MINIMIZE IMPACT OF TENNIS CONDOMINIUM AND
CLUB CONDOMINIUM FROM ADJACENT OFF SITE PROPERTY

Key Biscayne Hotel. Hand-drawn sections in ink on vellum,
with type text added manually.

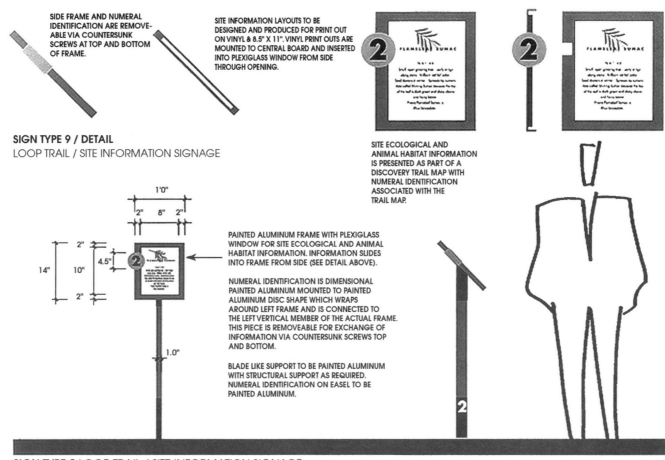

SIDE FRAME AND NUMERAL IDENTIFICATION ARE REMOVE-ABLE VIA COUNTERSUNK SCREWS AT TOP AND BOTTOM OF FRAME.

SITE INFORMATION LAYOUTS TO BE DESIGNED AND PRODUCED FOR PRINT OUT ON VINYL & 8.5" X 11". VINYL PRINT OUTS ARE MOUNTED TO CENTRAL BOARD AND INSERTED INTO PLEXIGLASS WINDOW FROM SIDE THROUGH OPENING.

SIGN TYPE 9 / DETAIL
LOOP TRAIL / SITE INFORMATION SIGNAGE

SITE ECOLOGICAL AND ANIMAL HABITAT INFORMATION IS PRESENTED AS PART OF A DISCOVERY TRAIL MAP WITH NUMERAL IDENTIFICATION ASSOCIATED WITH THE TRAIL MAP.

PAINTED ALUMINUM FRAME WITH PLEXIGLASS WINDOW FOR SITE ECOLOGICAL AND ANIMAL HABITAT INFORMATION. INFORMATION SLIDES INTO FRAME FROM SIDE (SEE DETAIL ABOVE).

NUMERAL IDENTIFICATION IS DIMENSIONAL PAINTED ALUMINUM MOUNTED TO PAINTED ALUMINUM DISC SHAPE WHICH WRAPS AROUND LEFT FRAME AND IS CONNECTED TO THE LEFT VERTICAL MEMBER OF THE ACTUAL FRAME. THIS PIECE IS REMOVEABLE FOR EXCHANGE OF INFORMATION VIA COUNTERSUNK SCREWS TOP AND BOTTOM.

BLADE LIKE SUPPORT TO BE PAINTED ALUMINUM WITH STRUCTURAL SUPPORT AS REQUIRED. NUMERAL IDENTIFICATION ON EASEL TO BE PAINTED ALUMINUM.

SIGN TYPE 9 LOOP TRAIL / SITE INFORMATION SIGNAGE

Auburn Hills. Digital base rendered in Adobe Photoshop. The image is imported into Quark Express for the addition of text and titles.

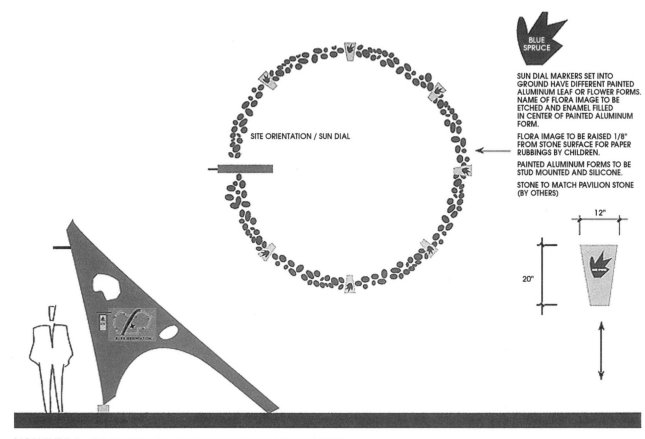

BLUE
SPRUCE

SUN DIAL MARKERS SET INTO
GROUND HAVE DIFFERENT PAINTED
ALUMINUM LEAF OR FLOWER FORMS.
NAME OF FLORA IMAGE TO BE
ETCHED AND ENAMEL FILLED
IN CENTER OF PAINTED ALUMINUM
FORM.

FLORA IMAGE TO BE RAISED 1/8"
FROM STONE SURFACE FOR PAPER
RUBBINGS BY CHILDREN.

PAINTED ALUMINUM FORMS TO BE
STUD MOUNTED AND SILICONE.

STONE TO MATCH PAVILION STONE
(BY OTHERS)

SITE ORIENTATION / SUN DIAL

12"

20"

SIGN TYPE 6 SITE ORIENTATION / GNOMEN AND SUN DIAL CONCEPT

Auburn Hills. Digital base rendered in Adobe Photoshop. The
image is imported into Quark Express for the addition of text
and titles.

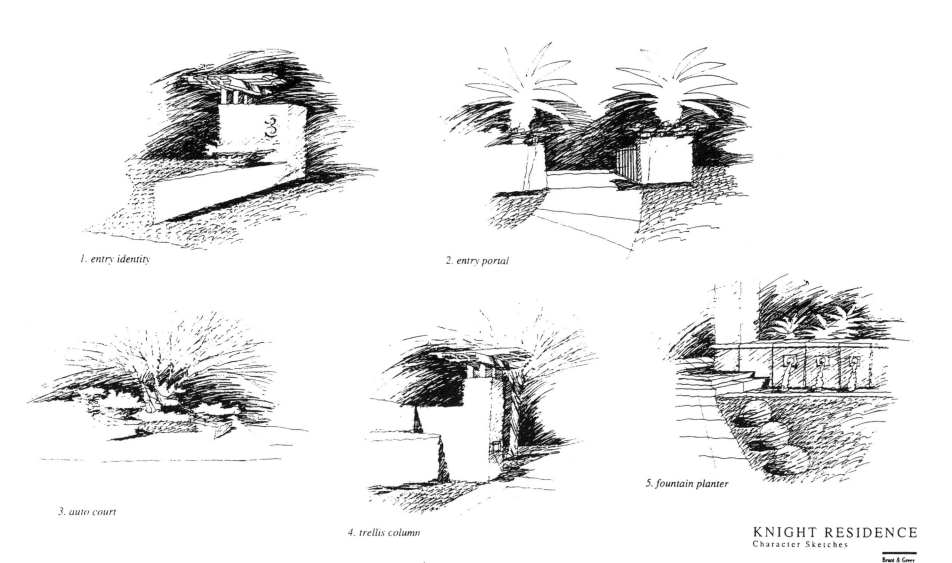

1. entry identity

2. entry portal

3. auto court

4. trellis column

5. fountain planter

KNIGHT RESIDENCE
Character Sketches

Brant & Greey
Landscape Architecture
1110 E. Missouri, Suite 120
Phoenix, Arizona 85014
602.253.4040 Fax 253.4040

1.5.95

Knight Residence. Freehand in ink on vellum with computer-
generated text and titles.

6. patio garden

7. sculpture area

8. splash blocks

9. pool edge

10. cactus garden

KNIGHT RESIDENCE
Character Sketches

Brunt & Greey

1.5.95

Knight Residence. Freehand in ink on vellum with computer-generated text and titles.

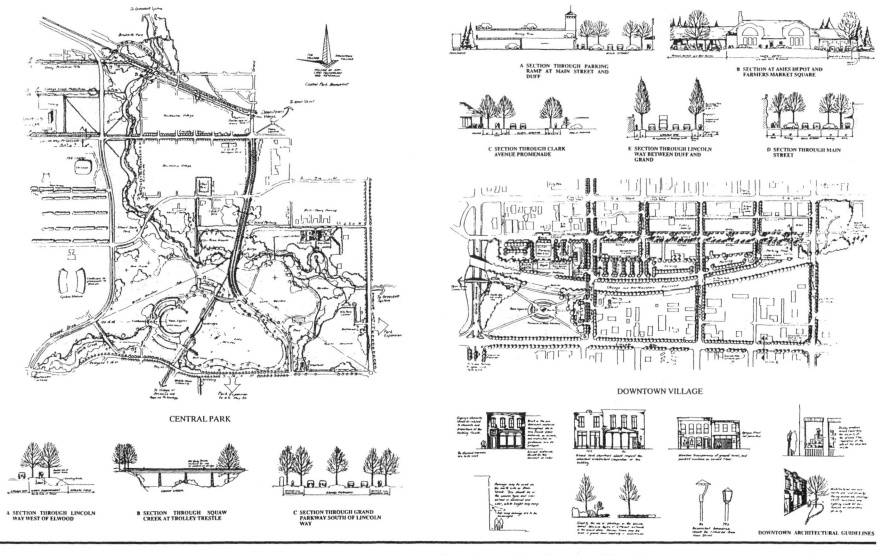

CENTRAL PARK

A SECTION THROUGH PARKING RAMP AT MAIN STREET AND DUFF

B SECTION AT AMES DEPOT AND FARMERS MARKET SQUARE

C SECTION THROUGH CLARK AVENUE PROMENADE

E SECTION THROUGH LINCOLN WAY BETWEEN DUFF AND GRAND

D SECTION THROUGH MAIN STREET

DOWNTOWN VILLAGE

A SECTION THROUGH LINCOLN WAY WEST OF ELWOOD

B SECTION THROUGH SQUAW CREEK AT TROLLEY TRESTLE

C SECTION THROUGH GRAND PARKWAY SOUTH OF LINCOLN WAY

DOWNTOWN ARCHITECTURAL GUIDELINES

A S E N S E   O F   P L A C E

SASAKI ASSOCIATES, INC.
Dallas, Texas
July 23, 1990

Freehand in ink on mylar with computer-generated text and titles.

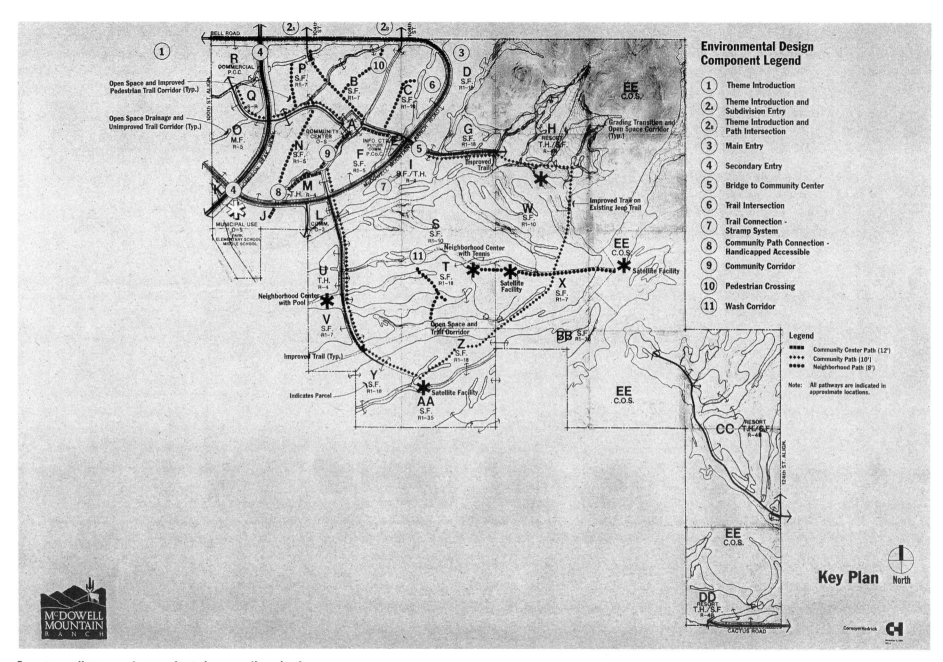

Environmental Design Component Legend

1. **Theme Introduction**
2A. **Theme Introduction and Subdivision Entry**
2B. **Theme Introduction and Path Intersection (Typ.)**
3. **Main Entry**
4. **Secondary Entry**
5. **Bridge to Community Center**
6. **Trail Intersection**
7. **Trail Connection - Stramp System**
8. **Community Path Connection - Handicapped Accessible**
9. **Community Corridor**
10. **Pedestrian Crossing**
11. **Wash Corridor**

Legend
- Community Center Path (12')
- Community Path (10')
- Neighborhood Path (8')

Note: All pathways are indicated in approximate locations.

Key Plan North

McDowell Mountain Ranch. Color pencil on kraft paper over freehand base drawing. The text and titles are computer generated and applied using sticky-back material.

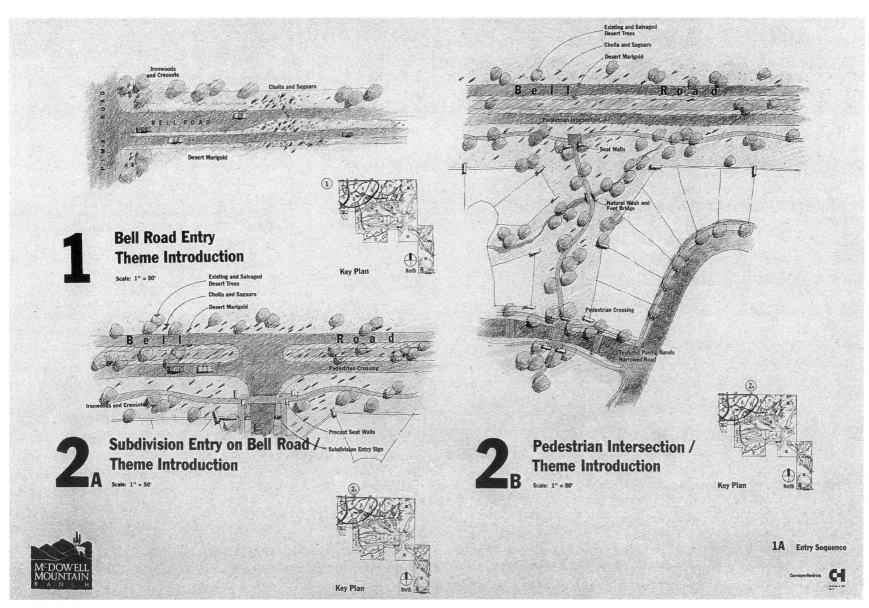

1 Bell Road Entry
Theme Introduction
Scale: 1" = 50'

Ironwoods and Creosote
Cholla and Saguaro
BELL ROAD
Desert Marigold
PIMA ROAD

Key Plan
North

2A Subdivision Entry on Bell Road /
Theme Introduction
Scale: 1" = 50'

Existing and Salvaged Desert Trees
Cholla and Saguaro
Desert Marigold
Bell Road
Pedestrian Crossing
Ironwoods and Creosote
Precast Seat Walls
Subdivision Entry Sign

Key Plan
North

2B Pedestrian Intersection /
Theme Introduction
Scale: 1" = 50'

Existing and Salvaged Desert Trees
Cholla and Saguaro
Desert Marigold
Bell Road
Pedestrian Intersection
Seat Walls
Natural Wash and Foot Bridge
Pedestrian Crossing
Textured Paving Bands Narrowed Road

Key Plan
North

1A Entry Sequence

McDowell Mountain Ranch. Color pencil on kraft paper over freehand base drawing. The text and titles are computer generated and applied using sticky-back material.

247

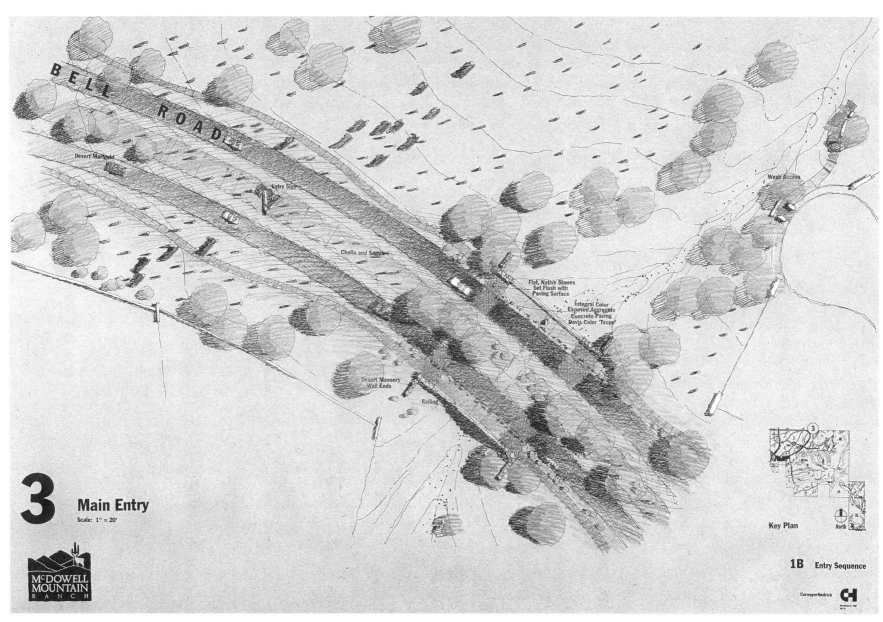

BELL ROAD

Desert Marigold

Entry Sign

Cholla and Saguaro

Flat, Native Stones
Set Flush with
Paving Surface

Integral Color
Exposed Aggregate
Concrete Paving
Davis Color 'Taupe'

Wash Access

Desert Masonry
Wall Ends

Railing

3 **Main Entry**
Scale: 1" = 20'

McDOWELL
MOUNTAIN
R A N C H

Key Plan

North

1B Entry Sequence

Cornoyer Hedrick

McDowell Mountain Ranch. Color pencil on kraft paper over
freehand base drawing. The text and titles are computer
generated and applied using sticky-back material.

Seven Arrows. Freehand in ink on mylar over freehand base drawing.

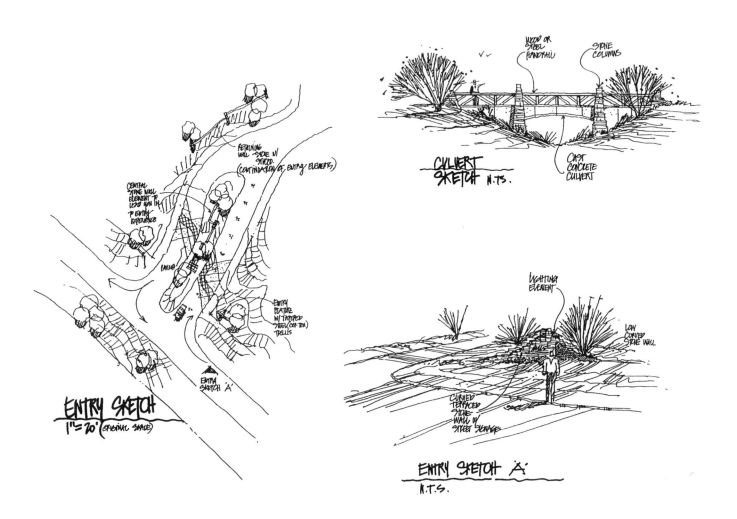

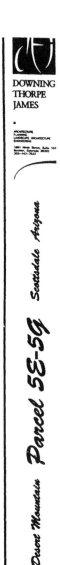

Desert Mountain. Freehand in ink on mylar over freehand base drawing.

Pool Area Perspective. Color marker on presentation blackline over hand-drawn base.

▌U.S. Fish and Wildlife. Freehand in ink on vellum.

Northern Illinois University. Watercolor paint and color pencil on watercolor paper over combination of hard-line and freehand base perspective.

Watercolor paint and color pencil on watercolor paper over freehand base perspective.

Watercolor paint and color pencil on watercolor paper over combination hard-line and freehand base perspective.

Watercolor paint and color pencil on watercolor paper over combination hard line and freehand base perspective.

Watercolor paint and color pencil on watercolor paper over combination hard-line and freehand base perspective.

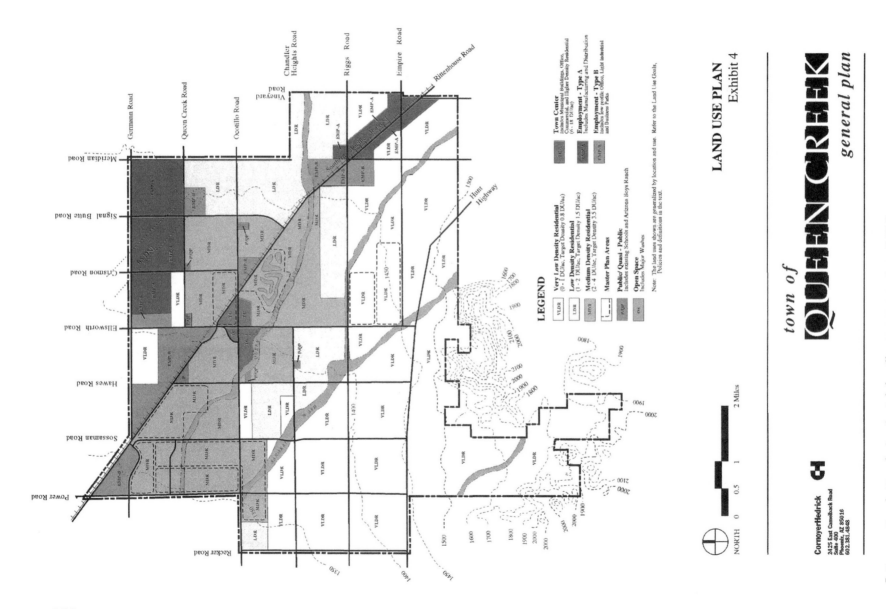

LAND USE PLAN
Exhibit 4

town of
QUEEN CREEK
general plan

CornoyerHedrick
2425 East Camelback Road
Suite 400
Phoenix, AZ 85016
602.381.4848

NORTH

0   0.5   1   2 Miles

Queen Creek. Rendering in Adobe Illustrator over AutoCADD base.

Tosco Daycare. Hard-line in ink on vellum with color marker
and color pencil on presentation blackline.

Resort entry. Color pencil and watercolor paints on presentation blackline.

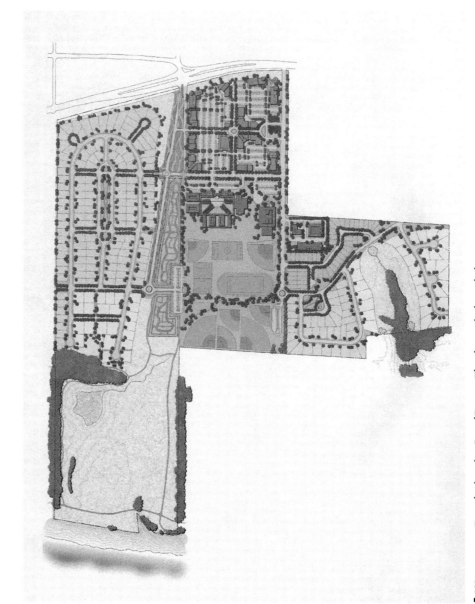

Wavecrest. Rendering in CorelDraw. The base is hand drawn over a screened CADD plot, then scanned for rendering.

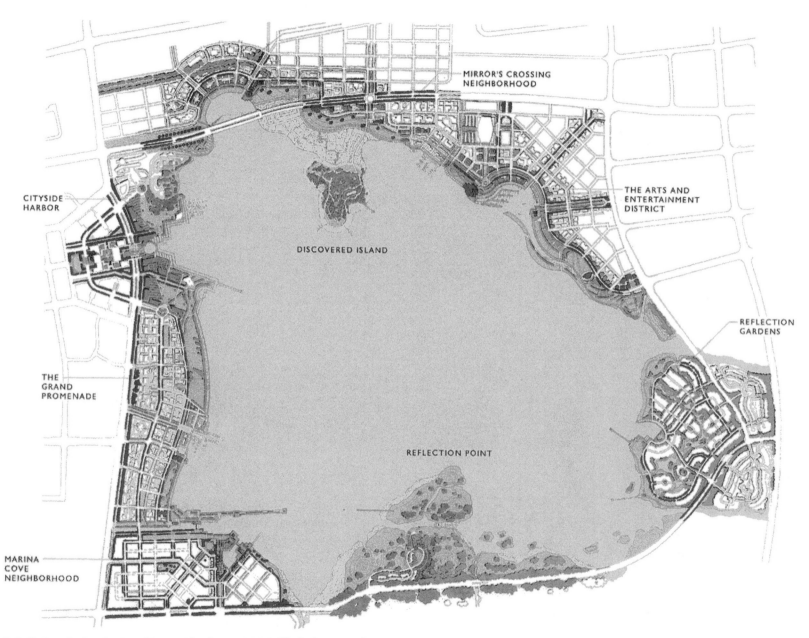

MIRROR'S CROSSING
NEIGHBORHOOD

THE ARTS AND
ENTERTAINMENT
DISTRICT

CITYSIDE
HARBOR

DISCOVERED ISLAND

REFLECTION
GARDENS

THE
GRAND
PROMENADE

REFLECTION POINT

MARINA
COVE
NEIGHBORHOOD

Jinji. Rendering in CorelDraw. The base CADD file is imported
into CorelDraw for rendering.

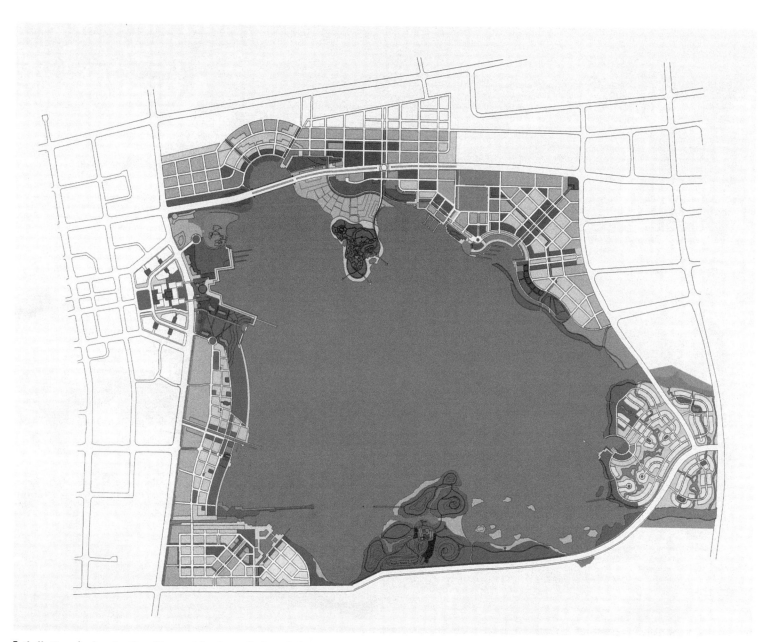

Jinji. Rendering in CorelDraw. The base is hand drawn over a
screened CADD plot, then scanned for rendering.

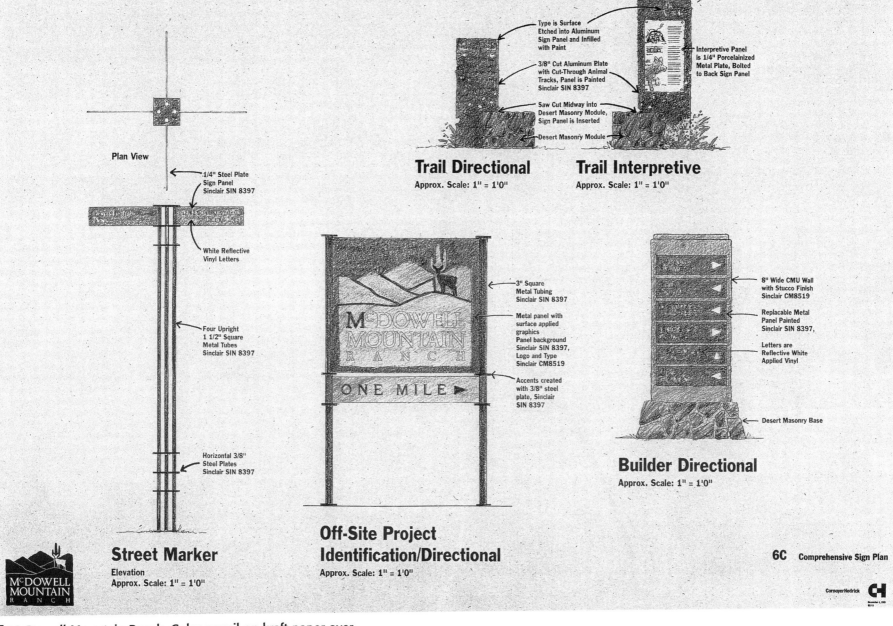

Plan View

1/4" Steel Plate
Sign Panel
Sinclair SIN 8397

White Reflective
Vinyl Letters

Four Upright
1 1/2" Square
Metal Tubes
Sinclair SIN 8397

Horizontal 3/8"
Steel Plates
Sinclair SIN 8397

Street Marker
Elevation
Approx. Scale: 1" = 1'0"

Type is Surface
Etched into Aluminum
Sign Panel and Infilled
with Paint

3/8" Cut Aluminum Plate
with Cut-Through Animal
Tracks, Panel is Painted
Sinclair SIN 8397

Saw Cut Midway into
Desert Masonry Module,
Sign Panel is Inserted

Desert Masonry Module

Interpretive Panel
is 1/4" Porcelainized
Metal Plate, Bolted
to Back Sign Panel

Trail Directional
Approx. Scale: 1" = 1'0"

Trail Interpretive
Approx. Scale: 1" = 1'0"

McDOWELL MOUNTAIN RANCH

ONE MILE ▶

3" Square
Metal Tubing
Sinclair SIN 8397

Metal panel with
surface applied
graphics
Panel background
Sinclair SIN 8397,
Logo and Type
Sinclair CM8519

Accents created
with 3/8" steel
plate, Sinclair
SIN 8397

8" Wide CMU Wall
with Stucco Finish
Sinclair CM8519

Replacable Metal
Panel Painted
Sinclair SIN 8397,

Letters are
Reflective White
Applied Vinyl

Desert Masonry Base

Builder Directional
Approx. Scale: 1" = 1'0"

Off-Site Project
Identification/Directional
Approx. Scale: 1" = 1'0"

6C Comprehensive Sign Plan

McDowell Mountain Ranch. Color pencil on kraft paper over freehand base drawing. The text and titles are computer generated and applied using sticky-back material.

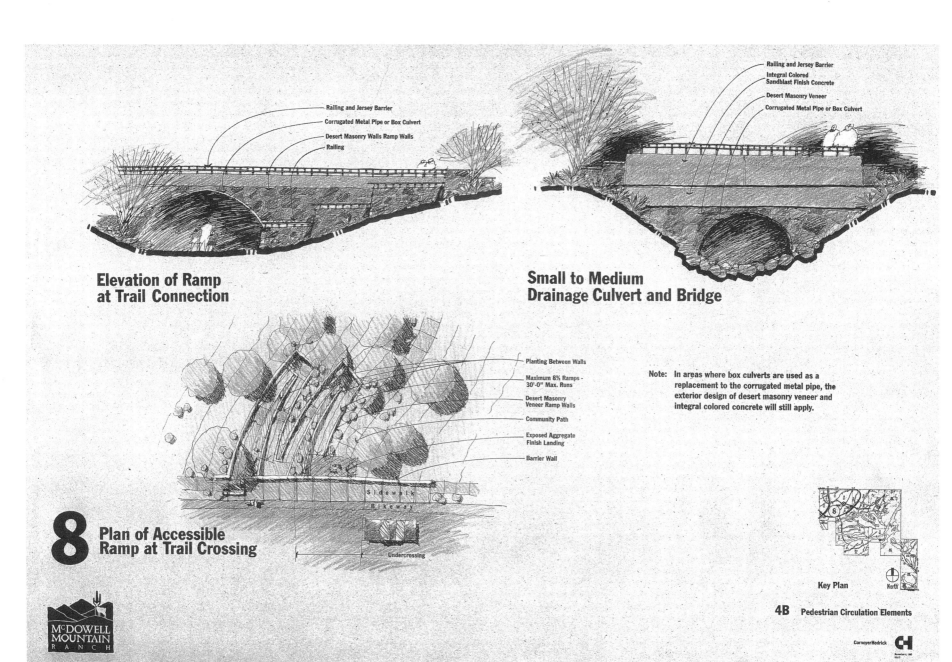

**Elevation of Ramp
at Trail Connection**

- Railing and Jersey Barrier
- Corrugated Metal Pipe or Box Culvert
- Desert Masonry Walls Ramp Walls
- Railing

**Small to Medium
Drainage Culvert and Bridge**

- Railing and Jersey Barrier
- Integral Colored Sandblast Finish Concrete
- Desert Masonry Veneer
- Corrugated Metal Pipe or Box Culvert

**8 Plan of Accessible
Ramp at Trail Crossing**

- Planting Between Walls
- Maximum 8% Ramps - 30'-0" Max. Runs
- Desert Masonry Veneer Ramp Walls
- Community Path
- Exposed Aggregate Finish Landing
- Barrier Wall

Sidewalk
Bikeway

Undercrossing

Note: In areas where box culverts are used as a replacement to the corrugated metal pipe, the exterior design of desert masonry veneer and integral colored concrete will still apply.

Key Plan

North

4B Pedestrian Circulation Elements

CornoyerHedrick

McDowell Mountain Ranch. Color pencil on kraft paper over freehand base drawing. The text and titles are computer generated and applied using sticky-back material.

INDEX